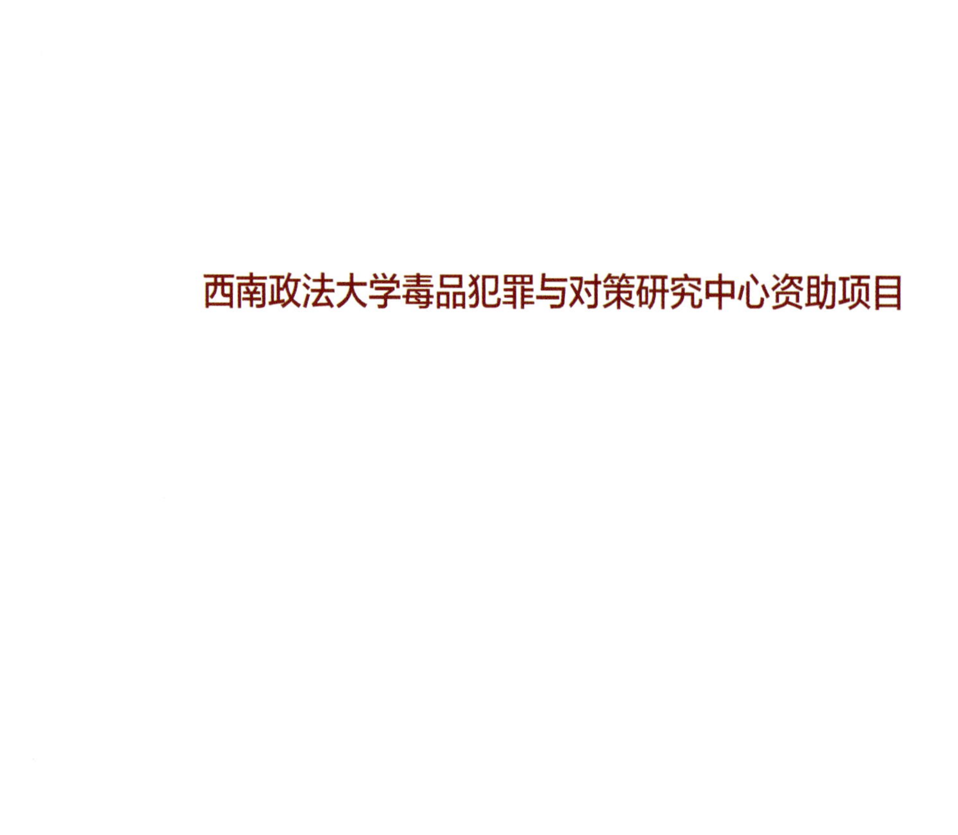

西南政法大学毒品犯罪与对策研究中心资助项目

国际犯罪学大师系列
GUOJI FANZUIXUE DASHI XILIE

学术顾问：付子堂

国际犯罪学大师论恐怖主义犯罪

Master Criminologists on Anti-terrorism

主编◎刘建宏

人民出版社

主编简介

刘建宏　博士

Jianhong Liu

刘建宏，西南政法大学讲座教授，博士生导师，博士后导师。出生于中国，在南开大学取得硕士学位后于 1988 年赴美留学。于 1993 年春获美国纽约州立大学博士学位，之后在美国任教多年，于 2002 年获终身正教授，2007 年起担任澳门大学教授。主要研究领域为比较犯罪学、比较刑事司法、毒品犯罪、社会科学方法论与社会统计学等。

刘建宏教授是国际知名的犯罪学教授，当选为众多国际著名犯罪学组织的领导。于 2009 年当选亚洲犯罪学学会创始会长并于 2013 年再次当选（2009–2015），目前担任国际犯罪学学会学术委员会主席 (2014–2019)、亚洲犯罪学学会会员大会主席 (2016–2019)、世界著名学术组织“坎贝尔合作组织刑事司法指导委员会”委员 (2009–) 等国际学术领导职务。担任《亚洲犯罪学杂志》主编 (Springer publishing)、《亚洲犯罪学及刑事司法研究》系列丛书主编（Springer Publishing），另外担任近 20 部犯罪学杂志包括著名的《英国犯罪学》杂志 (British Journal of Criminology) 等 5 种 SSCI 杂志的编委。

刘建宏教授著作颇丰，其独著、主编及合编学术著作 29 部，发表学术杂志文章 66 篇（其中 SSCI 37 篇）及学术书籍章节 34 篇。刘建宏教授是亚洲犯罪学的领军学者，他提出的亚洲范式和关系主义司法理论为亚洲犯罪学的发展提供了重要的理论支持。

刘建宏教授曾与美国犯罪学学会副会长麦斯纳教授等共获美国国家科学研究基金奖〔US National Science Foundation (SES–0351014) 2004〕在中国进行犯罪学研究。

2006 年获美国国务院福布来特学者奖 (Fulbright Scholar Award, from USA Fulbright Commission 2006－2007)。2011 年 7 月应世界经济论坛主席施瓦布 · 克劳斯教授邀请参加世界经济论坛智库“ 全球议程委员会有组织犯罪委员会 ”研究全球热点问题，为各国各界提供政策咨询建议。2011 年应联合国亚太中心邀请担任顾问主持东亚及太平洋地区海洛英走私研究项目。2015 年由斯德哥尔摩犯罪学基金会任命为“ 斯德哥尔摩犯罪学奖 ”的专家提名者。2015 年担任欧洲研究委员会的基金审查员 (Grant Reviewer)。2016 年度获美国犯罪学学会授予“ 弗里达 · 艾德勒杰出学者奖 (Freda Adler Distinguished Scholar Award) ”，以表彰他在国际犯罪学领域的贡献和杰出的学术成就。

刘建宏教授长期活跃在国际前沿学术领域，在众多所国际著名大学兼任教授、研究员等学术职务。应邀担任重要会议主旨发言 (Keynote speaker) 几十次。刘建宏教授在他的学术活动中努力消除西方社会对中国的偏颇认识，对积极促进中外学者合作交流做出了重要贡献。

Preface

Louise Shelley

China's role as a permanent member of the Security Council of the United Nations strong has given it the opportunity to respond to global terrorism. The UN Security Council, since December 2014, has unanimously adopted several measures against terrorism, particularly, in regards to terrorist financing. China has contributed to the UN's leadership in this area because it comprehends the importance of the terrorist threat not only for individuals but also for global political stability and international trade. The increased threat of global terrorism has become apparent because of the rise of ISIS. ISIS is not just a problem for the Middle East because it has recruited fighters from diverse regions of the world and has claimed responsibility for attacks committed in North America, Europe, Africa and Asia. Therefore, terrorism is a global threat in a way that has not been seen previously.

Terrorism's costs are often evaluated primarily in political termsbut terrorist acts also have significant economic as well as human costs. Terrorism disrupts the global economy and international trade. Acts of terrorism threaten shipping routes, increase the risks and costs of airplane travel and reduces tourism. With terrorism's impacts on transport networks, supplies of raw materials may be disrupted and the ease and costs of international trade is increased.

The essays included in this collection were produced for a major conference on terrorism held in Hangzhou at the Zhejiang Police College in June 2015. This conference brought together foreign experts with Chinese thinkers on the topic who provided important commentaries on this important topic. Following this stimulating exchange, the initial papers were revised by the western scholars taking into account the important points raised by Chinese analysts. The papers presented here reflect more developed arguments, and the essays in this collection show that more than legitimate trade is affected. Not only is licit trade undermined by terrorism but illicit trade is an important funding source for the perpetuation of terrorism.

Much scholarship produced on terrorism looks at the national security challenge posed by terrorism. Because these papers are the result of a conference conducted at a major law enforcement institution, they focus more on the intersection of crime and terrorism. They highlight the fact that not only are terrorist acts criminal but that criminal activity helps drive terrorism in many regions of the world. This is particularly the focus on the essays by Professors Savona and Shelley.

The first part of the book provides two broad essays focusing on core elements of contemporary terrorism. Professor Shelley's contribution focuses on the interaction of crime, corruption and terrorism. She suggests that the interaction of these three phenomena have destabilizing impacts and the consequences of terrorism are often felt far from the initial point of interaction of the three components of the "dirty entanglement" (crime, corruption and terrorism).Shelley points out that while transnational crime is an increasingly significant problem, terrorism has become ever more dependent on crime both for its financing as well as the logistics of its operations. Terrorism, like transnational crime, is one of the most negative consequences of globalization. Globalization has facilitated increased movement of goods and people, new and enhanced forms of communication and has made it possible to hide the illicit in the global supply chains for licit goods. ISIS may be the most active terrorist organization until now. It exploits the cracks in the global financial system but it is only one of many terrorist organizations thathas done this in recent years.

ProfessorViano's contribution, the second essay in part one provides a sweeping introduction to contemporary jihadi terrorism. He examines the role of religion, finance, recruitment and global politics in the development of this terrorism. As a scholar with a strong grounding in theology, he is able to analyze the way that ISIS manipulates elements of the Islamic faith to recruit and mobilize individuals. He points out that the construction of the so called "Caliphate" is a strong draw for both male and female recruits to ISIS. Professor

Viano also looks at the "lone wolf" terrorism that is random and contrasts this with collective acts of terrorism. He also examines the financial flows to terrorist groups, a perspective that will be analyzed in greater depth in part 2 of the book.

The second part of the book examines the diverse forms of illegal activity that fund contemporary terrorism, especially analyzing the focus on financial support for ISIS. Professor Savona and Ms.Pecile look at different conflicts in the global community and the illicit trade that perpetuates these conflicts. Their case analysis focuses on diverse regions of the world. They look at the criminal activity that funds Boko Haram in Nigeria, the ISIS exploitation of oil and antiquities and the heroin business in Afghanistan and the drug trade in Syria. In all these cases, illicit trade has helped perpetuate these conflicts. They suggest that the reduction of opportunities for this trade is an effective way to counter terrorism.

Professor Shelley's chapter on the funding of ISIS points out that ISIS is not the first terrorist group to use diversified forms of illicit activity, to seek to take advantage of geographic opportunities and to tax the cross-border flow of goods. What is distinctive about ISIS is their ability to generate hundreds of millions of dollars in annual revenues that has allowed them to sustain a large military force and provide some services in the territory they now occupy. Terrorists need to secure supply chains, recruit personnel and must obtain the professional services that they need to finance their operations. ISIS is shown to have emerged from al-Qaeda of Iraq and the Saddam Hussein's Baathist government and used the corruption and criminal activity of previous regimes to its advantage. Countering the financing of ISIS requires more than a military perspective but a whole of society approach including the business community and citizens, researchers and the media to educate citizens.

The last chapter in the collection, also by Professor Shelley, focuses on the WMD trade that operates on a different economic logic——one based not on volume but on scarcity and risk. The illicit trade in WMD leads to the ultimate asymmetric threat. A WMD attack of any kind—nuclear, biological, or chemical——could have many serious and long-term consequences. This threat has become an increasing concern as ISIS has had proximity to the chemical weapons of Syria and ISIS has shown an interest in other forms of WMD. Therefore, the United Nations Security Council in Resolution 2195 has affirmed that the arms trade is an element of the convergence of crime and terrorism. It is possibly the most dangerous convergence that we face because it could undermine the sustainability of the planet, lead to greater loss of human life than most terrorist attacks and could long have long term health consequences for those who reside in regions where WMD has been deployed.

In conclusion, this collection on terrorism, that represents work written by leaders in the international criminological community show that terrorism is not a distinct problem. But unlike other terrorism studies that focus on its political and security implications, this collection should help a Chinese community understand in greater depth why an understanding of crime is an important tool in understanding contemporary terrorism. Moreover, criminological insights can help provide important tools to combat the global problem of the rise of terrorism.

序言（中文版）

路易丝·谢利

中国作为联合国的常任理事国，有给全球恐怖主义以强烈回应的可能。2014 年 12 月，联合国安理会一致同意要采取一些措施来打击恐怖主义，尤其是要打击恐怖主义的融资。中国帮助联合国提升了在该领域的领导能力，因为中国已经认识到恐怖主义不仅威胁着各个国家，同时也威胁着全球的政治稳定以及国际贸易。由于 ISIS 的崛起，不断增长的全球恐怖主义威胁正在变得愈加显著。ISIS 不只是中东地区的问题，因为 ISIS 雇佣的士兵来自世界各地，而且它还宣称自己对北美、欧洲、非洲和亚洲的恐怖袭击负责。因此，恐怖主义是一个前所未有的全球性威胁。

我们往往从政治方面来评估恐怖主义带来的损害，但是恐怖行为也会造成明显的经济损失和人力资源的损害。恐怖主义造成了全球经济以及国际贸易的混乱。恐怖行为对航运路线构成了威胁，它提高了航空旅游的风险以及花费，还导致了旅游业的低迷。由于恐怖主义对运输网络造成的影响，原料供应可能会中断，同时国际贸易的贸易总量将减少而贸易成本将增加。

本次征集的论文来自于 2015 年 6 月在杭州的浙江警察学院举行的重要会议。该会议着重讨论了恐怖主义问题。会议中，该领域的国外专家和中国学者齐聚一堂，对于这个重要问题展开了深入的论述。在这场颇具启发性的意见交换之后，西方学者综合了中国研究人员提出的重要观点对原稿进行了修改，使这些文章的观点更为成熟。从此次征集的论文来看，其造成的影响不只限于合法贸易。在合法贸易遭受恐怖主义破坏的同时，非法贸易成为恐怖主义得以存续的重要资金来源。

在恐怖主义造成国家安全方面的挑战这一问题上,目前已经有了大量的学术成果。因为本次会议是由执法机关主办的,所以收录的这些论文将视角放在了犯罪与恐怖主义的交叉领域。这些论文不仅突出了恐怖分子实施犯罪活动的事实,还强调了在全球许多地区,犯罪活动都推动了恐怖主义的发展。萨沃纳教授以及谢利教授的文章尤其关注这一方面。

本书的第一部分提供了两篇概括性论文,它们着眼于当代恐怖主义的核心要素。其中谢利教授的论文关注了犯罪、腐败和恐怖主义的交互作用。她认为,这三种现象的交互作用导致了动荡,也使得恐怖主义造成的危害,在"肮脏的纠缠"的三大要素(犯罪、腐败和恐怖主义)交互作用之后有了巨大的提升。谢利教授指出,跨国犯罪渐渐成为一个重要的问题,而与此同时,如今的恐怖主义更加依赖犯罪来获取资金进行物资流动。恐怖主义和跨国犯罪一样,也是全球化所带来的最主要的负面后果之一。全球化促进了商品和人口的流动,导致更为强大的新型交流方式的产生,也使得非法活动隐藏到合法货物的全球供应链之中成为可能。ISIS 可能是迄今为止最为活跃的恐怖组织之一。ISIS 利用着全球经济系统的漏洞,然而它却只是近些年来这样做的众多恐怖组织中的一个。

第一部分的第二篇文章来自维亚诺教授,该文章对当代宗教极端恐怖主义进行了全面的介绍。他探讨了宗教、金融、征兵和全球政策在该种恐怖主义发展中所扮演的角色。作为一个有着深厚宗教学背景的学者,他能够对 ISIS 通过篡改部分伊斯兰信仰来对征兵和动员的行为进行分析。他指出,建立所谓"阿拉伯帝国"是驱使男性和女性加入 ISIS 的重要动力。同时,维亚诺教授也注意到了那些带有随机性的"独狼式"恐怖主义,并将这种恐怖主义与集体性的恐怖行为进行了比较。他还探讨了恐怖组织资金流的问题,而这个问题将在本书的第二部分进行更深入的分析。

本书的第二部分主要探讨了那些为当代恐怖主义提供资金的各种非法活动,并着重分析了 ISIS 的财政支撑情况。萨沃纳教授与珀西勒女士的文章着眼于国际社会中的各种冲突以及使这些冲突得以延续的非法贸易。他们的案例分析以全球的各种区域为重点。他们着眼于向尼日利亚的极端组织提供资金的犯罪活动,以及 ISIS 的石油和古文物的开发利用,还有阿富汗的海洛因贸易和叙利亚的毒品贸易。在所有这些案例中,非法贸易都为冲突的持续提供了帮助。他们提出,减少这些贸易的机会是打击恐怖主义的一种有效途径。

谢利教授在文章中对于 ISIS 的经费进行了专门的讨论。她指出,ISIS 并不是第一个利用非法活动来赚取经费的恐怖组织,也不是第一个寻找自身的地理条件优势并向过境货物流收税的恐怖组织。ISIS 的与众不同之处在于其能够得到亿万美元的年收入，这使得他们可以维持规模庞大的军事力量并向其控制区域提供一些服务。恐怖分子需要保护自己的供应链、进行人员招募，同时他们必须获得专业的服务来为其自身运作提供资金。ISIS 已经从伊拉克"基地"组织和萨达姆·侯赛因的复兴党政府中脱离了出来，他们利用先前政权的腐败和犯罪行为来形成自己的优势。打击 ISIS 的资金筹集活动不仅需要军事途径，更加需要整个社会的努力，包括工商业界、市民、研究人员，以及媒体对人民的教育。

本次收录的最后一篇文章也来自于谢利教授，她将目光放在了大规模杀伤性武器贸易上，这种贸易有着不一样的经济逻辑——它并不以贸易物的需求数量为存在基础而是以该贸易的稀缺性与风险性为存在基础。大规模杀伤性武器的非法贸易导致了最终的非对称性威胁。不论是核武器、生物武器、化学武器，任何形式的大规模杀伤性武器袭击都会带来严重而长期的后果。考虑到 ISIS 已经十分接近获取叙利亚化学武器这一目标，同时 ISIS 也显示出对其他类型的大规模杀伤性武器的兴趣，大规模杀伤性武器袭击的威胁正在增加。因此，联合国安理会在 2195 号决议中肯定了军火贸易是衔接犯罪与恐怖主义的一个重要因素。这可能是我们所面临的最为危险的一种衔接形式，因为它会破坏地球的可持续性，其所造成的死亡比大多数的恐怖袭击还要更加巨大，并且它还会对那些生活在被部署了大规模杀伤性武器的区域中的人们造成长期的健康危害。

总的来说，本次收录的关于恐怖主义的文献体现了国际犯罪学界领军人物的主要学术成果，并显示出恐怖主义并不是一个清晰的问题。但是不同于其他那些只关注恐怖主义的政治和安全影响的恐怖主义研究，本次收录的论文能够帮助中国社会更深刻地认识到为什么理解犯罪可以成为理解当代恐怖主义的重要方式。此外，犯罪学的视野也能够为我们提供一些重要的工具来打击恐怖主义这一国际问题。

目　录

一、问题的概念化

Part I　Conceptualizing the Problem

二、案例研究

Part II Case Studies

引言:恐怖主义——我国犯罪学的新挑战

刘 建 宏

作为一种日益严重的"非传统安全威胁",恐怖主义犯罪已经逐渐演变成为迫切需要国际社会共同严肃面对的又一重大挑战。恐怖主义犯罪严重损害着国际社会的和平发展以及国际政治经济秩序;严重威胁着受害国家或地区的政权及社会稳定;严重危害着一般民众的生命财产安全;在社会层面造成了极大的恐慌,严重降低了一般民众的日常生活质量。因此,控制恐怖主义的蔓延态势、降低恐怖主义犯罪的威胁、铲除恐怖主义滋生的土壤已经成为包括中国在内的许多国家和社会的共同关切,因而"只有采取持久、全面的对策,促使所有国家及国际和区域组织积极参与和协作,遏制、削弱、孤立恐怖主义威胁并使其失去能力,才能战胜恐怖主义"(United Nations,2014,2015)。但是,在经济全球化、世界一体化趋势的大潮冲刷之下,人类社会发展的不均衡态势并未从根本上得到遏制,在风云变幻的国际关系与地缘政治中不可避免地存在着一些尚待调和的矛盾和利益冲突,因而恐怖主义组织在这些间隙地带总能较为容易地获得生存空间并逐渐发展,获取当地或外界的某些力量或明或暗的支持,进而与特定的政治实体相对抗,危害无辜者的生命和财产安全。

进入21世纪以来,国际恐怖主义势力在世界各地制造了上百起针对平民的恐怖袭击事件,造成了严重损害和后果。2001年发生在美国的"9·11"恐怖事件震惊了整个国际社会,造成了包括几十名华人在内的重大人员伤亡和财产损失,给死难者家属和无辜平民留下了难以抹平的痛苦记忆。2015年11月13日发生在法国巴黎的恐怖主义袭击、2015年10月31日针对俄罗斯客机制造的空难事件、2015年11月18

日中国和挪威的两名人质被杀害等一连串的恐怖主义事件再次引起了国际社会的严重关切和同仇敌忾。实际上，除了联合国五大常任理事国之外，巴基斯坦、阿富汗、伊拉克、叙利亚等许多国家长期以来一直遭受着恐怖主义的威胁和侵害。

毫无例外，在恐怖主义日渐猖獗的国际大背景下，中国也不再是恐怖主义犯罪的真空地带。实际上，近些年来发生在中国的恐怖主义犯罪亦呈现出逐渐恶化的态势。近二十年来，在中国陆续发生了数百起恐怖袭击事件，造成了大量的平民死伤和财产损失。据统计，在 1992 年至 2001 年的十年间，"东突"恐怖组织在新疆维吾尔自治区境内制造了至少两百多起暴力恐怖案件，造成各民族群众、基层干部、宗教人士等 162 人丧生，440 多人受伤。进入 21 世纪以来，恐怖主义犯罪逐渐向其他地区蔓延，其中举国震惊的恐怖主义犯罪事件包括了 2008 年发生在西藏的"3·14"事件、2009 年发生在新疆的"7·5"事件、2013 年 10 月 28 日发生在北京的冲击金水桥事件、2014 年 3 月 1 日发生在云南昆明火车站的滥杀事件等。所有迹象表明，民族分裂势力、恐怖主义势力和宗教极端势力相互纠缠，已经对我国的国家安全、社会经济稳定、人民生命财产安全构成了现实的重大威胁。这不仅需要引起全社会的广泛关注和充分警惕，亦需要不断加强和加深国际合作、经验交流以及学术研究，以有效地应对恐怖主义犯罪的挑战。

然而，如何有效地利用国内法律和综合性措施应对恐怖主义犯罪的威胁，中国还缺乏必要的经验积累和深度的理论研究。从国际范围内来看，包括政治学、国际关系、历史学、社会学、人类学、刑法学等诸多学科已经开始关注恐怖主义犯罪这一特殊类型的犯罪形式（Roberts，2015）；其中作为唯一一门全景式认识犯罪、治理犯罪的社会科学，犯罪学理应为此作出自己独特的学术贡献。而且，犯罪学对恐怖主义犯罪问题的研究应当是超前的、科学的、实用的，而不应该是满足于个案的、反应的、纯理论的学术探讨或经验总结。当然，以犯罪学的理论和方法作为依托对恐怖主义犯罪进行的应用型研究并不是要取代那些负责安全、情报或侦查等工作的实战部门的具体经验和做法，而是希望两者之间形成有效的借鉴和交流，进而推动我们全面、理性、科学地了解恐怖主义犯罪产生的历史、文化、政治和社会原因，并提出有效的治理对策。遗憾的是，迄今为止，犯罪学在提供有助于人们认识和控制这一新型犯罪的知识和技术方面差强人意——那些建立在社会学或心理学基础之上的传统犯罪学理论无法完全胜任于分析和理解恐怖主义犯罪或恐怖主义分子；而基于新古典犯罪学思想的传统刑事司法措施或基于机会理论的情境预防措施也难以从根本上控制恐怖主义犯罪引起的物质损失和精神创伤（Von，2011）。

为了取得国际反恐合作的更大成功，首先需要在恐怖主义犯罪的界定上凝聚更加广泛的国际共识。遗憾的是，目前各国政府以及学术界对于恐怖主义犯罪的概念仍旧没有取得公认的、一致的定义。其中一个重要的障碍就是如何界定恐怖主义犯罪不仅是一个法律问题，在更多的方面表现为政治问题、宗教问题或历史问题。“它（恐怖主义，笔者注）是一个充满政治性的概念，……一个看起来是语义学的问题，本质上却是不同意识形态的冲突，意味着我们是否把某个事件视为恐怖主义取决于我们的政治观点”（何秉松，2001，p.54）。从世界范围内来看，某些政府倾向于将针对本国的某些政治性暴力事件定义为恐怖主义犯罪，但是却有选择地将针对其他国家或社会的类似暴力事件定义为恐怖主义犯罪或非恐怖主义犯罪，其中考量的标准主要是当时的政治利益而非科学上的定义。换而言之，不但在学术界对于恐怖主义犯罪的内涵和外延还没有达成足够充分的共识，而且在世界范围内对于特定恐怖主义组织的具体认定过程中也不可避免地被掺杂进了许多其他错综复杂的因素。

正是由于恐怖主义犯罪具有的政治属性，因此在定义恐怖主义犯罪时，客体本位的犯罪定义通常不得不让位于主体本位的犯罪定义。主体本位的犯罪定义更加强调掌握着话语权的定义者的适格与主导地位，他们的利益诉求和价值取向决定了他们将何种行为定义为恐怖主义犯罪，而将另外的在行为特征上相似或相同的活动并不定义为恐怖主义犯罪。从世界范围内来看，在认定国内恐怖主义与国际恐怖主义犯罪时采取双重或多重标准就变得格外普遍和平常。对具体的恐怖活动或组织是否应该被认定为恐怖主义犯罪或恐怖主义组织，不同的政府组织和政治势力乃至具有不同政治观点和宗教信仰的普通民众可能有着完全不同的观点。因此，相比于定义其他类型的犯罪或跨国有组织犯罪，对于恐怖主义犯罪的定义要取得共识，特别是在国际范围内取得足够的共识将显得更加困难、更加复杂。特别是，当民族分裂分子或宗教极端分子将恐怖犯罪活动作为其实现政治目的的主要手段时，其他政治势力对此的默许甚至或明或暗的支持为有效打击此类恐怖主义犯罪增添了巨大的变数。

但是，这并不是说国际社会和学术界对于恐怖主义犯罪的概念完全没有共识（Schmid，2012；Schmid，Jongman，& Horowitz，1988）。王牧（2003，p.16）指出，“恐怖主义有两个最基本的特征，这就是：政治目的和暴力手段。这两个基本特征决定了恐怖主义的最本质的方面。”Saleem and Azam Tahir（2013）对西方语境下对恐怖主义犯罪的 23 种定义进行了荟萃分析，提出了恐怖主义犯罪的三个特征——暴力或威胁使用暴力、政治目标、针对平民。笔者认为，恐怖主义犯罪在行为上具有的共同特征至少应该包括以下四点：

1. 政治指向相对明确

如前所述，恐怖主义犯罪具有政治犯罪的基本特征。但是，另一方面，由于恐怖主义犯罪具有严重的反人类性质，其社会危害性往往超出某个政治实体的范围，因此在国际实践中并不将恐怖主义犯罪作为一般的政治犯罪加以对待。例如，在国际法的框架下，恐怖主义犯罪是一种可引渡罪。如不能引渡，则必须起诉。但是应该看到，尽管恐怖主义犯罪具有滥杀的倾向，但是从其政治指向来说，一般是较为具体而明确的。正因如此，在当前的国际政治形势下，恐怖主义组织可以充分利用各种政治势力的矛盾或敌对关系以获得相应的生存空间。

2. 武装性质

恐怖主义组织或个人实施恐怖犯罪的主要手段就是暴力或以暴力相威胁，但是它与一般的暴力犯罪有着很大的不同。为了达到恐怖的效果，恐怖主义组织往往需要制造、购买和使用杀伤力更大的武器，其中最为常见的恐怖袭击武器就是枪支与炸弹。尽管在不同的国家或社会，恐怖主义组织的武装程度有所不同，但是它们为了在与政府和一般民众对抗的过程中尽可能地保持自身的优势，总会不择手段地武装自己。国际范围内愈演愈烈的军火走私贸易为恐怖主义组织提供着充分的武器装备和技术支持。

3. 有组织性

尽管有些犯罪学家认为恐怖主义犯罪与有组织犯罪有着很多不同，但实际上“恐怖主义犯罪几乎具有有组织犯罪的所有特征”（Ferreira，1997，p.120）。即便在“独狼式”的恐怖袭击中，犯罪分子通常与某个恐怖组织具有较为紧密的互动关系或直接隶属于某个恐怖组织。但是，某些恐怖主义并不一定具有传统意义上稳定的、坚固的组织结构，因此消灭某些所谓“头目”并不一定具有宣称的决定意义。以“基地”组织为例，美国政府坚持认为这一恐怖组织有着严密的组织结构，拉登就是其中级别最高的“一号头目”，当然还有“二号”、“三号”等。甚至有些“专家”给出了“基地”组织的成员数量估计，认为大约在1200名。但是，随着西方国家反恐战争的深入，所谓的“基地”头目被一一铲除，被关押的“基地”组织成员数量也越来越多，但是可以看到被“基地”组织宣称负责的恐怖袭击并未销声匿迹，甚至一度愈演愈烈。由此可以推断，恐怖主义的组织架构和严密程度并不一定类似于人们熟知的企事业单位或政府机关，而且不同的恐怖主义组织在组织性上也可能存在着巨大差异。

4. 滥杀平民

尽管恐怖主义犯罪的政治指向较为明确，但是为了在社会层面上制造更大的恐慌，而且在政治上居于显要地位的政府部门或敏感机关等重要部门一般都会存在着更为严密的防卫或保卫力量，因此恐怖主义组织存在着故意或放任滥杀平民的倾向（Elbakidze & Jin，2012）。无论是发生在美国的“9·11”事件，还是发生在中国北京的冲击金水桥事件，以及发生在法国巴黎的爆炸事件都无一例外地造成了大量的无辜平民伤亡。从这个意义上而言，恐怖主义明显地具有反人类、反社会的性质，理应受到人类社会的一致谴责和抵制。例如，自杀式的炸弹袭击在中东地区屡见不鲜，但是普通民众往往仅仅凭借刻板印象简单地认为袭击者都是宗教狂热分子或异教徒，他们的极端行为都是受到了各自宗教教义的极端曲解所致。但是实际上人们往往忽略或在潜意识中不愿承认宗教上的极端也通常掺杂了由于政治上长期的不公平而导致的极端负面情感（Richards，2015）。宗教与政治的关系错综复杂，一成不变的是，包括了宗教极端主义的各种恐怖主义组织总是试图以暴力滥杀无辜平民造成社会恐慌进而达到政治目的。因此，宗教界的有识之士及普通的信教群众与世俗社会一样对于恐怖主义犯罪深恶痛绝。

恐怖主义的存在和发展有着错综复杂的历史、社会、政治以及宗教等诸多方面的深层次原因（Coggins，2015）。关于产生一般犯罪的历史条件和社会条件，马克思有一段著名的论述："犯罪——孤立的个人反对统治阶级的斗争，和法一样，也不是随心所欲地产生的。相反，犯罪和现行统治都产生于相同的条件。"相比于一般犯罪，恐怖主义产生、存在和发展的原因、条件更加错综复杂，因而传统的犯罪原因理论难以单独承担解释恐怖主义原因并指导相应的实践对策的重任。因此，犯罪学家必须充分借鉴历史学、社会学、宗教学、国际政治学、法学等其他相邻学科的研究成果和国际范围内打击和治理恐怖主义犯罪的正反两方面的经验教训，才有可能为科学地研究恐怖主义犯罪、理性地治理恐怖主义犯罪提供必要的智识基础。为此，本书收录并翻译了国际犯罪学界三位大师的五篇论文，希望为国内同行提供必要的借鉴。

显然，恐怖主义组织并不能从其常见的恐怖袭击活动中获得足够的经济利益，因而它们必然需要借助其他犯罪活动或与其他犯罪组织、群体或个体相互勾结以建立经济基础。谢利教授在其论文《犯罪、腐败和恐怖主义之间的关系》中借用量子力学中的术语将三者之间的关系界定为"肮脏的纠缠"。谢利教授提醒我们，恐怖主义犯罪通常与跨国有组织犯罪、当地的政府腐败和公司腐败等传统类型的犯罪有着错综复杂的关联，而且一旦三者纠缠在一起，其危害后果将远远超过每种犯罪单独造成的损失。因此，"国际社会应该更多地关注腐败问题，来限制跨国犯罪和恐怖主义。腐败作为问题的核心元素，却总是常常为人们所忽视。"这样的警示提醒着我们在恐怖主义犯罪猖獗的地区，不能忽视当地的腐败犯罪或有组织犯罪等传统类型的犯罪，应当有意识地深入调查并斩断它们之间的纠缠关系，消除它们之间的共生现象。

恐怖主义组织为了最大程度地制造恐怖效应，继而达到自身的政治目的，在犯罪手段的选择上无所不用其极。其中最令世人担忧的一种可能就是恐怖分子借助其他犯罪分子通过某种渠道获得包括生化武器甚至是核武器在内的大规模杀伤性武器。谢利教授在《非法核贸易:行为主体和新兴趋势》一文中给我们敲响了警钟。“非法核材料贸易以及对这种贸易的资助都是由各种罪犯与腐败人士进行的。因此,其他情况下产生的某些犯罪学理论与概念有助于让我们理解犯罪人,以及那些令非法核贸易更为便利的条件与关系网络。”谢利教授在此提醒我们包括腐败等传统类型的犯罪以及当地的社会解组状况可能为恐怖主义分子获取更具毁灭性的武器提供了便利。因此,传统的犯罪学理论以及情境犯罪预防技术在帮助我们认识恐怖主义犯罪的发生机制以及治理此类犯罪方面大有用武之地。

案例分析的方法可以让我们深入地了解特定恐怖主义组织的发展历程,并为当今国际社会应对特定恐怖主义组织的威胁提供具体化的指导。ISIS 就是当前最为活跃的恐怖主义犯罪的代表组织。谢利教授在《恐怖主义商业:基于 ISIS 的个案分析》一文中敏锐地观察到,“ISIS 之所以能成功获取人员、武器及资金,是因为它发挥着企业的功能。事实上,它是已知的最为有效的恐怖主义企业。”因而,“打击恐怖主义就要像打击一个商业竞争对手一样。这要求我们的政策不只是依靠军事力量,还要依靠政府部门之间以及政府部门与私营部门之间的相互合作。”谢利教授进一步预言,“将 ISIS 作为企业来进行打击可能将是今后打击恐怖主义的一个主要模式。”与此相呼应的是,在联合国层面上,安理会分别在 2014 年 11 月和 2015 年 2 月通过的 2195 号决议和 2199 号决议均特别强调了切断恐怖主义融资渠道以及冻结其资金、金融资产或经济资源等手段的重要性。

类似地,萨沃纳与珀西勒在他们的论文《打破冲突、非法贸易条件与犯罪组织或恐怖组织的动态发展所组成的循环圈》中通过分析三个具体的案例,有力地论证了“薄弱的法律制度以及准国家的失败是导致恐怖组织成功的两个初始条件”、“非法贸易是恐怖主义发展的中心”。他们在结论部分指出,“减少机会的方法才是解决犯罪组织与恐怖组织不断蔓延的根本之道,也是打破冲突、非法贸易条件、犯罪组织与恐怖组织之间的恶性循环的唯一选择。”

国际犯罪学会主席埃米利奥 · C.维亚诺在《正在增长的恐怖主义:认识其原因,达到有效预防和成功防御》一文中雄辩地指出,尽管防护性的项目和措施颇有价值,但是“从长远来看,所有这些项目在持续且有效地减少全球恐怖主义威胁方面,都不是非常成功”。借鉴埃博拉病毒防治等流行病学的经验,维亚诺教授指出,“如果恐怖主义更可能是一个政治现象而非宗教现象的话,那么我们就必须从政治观念、政治现实以及政治问题方面着手来预防和打击恐怖主义。”因此,“在极端分子和其可能的支持者之间制造裂痕和阻隔,在某些时候还是有可能的也是可以完成的。致力于处理那些合理的怨愤，并同时为政治上的差异寻求一个中间地带，这些努力不能也不应该被理解为是试图去向极端主义者和原教旨主义者妥协。我们更应该说，这是一个能够减少政治压迫、政治对立以及政治上的种族歧视的有效工具，最重要的是，它能降低极端主义者以及暴力手段对于那些恐怖主义支持者的诱惑力和吸引力。”

的确，正如中国的一句谚语所言，“得民心者得天下”——民心的向背才是反恐能否真正取得成功的最终决定因素。恐怖主义组织以及反恐的力量有时会将一时的“成功”作为重大成果而沾沾自喜甚至“胜利”。然而，毫不奇怪的是，当恐怖主义组织宣称获得重大“成功”之时，往往就是其自我毁灭的开始。“多行不义必自毙”，恐怖主义者的倒行逆施必然会促进国际范围内反恐力量的广泛合作和强烈反应，进而加速恐怖主义组织的灭亡进程。例如，策划了“9·11”事件的“基地”组织、残暴统治阿富汗长达数年之久的塔利班集团，最终走向了命中注定的末路。但是，另一方面，反恐力量有时也会基于某些局部的胜利作出过分乐观的估计。当西方的政治人物和一般民众在庆祝“基地”组织的头号人物拉登被打死，乃至某些“极权”政府被推翻等重要事件之时，人们却遗憾地看到在全球范围内恐怖主义的威胁并未随着这些所谓的“胜利”而销声匿迹，反而呈现出愈演愈烈的恶化态势。

只有理性而科学地研究恐怖主义产生及不断恶化的深层次原因并逐步加以消除，才能从治本的层次上遏制恐怖主义的现实威胁。简而言之，人类社会的普遍发展与共同繁荣是消除恐怖主义的社会经济基础，因此通过社会发展来预防包括恐怖主义在内的所有形态的犯罪必须被提高到应有的顶层设计高度并切实得到加强和落实。十余年来国际范围内的反恐战争的经验教训足以表明在反恐工作中坚持国际合作、标本兼治、加强社会经济协调发展的重要性和紧迫性。尽管从根本上治理恐怖主义犯罪的深层次原因绝非易事，但是真正反对恐怖主义的各国政府必须正视这些深层次原因，切实有效地作出努力。

总之，反恐力量也需要从意识形态、信仰体系、社会公平、经济发展、文化共荣等方面争取更广泛、更深层的民意支持。单纯的军事打击或高压统治不可能真正地、长久地消除恐怖主义滋生的社会、经济和文化基础。因此，一方面，要针锋相对地打击那些冒头的恐怖主义犯罪组织及其具体的恐怖主义行动；另一方面，必须从更高远的战略角度广泛地争取民众的真正支持，坚持人民反恐的理念和方向，消除恐怖主义发生和发展的土壤。只有坚持标本兼治、切实提高社会治理的能力和效率、促进社会经济的和谐发展，才能从根本上赢得民心，取得反对恐怖主义斗争的最终胜利。

一、问题的概念化

Part I Conceptualizing the Problem

犯罪、腐败和恐怖主义之间的关系

路易丝·谢利(Louise Shelley)①

犯罪、腐败与恐怖主义之间的相互作用,引用量子物理学的术语“纠缠”(entanglements)来比喻,称其为“肮脏的纠缠”(dirty entanglements)。② 一旦这三种元素相互作用,其产生的后果将大大超过作用之初。这个问题促成了当今世界极不稳定的局面。世界不稳定的一部分原因在于,伴随大量的非法移民、流离失所的人群,以及一个从西非出发,穿越北非,直至中东和巴基斯坦,并可能进一步向中亚延伸的大范围不稳定弧带的存在。2015 年已成为自第二次世界大战以来最不稳定的年份。在这些区域中,肮脏的纠缠导致的后果正在扩增,变得比相互作用之初更为严重。因此,我们目前正在研究的是我们大家都必须努力解决的全球问题。

幸运的是,我们都是联合国大家庭的一分子,而联合国正在日益积极地打击跨国犯罪并且破坏其与恐怖主义的联系。跨国犯罪可以不依靠恐怖主义而存在,但恐怖主义却不能脱离犯罪和跨国犯罪而生存。而腐败一直是有组织犯罪得以实施的关键。因此,正如联合国安理会在 2195 号决议中所认定的那样,如今这已经成为实施跨国犯罪与腐败的关键。③

---

① 路易丝·谢利(Louise Shelley),美国乔治·梅森大学公共政策与国际关系学院教授,奥马尔·L.和南茜赫斯特讲席教授,恐怖主义、跨国犯罪和腐败研究中心主任。

② Louise Shelley, *Dirty Entanglements: Corruption, Crime and Terrorism*, Cambridge: Cambridge University Press, 2014.

③ http://www.un.org/en/sc/documents/resolutions/2014.shtml, December 19, 2014.

在过去的二十年，跨国犯罪数量急剧增长。而如今，跨国犯罪的急剧增长，令我们无法再忽视其存在。在2004年联合国安理会的决议与宣言中，跨国犯罪只出现了4次，而到了2014年，这一数字已经超过30次。这表明，在过去的10年里，跨国犯罪的援引率增长了8倍，并且其中绝大多数出现在比宣言更具分量的决议中。① 这种增长并不是突然出现的，而是随着对该问题关注度的逐年提升而逐渐产生的。这表明，联合国在对威胁安全的首要问题的认识上有了巨大的转变。中国作为安理会的成员之一，在构建相关的框架体系方面能起到重要的作用。

对跨国犯罪的关注是必要的，因为在全球化、自由贸易、科技和松散的金融法规的共同作用下，世界上已经产生了一些堪称有史以来最强大、最高效的犯罪网络。现在，不论是在发达国家还是在发展中国家，许多国家和地区都逐渐把跨国犯罪视为一种安全威胁。② 在发展中国家，跨国犯罪所带来的影响可能是最为剧烈的，因为那里缺乏打击这一威胁的社会能力以及政府能力。

跨国犯罪对诸多方面造成了挑战：政治安全、经济体制、国家及其公民的福祉。跨国犯罪这样一个威胁是由那些或独立于国家或已经融入国家或对国家有强烈影响的非国家行为者造成的。大量的研究表明，跨国犯罪是一种非对称威胁，因为其造成的损害与其组织的规模、资金不成比例。跨国犯罪与恐怖分子联系的日益密切也增加了我们的安全挑战。

最大的跨国犯罪网络运作于多个大洲，拥有几十亿美元的年营业额，它能威胁整个国家甚至是整个地区。这些关系网络常常运作于发达国家、发展中国家和冲突地区。它们的功能横跨了洲际供应商、消费者和金融中心三个方面。

有的现代罪犯管理着那些拥有先进技术的高效的全球供应链。为了能够高效运作，他们特别喜欢利用那些拥有良好运输系统、交通设施和基础设施的国家。许多犯罪组织也存在合法的商业利益。因此，他们总是以合法形式来掩盖其违法活动。他们经常进行分包和转包，就像一般的商业公司那样。

起诉那些聪明的跨境犯罪者们是极其困难的。他们能通过执法与监管的漏洞来获取利润，并同时将违法行为隐藏在复杂的供应链中。虽然联合国提供了一套框架体系来定义跨境犯罪，但要想确保有效地抑制住这一日渐严重的问题，还得取决于各国的机制。而犯罪者们正利用了各国间缺乏统一立法这一点。

---

① Ugi Zvekic,"Reinforcing Multilateral Approaches to Transnational Organized Crime by Strengthening Local Ownership and Accountability",Global Initiative Against Transnational Organized Crime,2015,3.

② http://www.globalinitiative.net/programs/towards-a-global-strategy/; Strategy to Combat Transnational Organized Crime,https://www.whitehouse.gov/.../transnational-crime/strategy.

一、对腐败界定的缺失

尽管经过了多年的尝试,联合国还是无法对腐败的概念进行界定。迄今为止,没有任何国际公约涉及这一课题。不同的国际机构对腐败有不同的界定,有些比较狭窄,而有些则比较宽泛。在较为宽泛的界定中,腐败并不只限于政府人员。由于跨国犯罪总是频繁地与商界相交叉,所以为了避免对我们分析造成限制,不对腐败的定义进行限缩似乎十分重要。世界银行将腐败界定为"为了私利滥用公职"。但这个定义太过狭窄,它没有包括私人主体的腐败行为。亚洲发展银行对腐败的界定包含了私人主体。[①] 笔者认为这个界定更为合适,因为如此我们就可以把那些工作在银行里的银行职员所进行的,为贩毒集团或是各种恐怖组织进行的洗钱行为,认定为腐败行为。

腐败是一个复杂的现象,在地方、国家乃至全球层面都有存在。[②] 腐败所带来的影响,会随涉及的领域和环境的不同而产生差异,但是不论在何种环境中,腐败都是犯罪、恐怖主义和其他社会疾病得以发展和存续的重要因素。我们可以把腐败看作促使有组织犯罪、暴力犯罪和恐怖主义增长的孵化器。[③] 而这一认识反过来说也同样成立。和社会的动荡一样,犯罪也培育着腐败。所以,我们对抗的所有这些,都是十分复杂并且能够自我强化的。

二、联合国如何界定跨国犯罪

联合国认为跨国有组织犯罪是指,由三人或多人所组成的、在一定时期内存在的、以实施一项或多项严重犯罪为目标的犯罪集团,其为了获得直接或间接的经济或物质利益而进行的一切活动。这一定义出自 2001 年联合国通过的跨国有组织犯罪公约。[④]

---

① Asian Development Bank, Anticorruption: Our Framework and Strategies, 1998, http://www.adb.org/documents/anticorruption-policy.

② Robert Klitgaard, *Controlling Corruption*, Berkeley: University of California Press, 1988.

③ Martha Elena Badel Rueda, *Costos de la corrupción en Colombia*, República de Colombia Departamento Nacional de Planeación Unidad de Análisis Macroeconómico, Documento 111, May 24, 1999, 62.

④ http://www.unodc.org/unodc/en/treaties/CTOC/index.html.

严重犯罪指任何构成可受到最高至少四年监禁刑的犯罪行为。贩卖人口与贩毒都是典型的严重有组织犯罪,然而对贩毒的刑罚总是远远重于贩卖人口。

同时,有组织结构的集团是指,并非是为了立即实施一项犯罪而随意组成的集团,而是具有某种明确的组织结构的团体。一些有组织犯罪集团呈现高度的结构化,并伴有固定的教化仪式,例如西西里岛的黑手党组织。① 而另一些则更不固定、更加灵活,但仍具有明确的领导和下属划分。

有以下四种情形之一的有组织犯罪可以认为是跨国有组织犯罪:

1)在一个以上国家实施犯罪——例如,在一个国家种植毒品,在另一个国家进行加工,然后贩卖到第三个国家的情形。

2)虽在一国实施,但其准备、筹划、指挥或控制的实质性部分发生在另一国的犯罪——例如南非的非法搜猎犀牛的行为,其依靠犯罪网络穿越莫桑比克边境将犀牛角运至越南。

3)虽在一国实施,但涉及在一个以上国家从事犯罪活动的有组织犯罪集团——例如意大利黑手党或者中国的三合会,他们有覆盖全球的多国犯罪网络。

4)虽在一国实施,但对于另一国有重大影响——例如假冒香烟的行为,它会对合法的烟草公司和公民的健康带来损害。而且这种行为也为世界上许多地方的恐怖主义提供了重要的资金来源。

虽然我们对跨国犯罪有了一个共同的界定,但要想解决它依然存在困难,因为我们只能依据国内法来打击跨国犯罪,但是罪犯却是在全球范围实施着犯罪。如果一个尼日利亚的欺诈者通过网络欺骗了法国、澳大利亚和美国的信用卡用户,那么这起犯罪的实施地应该算是哪里呢?若抛开管辖权问题,谁会有起诉的积极性呢?在现实世界中情况只会更加复杂,如此一来,犯罪分子就能掩藏自己的赃物来源,而中间商也可以声称自己毫不知情。

自冷战结束,苏联解体,犯罪的全球化开始不断加速。冷战的结束和超级大国冲突的终结,导致了全球许多地区之间那些发挥隔离作用的边界开始崩溃。大规模的超级大国冲突被许多更小的地区冲突所替代。这些冲突导致了跨国犯罪的兴起,因为这些犯罪活动被用来维持冲突的继续。犯罪提供了购买武器和维持军事力量的资金。从这些冲突地区逃离的大量移民导致近十年来偷渡与人口走私的兴起。

全球化的这些"阴暗面"(dark side)给世界各国带来了巨大的挑战——没有哪个现代国家可以避免这一威胁。跨国犯罪网络之所以能够在全世界成功运行是因为他

---

① Jane and Peter Schneider, Reversible Destiny: Mafia, Antimafia, and the Struggle in Palermo Berkeley and Los Angeles, University of California Press, 2003.

们可以做到以下几点:1)通过操纵全球金融系统和交易系统中的那些松散的规则来进行金钱和财产的转移;2)利用法律制度和立法的空白,以及多边地区犯罪监控的复杂性;3)利用政府间的不信任与缺乏联系;4)利用那些有着卓越的运输系统、交通设施和金融服务的关键地区里的基础设施;5)通过复杂的供应链来隐藏犯罪活动;6)利用网络空间形成自己的优势。

三、跨国有组织犯罪有多严重

根据联合国的调查,早在20世纪80年代,麻醉品交易就至少占到了全球经济的2%,这等同于钢铁和纺织品的国际贸易量。[①] 从那以后,世界上许多地区变成了毒品的生产地和销售市场,这使得毒品问题变得更加严重。然而,正如我们随后要讨论的,跨国罪犯与恐怖分子已经极大地拓展了自己的经营活动范围,变得更多样化,不再仅仅局限于贩毒这一种。

跨国犯罪者们的大量经济活动所产生的危害并不是均匀地分布于各个地区。对于冲突区域和那些缺乏法律治理且没有能力处理这一问题的国家,其产生的危害更加严重。这些非法贸易带来的后果十分严重,它会暗中破坏地球的可持续性,也会通过假药和有毒有害食品来残害消费者,还会暗中破坏国家的发展。

毒品贸易与其他形式的非法贸易的衔接,给中国带来了特殊的问题。正如某官方报告的那样,非洲的贩毒嫌疑人已经成为巴基斯坦毒枭的代理人。[②] 我们研究中心——TraCCC,在研究非洲象牙的非法贸易及其与毒品贸易的关联时,也发现了同样的现象。我们的研究揭示,这是一个肮脏的纠缠现象,因为其联系着跨国犯罪与恐怖主义,正如巴基斯坦毒枭既与恐怖活动有所牵连,又同时从腐败中获得帮助。因此,毒贩通过收益颇丰的象牙贸易而变得富有,这也使得他们拥有更强的能力来经营毒品行业。

在阿富汗,跨国罪犯、腐败官员和恐怖组织都从事着非法活动,这导致了该国有着世界上犯罪化最严重的经济。在过去十年中的一些时候,阿富汗经济中至少50%是依靠于贩毒、非法木材贸易以及对贸易路线上的在途商品进行勒索所产生的犯罪

---

① United Nations International Drug Control Programme, World Drug Report, Oxford: Oxford University Press, 1997.

② Zhang Yan, "Police Face Hard Fight over Drugs", China Daily USA, June 25, 2015, usa.chinadaily.com/cn/china/2015-06/25/content_21097666.htm.

收益。[1]

当跨国犯罪组织控制了如此大比重的经济，投资就会失去作用。中美洲是世界上暴力情况最严重的地区之一，据世界银行估计，在这里暴力犯罪造成了大约 8%的经济损失。[2]

由于跨国有组织犯罪和恐怖主义组织的运作都依赖于腐败，所以只要这些组织以某个国家作为基地并进行运作，那么该国的腐败就会日趋严重。虽然腐败问题在发展中国家最为显著，但问题的根源并不仅仅出在发展中国家的身上。发达国家的腐败，尤其是在金融市场之中的腐败，为非法资本提供了洗钱的可能，这使得跨国犯罪组织得以持续运作。[3]

犯罪分子与恐怖分子的合作遍及全球各地，这意味着我们需要携手来共同面对这一问题。因此，我们不仅需要一起构建法律体系，还需要共同研究相应的对策。

四、国际社会该如何打击跨国有组织犯罪和恐怖主义

针对跨国犯罪的联合国决议

1988 年，联合国通过了《联合国禁止非法贩运麻醉药品和精神药物公约》（也称《维也纳公约》），以帮助世界各国合力打击麻醉品交易。[4] 但该公约只关注了跨国犯罪的一个方面，其作用十分有限。

因此，在 2001 年，联合国通过了《打击跨国有组织犯罪公约》。现在，大多数国家都签署了这一公约。该公约的通过是联合国在这一领域 25 年工作中取得的最高成就。25 年前，当联合国第一次使用"跨国犯罪"这个词时，它包括了 18 种以政治、经济为目的的重要的跨边境犯罪，比如恐怖主义、劫机以及跨国有组织犯罪活动。[5]

近年来，联合国将更多的注意力投入到了一些更重要的跨国犯罪行为，比如毒品、偷渡、非法交易、非法国际枪支贸易，最终联合国不仅通过了《打击跨国有组织犯罪公约》，还通过了针对偷渡移民、贩卖人口、非法制造、贩卖军火的相关协议。[6] 联

---

① Louise Shelley, *Dirty Entanglements*: *Corruption*, *Crime and Terrorism*, Cambridge: Cambridge University Press, 2014, 238-44.

② Central American Unit, World Bank, Crime and Violence in Central America, Vol.II, 2010, 28.

③ J.C.Sharman, The Money Laundry Regulating: Criminal Finance in the Global Economy, Ithaca: Cornell University Press, 2011.

④ https://www.unodc.org/unodc/en/treaties/illicit-trafficking.html.

⑤ http://www.unodc.org/unodc/en/treaties/CTOC/index.html.

⑥ http://www.unodc.org/unodc/en/treaties/CAC/index.html.

合国对跨国有组织犯罪的定义十分全面，它明确了犯罪组织的大小、持续时间及其跨国性质问题。该定义能够适用于大量的犯罪主体与犯罪结构，同时也考虑到了各种犯罪集团的不同组织结构，因为一些犯罪集团的组织结构可能与传统等级森严的黑手党组织或是基于种族的传统犯罪集团有很大的不同。

该公约将参与有组织犯罪集团、洗黑钱以及牵涉跨国犯罪的腐败行为均判定为犯罪。公约支持政府采取措施以没收犯罪所得。公约提倡各国联合起来共同处理跨国有组织犯罪。

该联合国公约为各国打击跨国有组织犯罪、恐怖主义以及采集和共享有关数据提供了一个框架。公约还提出，不论在全球的任何地方，集团犯罪的收益都是非法的。这条可适用于走私麻醉品、贩卖人口、走私武器、走私大规模杀伤性武器，以及走私野生动植物制品，如象牙、犀牛角和其他制品。

针对恐怖主义的联合国决议

2014 年 12 月，联合国安理会一致表决通过了 2195 号决议。该决议由乍得发起，其主要关注恐怖主义、跨国犯罪以及那些帮助维持冲突进行并暗中破坏世界秩序的非法贸易活动这三者之间的关系。[①] 如今，该决议已然成为一股对联合国内部结构以及许多国家进行变革的力量。随着全球社会都转而将解决恐怖主义作为首要问题，弄清非法贸易的动力及其影响范围就显得十分必要了。

该决议指出，许多乃至绝大多数的恐怖组织都依赖着跨国犯罪活动。恐怖主义、跨国犯罪、腐败是相互联系的。恐怖主义、暴力极端主义和跨国犯罪的相互依存可能会导致冲突的升级并维持冲突的进行。恐怖主义依靠着多种形式的犯罪活动。在阿富汗、巴尔干半岛地区以及现在的伊拉克与叙利亚，国际社会都看到了这个情况。而在非洲这也是一个严重的问题，因此乍得才会努力发起这一决议。

联合国安理会 2195 号决议确定了多种支持恐怖主义的非法贸易形式，主要有：非法买卖武器、人口、毒品、人工制品；自然资源的非法贸易，如黄金、贵重金属、石材、矿物、野生动植物、碳和石油；掳人勒赎，如勒索、抢银行；等等。[②]

因此，商品的全球贸易可能会为恐怖主义筹集资金提供帮助并加速另一个地区的动荡。在土耳其和欧洲销售的伊拉克古文物为 ISIS 筹集资金提供帮助就是其中的一个例子。销售于美国和亚洲的野生动植物制品贸易，如象牙的买卖，为非洲的政府动荡和恐怖主义提供了资金。在俄罗斯和欧洲销售的海洛因为阿富汗的恐怖主义提供资金。

---

① http://www.un.org/en/sc/documents/resolutions/2014.shtml, December 19, 2014.

② http://www.un.org/en/sc/documents/resolutions/2014.shtml, December 19, 2014.

2015年2月,联合国安理会通过了2199号决议。该决议要求成员国不仅要关注那些为恐怖组织——ISIS提供资金的犯罪,还要特别关注那些支持自称“伊拉克和大叙利亚伊斯兰国”或是ISIS激进分子的贸易活动以及通过贸易进行的洗钱行为。[①] 伊拉克自古以来就是贸易的中心。世界上最早出现的古文献就是美索不达米亚的泥板,而其中的许多内容都与贸易有关。甚至汉谟拉比法典也提到了失窃货物或受保护货物的贸易。[②] 因此,自我们有成文法律以来,对非法贸易的打击就已经存在。

ISIS

这份2015年2月通过的决议反映了ISIS像企业一样运行的事实。我们需要摆脱恐怖主义融资这一狭隘的概念,转而接受“恐怖主义商业”(business of terrorism)这一概念。

ISIS是恐怖分子像商人一样存在的典型例子。恐怖分子如果要像商人一样生存,则需要进行产品组合——一些专业的服务——来进行成本效益分析、制定纳税策略、监督供应链并寻找自己的战略联盟、竞争优势、临时目标,同时进行创新并引进现代技术。而且就像商人一样,可以通过与其竞争对手进行交易来打击他们。

确实,目前ISIS在许多方面都与商人相似。他们有多种收入来源,也会搜寻和发展新的利润线,同时也会关注自己的产品优势和竞争优势。在进入伊拉克之前,ISIS就一直在叙利亚进行石油走私。油田的诱惑可能是他们扩大经营的原因之一。ISIS的运行模式与跨国企业类似。它拥有多种商业模式,能够通过石油、绑架、抢银行、走私古董、勒索以及其他犯罪来获利。它还拥有一个全球范围的征兵策略,以此来吸引美国、欧洲、亚洲和其他中东地区的士兵。ISIS有专业的媒体战略措施来传达信息,招募人员与支持者。虽然ISIS具有企业的功能,但在其运作中,意识形态依旧发挥着重要的作用。在意识形态的作用下,ISIS只需支付低于该区域市场价的薪水,就能让战士们为其战斗。[③]

ISIS通过收购油田、向周边国家出售石油、穿越周边国家进行石油贸易所产生的收益,已经获得了极大的关注。但是一些普通的恐怖分子生意,如走私、绑架、勒索、抢劫,也是赚钱渠道之一。更何况贩卖假烟、药品、手机、古董及外国护照还能获得更多的金钱。将上述商品中的部分商品从叙利亚走私到土耳其的犯罪活动数量已经有

---

① “Security Council Approves Resolution Targeting Sources of Funding for ISIL”,http://www.un.org/apps/news/story.asp? NewsID=50067#.VdUyFqa6Ve8.

② http://www.commonlaw.com/Hammurabi.html.

③ Jacob N.Shapiro and Danielle F.Jung,“The Terrorist Bureaucracy:Inside the Files of the Islamic State in Iraq”,Boston Globe, December 14, 2014, https://www. bostonglobe. com/ideas/2014/12/14/the-terrorist-bureaucracy-inside-files-islamic-state-iraq/QtRMOARRYows0D18faA2FP/story.html.

了剧烈地提升。按现在的情况估计,自 ISIS 兴起以来,走私燃料数量已增至三倍,走私香烟数量也有所增长,走私手机数量已经翻了五倍。[①] ISIS 会根据国家所在的地域和古董的类型,对走私古董课以 20%到 50%的赋税。[②] 在进入叙利亚之前,外国士兵会在土耳其售卖自己的护照,这能产生数千美元的收益。在进入叙利亚之后,这些收益就可以为他们自己和 ISIS 提供资金。[③] 这些形式的非法贸易对恐怖分子有着特别的吸引力,因为这些非法贸易不会市场饱和、缺乏法规规制、竞争又少,并且比起那些被高度监控的犯罪,如武器交易和麻醉品交易,执法机关对其的关注度也不会很高。

ISIS 已经拥有了一些组装式的小型精炼厂,这些精炼厂价格低廉,容量低并且移动方便。这些可移动的精炼厂已经成为了爆炸行动的目标,但是他们中更多的却被保留了下来。

ISIS 的领导人也都是理性的商业人。他们寻求最佳的专业性服务来进行成本效益分析,并采用先进的技术在世界各地招募人员。ISIS 关注着那些低风险、高回报的犯罪。他们通过互联网进行高度复杂的招募活动并确保能够招到需要的人员。他们招募了许多有前科的人,因为这些人按照教义是"可任意处置的人"(disposable people),并且他们拥有着维持 ISIS 运作所需要的犯罪技术。

犯罪、恐怖主义与腐败的相互作用

联合国 2195 号决议指出,腐败也是犯罪与恐怖主义相互作用的一部分。这个结论和我在自己的新书《肮脏的纠缠:腐败、犯罪与恐怖主义》中所提出的结论相同。[④] 片面地分析犯罪与恐怖主义的相互作用,会使我们将今天所面临的威胁过度简单化。

一旦恐怖主义介入到犯罪与腐败这两种不稳定的现象中,那么问题的发展态势就会变得混乱且难以预见。而且犯罪、恐怖主义与腐败的相互作用还能够以一种不可预测的方式来整合各个因素所带来的影响。这类似于物理学中引力的三体问题,"虽然二体问题是可积分的,并且其解法也已经被完全搞懂了……但是三体问题的解法带有难以确定的复杂性,还远远没有被完全掌握。"这三种要素的相互作用极度频繁地发生于世界许多地区,这其中既包括发达国家也包括发展中国家。全球支撑网跨越了各大洲来吸收罪犯、恐怖分子和腐败官员。而且,这些支撑网依据长度的不同会有不同的组合。因此,在某个地方,恐怖分子可能正与罪犯合作,而同时在另一个地方,罪犯可能正

---

① http://blog.oup.com/2014/11/corruption-smuggling-turkey-government/.

② http://www.nytimes.com/2014/09/03/opinion/isis-antiquities-sideline.html.

③ Craig Cohen and Josiane Gabel, Global Flashpoints 2015: Crisis and Opportunity, Washington, D.C.: Center For Strategic and International Studies, 2015, 22.

④ Louise Shelley, *Dirty Entanglements: Corruption, Crime and Terrorism*, Cambridge: Cambridge University Press, 2014.

与腐败官员勾结来获得货运便利，而这些货物又将用来支持恐怖组织。①

学术研究已经从下面这些方面对罪犯与恐怖分子的相互作用进行了讨论：行为主体及行为方式、混合组织的形成、犯罪活动和恐怖活动的协调、造成二者趋同及相互转换所需的情景。但我不相信这些模型能够正确处理这一问题。这其中没有一个包含了腐败现象。因此，他们都过于简单地看待了相互作用。此外，他们也无法解决全球范围的问题，而在全球范围这些相互作用将实现其效能。所以，如果一个模型被开发出来是来量化一个被过于简单化看待的问题的，那么它将只会产生虚假的结果。

恐怖分子与犯罪集团的相互作用是一个十分罕见的现象。他们之间的相互作用更可能发生于不同组织的成员之间而不是组织与组织之间。否则，恐怖活动的其中一项任务很可能会外包给犯罪组织或是一个能够提供各种非法行为主体的辅助者。

犯罪与恐怖主义之间的相互作用总是发生在个体层面而非组织层面，然而，领导人可能会鼓励这种相互作用，例如在美国受到起诉的沙米尔·巴萨耶夫的案例。这个案例中，在对巴萨耶夫建立的资金单元所进行的洛杉矶调查里，一位俄罗斯北高加索地区别斯兰的校园袭击事件的策划者曾透露，其犯罪资金来源于美国的车臣恐怖组织。该案中，巴萨耶夫的使者抵达好莱坞，并与美国有组织犯罪成员一道进行了大规模的刑事欺诈。他们先是去买了一些SUV，然后谎称这些车被盗，之后去获取保险金，最后再将这些汽车运出美国运往高加索地区。② 这个案例并不典型，它不能作为罪犯与恐怖组织勾结的代表，但是，该案可以作为恐怖组织与犯罪组织相合作的代表，因为罪犯可能还没有认识到他们正在与恐怖分子合作。

对这个案件中从洛杉矶到俄罗斯北高加索地区的不同元素进行图解之后，我们发现，在这一漫长的路线中罪犯与恐怖分子呈现出不同的关系。下图为别斯兰袭击的资金路线图。在下面这么多点里，都只出现了肮脏的纠缠的三要素中的两个要素的相互作用。

洛杉矶的案例告诉我们，在那些弱小的冲突地区，犯罪与恐怖活动的关系常常依靠着那些存在于最发达社会的关系网络来支撑。这些位于最发达社会的关系网络提供了资金，有时还会提供后勤支持。在其他案例中，移民群体也可能会对恐怖组织提供直接的支持，他们有些是乐意为之，有些则是被暴力所胁迫。③

---

① Louise Shelley, *Dirty Entanglements: Corruption, Crime and Terrorism*, Cambridge: Cambridge University Press, 2014.

② Louise Shelley, *Dirty Entanglements: Corruption, Crime and Terrorism*, Cambridge: Cambridge University Press, 2014, pp.135-7.

③ Louise Shelley, *Dirty Entanglements: Corruption, Crime and Terrorism*, Cambridge: Cambridge University Press, 2014, pp.137-9.

从洛杉矶向在北高加索的车臣恐怖组织提供的资金

在其他情况中，犯罪组织和恐怖组织并不会相互合作，但是辅助者会为这两种组织提供便利。美国“9・11”事件之前，弗吉尼亚北部的机动车辆管理部门的情形就是一个很好的例子。该部门的腐败使来自拉丁美洲的非法移民得以获得汽车驾驶证，同时这也令“9・11”事件劫机者获得了驾驶许可。[①] 而辅助者是远比这些流出驾驶证的少数官员更加重要的人物。他们可能是提供武器的大型供应商，或者是能够同时为罪犯和恐怖分子管理重要的运输网的人。[②]

罪犯、腐败官员、恐怖分子的相互作用在世界的各种环境中都有发生，但一些场所会更有利于这些关系的存在。在拉丁美洲，阿根廷、巴西、巴拉圭三国的交界处是一个极为不祥的区域（见下图），各种犯罪组织与恐怖组织在此运作并相互影响。相互作用之所以会发生于此，是因为这里存在：高度的腐败，给维持治安造成困难的多边管辖权，以及许多移民群体。

罪犯与恐怖分子的相互作用更可能发生在：移民社区、监狱、大城市、港口、多边区域、自贸区以及冲突地区。特定地区的流动性强或人情冷漠，一些边界区的复杂性，一个地区同时存在罪犯、恐怖分子、腐败官员的极大可能性，例如监狱和港口，都解释了这些环境对罪犯与恐怖分子的相互作用的向心力。

能够阻止或阻碍有组织犯罪和恐怖分子之间联系的最重要的思路就是减少相互

---

① Louise Shelley, *Dirty Entanglements: Corruption, Crime and Terrorism*, Cambridge: Cambridge University Press, 2014, p.32.

② Doug Farah, “Fixers, Super Fixers, and Shadow Facilitators: How Networks Connect”, in Convergence: Illicit Networks and National Security in the Age of Globalization eds. Michael Miklaucic and Jacqueline Brewer, Washington, D.C.: Center for Complex Operations, 2013, 75- 96.

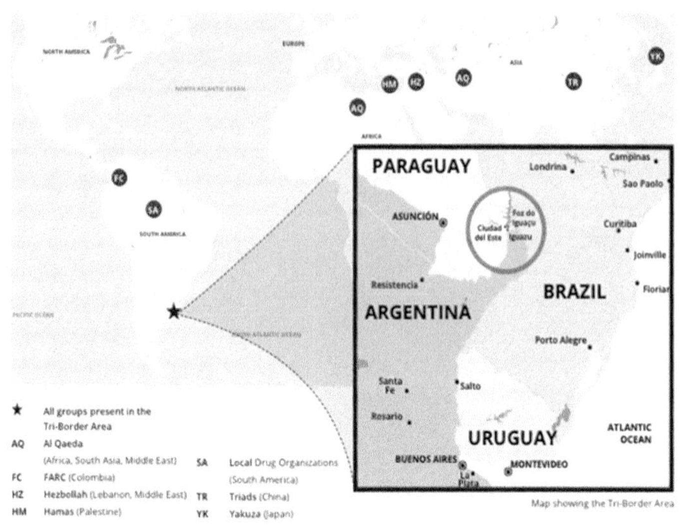

阿根廷、巴西、巴拉圭三国交界处的国际网络情况

作用的机会。在监狱中，分隔罪犯与恐怖分子的关键是限制其联系。犯罪人发展策略上的失败会导致这种相互作用自发地产生，正如伊拉克巴卡监狱被入侵之后所发生的那样。在当时的伊拉克巴卡监狱内，恐怖分子和为前萨达姆政权效力的官员被监禁在一起，该入侵事件导致了 ISIS 的形成。① 在欧洲，相互作用总是不经意发生，因为恐怖分子总是因一些轻微的犯罪而被逮捕，然后再与普通罪犯一起被关进监狱。当恐怖分子与普通罪犯一同监禁时，恐怖分子可以利用这一机会来招募这些被边缘化和被疏离的人来加入他们的事业。②

一个十分重要的现象是，罪犯和恐怖分子总在金融交易中进行互动。因此，确定他们可能进行互动的商业类型然后试着瓦解这些互动是十分重要的。例如，意大利的执法机关曾指出，他们在阿尔巴尼亚的商业伙伴不是一个普通的罪犯而是恐怖组织的成员。科萨·诺斯特拉组织从国家获取大量的收益，因此，他们中断了与该商业伙伴的业务关系，因为他们不想与破坏政府的恐怖分子有所关联。③ 这些相互作用对他们没有商业利益。

犯罪与恐怖活动的关系主要有两个弱点。长期进行犯罪活动的恐怖分子会变得

---

① See http://www.independent.co.uk/news/world/middle-east/camp-bucca-the-us-prison-that-became-the-birthplace-of-isis-9838905.html.

② Louise Shelley, *Dirty Entanglements: Corruption, Crime and Terrorism*, Cambridge: Cambridge University Press, 2014, 140.

③ Louise Shelley, *Dirty Entanglements: Corruption, Crime and Terrorism*, Cambridge: Cambridge University Press, 2014, p.153.

腐败并且缺乏意识形态。因此,仅仅把他们当成罪犯来打击,而不去处理意识形态方面的问题,也是可行的。

五、发达国家的犯罪与恐怖主义

发达国家中重要的城市中心区已经成为了恐怖袭击的目标。美国的"9·11"恐怖袭击、英国的恐怖袭击、西班牙马德里的地铁爆炸案①、日本东京的奥姆真理教恐怖袭击②以及最近的巴黎查理周刊遇袭事件,都已证实了该情况。

在这些袭击中,犯罪与腐败发挥着至关重要的作用。从毒品走私到信用卡诈骗与销售仿冒品,恐怖组织利用黑市来推进自己的事业,并同时模糊犯罪与政治活动的分界线。研究人员常常会遗漏恐怖袭击背后的犯罪与腐败问题,但是它们确实存在着。

正如我在《肮脏的纠缠:腐败、犯罪与恐怖主义》一书中所探讨的那样,犯罪辅助者帮助"9·11"劫持者获得他们留在美国所需的签证。华盛顿城郊的机动车辆管理局的腐败允许劫持者获得汽车驾驶证,从而让他们能够搭乘所要劫持的飞机。在马德里,恐怖分子在监狱之中彼此相遇。这些人全都有犯罪史。马德里地铁爆炸案背后的恐怖分子需要有自己的资金。虽然马德里的恐怖组织能够从"基地"组织那里获得初始资金,但这仅仅足够筹备袭击的成本并不足以来实施袭击。③ 作为替代,马德里的恐怖组织不得不利用头目艾哈米丹的毒品收益,来提升自己的犯罪能力。④ 通过这样,马德里袭击者最终购买了非法爆炸物并将之置于地铁之中。对在巴黎发生的查理周刊遇袭案和犹太超市袭击事件的调查表明,卡拉奇兄弟的成员之一,也是漫画家袭击者中的一人,其先前曾从事假冒球鞋的贩卖,还涉及走私香烟活动。⑤ 他也是在监狱里结识到准备袭击超市的恐怖分子的。⑥ 监狱的腐败给了恐怖分子进行

---

① Louise Shelley, *Dirty Entanglements: Corruption, Crime and Terrorism*, Cambridge: Cambridge University Press, 2014, 29-63.

② David E. Kaplan and Andrew Marshall, The Cult at the End of the World: The Terrifying Story of the Aum Doomsday Cult, from the Subways of Tokyo to the Nuclear Arsenals of Russia, New York: Crown Books, 1996.

③ Javier Jordán, "The Madrid Attacks: Results of Investigations Two Years Later", Terrorism Monitor 4, no.5 (March 9, 2006), http://www.jamestown.org/programs/gta/single/? tx_ttnews[tt_news] = 696&tx_ttnews[backPid] = 181&no_cache = 1.Category: Terrorism Monitor, Europe.

④ Elaine Sciolino, "Complex Web of Madrid Plot Still Entangled", New York Times, April 12, 2004.

⑤ Centre d'Analyse du Terrorisme, "Financement du Terrorisme La Contrabande et la contrefaçon de cigarettes", March 2015, http://www.cat-int.org/website/wp-content/uploads/2014/11/Focus-CAT-TF-Cigarette-Mars-2015.pdf.

⑥ Rukmini Callimachi and Jim Yardley, "From Amateur to Ruthless Jihadist in France Chérif and Saïd Kouachi's Path to Paris Attack at Charlie Hebdo", http://www.nytimes.com/2015/01/18/world/europe/paris-terrorism-brothers-said-cherif-kouachi-charlie-hebdo.html.

恐怖活动的可能。

发达国家对支持恐怖活动有着重要作用。正如我们先前讨论的洛杉矶案例一样，一个由罪犯与恐怖分子合作进行的汽车盗窃圈套为俄罗斯南部的车臣恐怖组织提供了资金。在密歇根州底特律市，烟草从税率较低的北卡罗纳州走私过来进行交易，而这些交易为恐怖组织提供了资金。①

现在，许多从欧洲征召来的外国士兵都有犯罪记录。他们中的一些人曾实施过轻微的犯罪行为，而另一些人则实施了更加严重的犯罪行为。对此有人猜测，许多国外士兵为了获取加入 ISIS 的旅费会进行一些轻微的非法贸易。

六、发展中国家的犯罪和恐怖主义

犯罪和恐怖主义对发展中国家的影响特别显著。边境地区的腐败和政府的腐败给了罪犯和恐怖分子得以运作的空间。不论是合法贸易还是非法贸易都会遵循同样的路径，即减少被侦查到的可能性。

其中较为发达的国家有足够的能力去观察和分析犯罪活动的聚集性、贸易路线的集中性，以及非国家行为者非法活动的聚集性。但是，发展中国家有限的能力使得上述特征之间的联系一直未受到阻碍。

跨国犯罪和冲突破坏了地区的稳定，使得这些组织可以在混乱的环境中得以运作。事实上，这些环境对他们的非法活动特别有益，所以他们也没有理由去化解冲突。

政治化的有组织犯罪集团、恐怖分子和那些对良好运转的国家不感兴趣的叛乱分子之间，可能存在着紧密的联系。这导致了政治环境的持续恶化。如果没有任何抑制因素对此进行阻止，那么这些组织就会衰退成只会实施掠夺和极端暴力行为的组织。ISIS 就是一个例证。在非洲我们能够明显看到，不同形式的非法贸易的汇聚，例如非法贩卖野生动物、武器、人以及烟草，使得整个非洲大陆变得动荡。而动荡与犯罪所带来的后果已经远远超过了相互作用之初。

七、作为服务提供者的恐怖分子和犯罪集团

在腐败的环境中，国家不能满足市民的需求。而在那些国家缺失的领域，非国家

① Centre d'Analyse du Terrorisme, "Financement du Terrorisme La Contrabande et la contrefaçon de cigarettes".

行为者就会介入其中。这些非国家行为者可以是非政府跨国组织，或者是非法的非国家行为者、恐怖分子，抑或是那些并非仅以市民福利为目的而向市民提供服务的跨国组织。通过取代缺失的国家，非法行为者会对人民造成巨大的侵害，而对那些拒绝侵害的人，非法行为者会通过暴力将其击退。①

犯罪组织的服务条款确保了市民不会脱离自己的社群。市民也不会和执法机关合作来摆脱其所在社群背后的犯罪组织，因为他们都因某些极其重要的服务而负债于这些犯罪组织。

当政府不提供基本的社会服务时，极端主义组织与恐怖主义组织就能够通过宣传反腐败运动来获得民众的支持。阿富汗塔利班组织就属此例。塔利班叛乱分子从鸦片经济中获得经济资本以及政治资本。② 在也门，腐败及其附属问题导致了公共服务的缺失、针对自然资源的拨款不足，以及灾难救援的难以到达。也门当下的动荡以及严重的暴力情况就是由这些所导致的。而这些也都是 AQAP 招募信息中的主要元素。正如有评论员报道的那样，“迄今为止，AQAP 一直表现出令人印象深刻的才能，他们仅仅用一个故事就将大量的抱怨完全地吸收了进去，而在这故事里，讨伐异教徒是解决国家各种危机的唯一途径。”③同样的，诸如阿布・沙耶夫组织（ASG）等都是通过利用市民对无处不在的腐败的厌恶和他们对为人民提供学校、公共交通、垃圾回收、医疗卡等的服务的重视，来进一步达成自己的政治目的。④

恐怖分子给予利益的原因不同于罪犯。提供社会服务不仅仅是在巴结他们所依赖的社群，而是能够帮助他们向人民灌输那些作为恐怖组织根基的意识形态。在西班牙巴斯克，ETA 组织发展并维持着青年、妇女、公会的支撑结构。⑤ 斯里兰卡的 LTIE 组织对非政府组织活动进行投资。⑥ AQAP 则将慈善工作放在了招募支持者之前。⑦

---

① Justin Magouirk, “Nefarious Helping Hand: Anti-Corruption Campaigns, Social Service Provision and Terrorism”, Terorrism and Political Violence, Vol.20, no.3, 2008, 356-75.

② UNODC, Addiction, Crime and Insurgency, 2009, 141, https://www. unodc. org/documents/data-and-analysis/Afghanistan/Afghan_Opium_Trade_2009_web.pdf.

③ Gabriel Koehler-Derrick, ed., A False Foundation? AQAP, Tribes and Ungoverned Spaces in Yemen, West Point, NY: Combating Terrorism Center at West Point, September 2011, 41, http://www. ctc. usma. edu/posts/a-false-foundation-aqap-tribes-and-ungoverned-spaces-in-yemen.

④ Erica Chenoweth and Jessica C.Teets, “To Bribe or to Bomb: Do Corruption and Terrorism Go Together?”, in Corruption, Global Security, and World Order, ed.Robert I.Rotberg, Washington, DC: Brookings Institution Press, 2009, 171.

⑤ B.Tejerina, “Protest Cycle, Political Violence and Social Movements in the Basque Country”, Nations and Nationalism 7, no.1(2001): 51-52.

⑥ Pierre Emmanuel Ly, “The Charitable Activities of Terrorist Groups”, Public Choice 131(2007): 181.

⑦ Peter Knoope, “AQAP: A Local Problem, a Global Concern”, August 20, 2013, http://icct. nl/publications/icct-commentaries/aqap-a-local-problem-a-global-concern? dm_i = 1ADT, 1SH80, 8J4SN9, 6E9R2, 1.

哥伦比亚 FARC 组织，在其最强盛时期，是公共设施，包括职业学校、卫生所和市政工程的主要提供者，它还通过铺设公路来提供基础设施。20 世纪 90 年代后期，通过对 15%的哥伦比亚人的调查显示，FARC 的服务有很高的使用率。①

八、结 论

犯罪、恐怖主义、腐败的相互作用，具有多样而复杂的关系。这些关系使得非法贸易和跨国犯罪在全球经济中承担了越来越大的份额，并且变成了许多国家和地区中的重要政治力量。如果那些破坏生活质量并被无辜市民所厌恶的腐败现象没有普遍存在的话，恐怖分子就无法招募合作者、发展自己的组织、维持宽广的供应网。

因此，国际社会应该更多地关注腐败问题，以此来限制跨国犯罪和恐怖主义。腐败作为问题的核心元素，却总是常常为人们所忽视。中国加入反腐败行动也表明了对腐败的腐蚀作用的重视。

我们需要减少和控制那些促使恐怖主义成长的非法贸易。毒品交易已经受到了大量的关注。如今，新型的大规模资金来源有偷渡和走私野生动植物制品，如象牙，以及走私古董。还有些资金支持来自于小物件的贸易——假冒衣服和运动鞋、走私香烟，以及其他小型的而不为执法部门所关注的犯罪活动。这在西欧和美国尤为显著。

在对跨国犯罪和恐怖主义的反馈上，我们需要停止烟囱效应（烟囱是一个孤立的垂直传导结构，缺乏平行沟通；烟囱效应指情报仅在上下两部门间纵向传递，不考虑具体环境，并缺乏横向部门间的沟通和协调），我们需要用综合的方式来解决相关的问题。我们也需要解决不同形式的非法活动的衔接而不是仅仅去关注某一种非法活动。对中国来说，要打击从非洲进入中国的国际毒品贸易，就必须同时将非法野生动物贸易作为目标，因为这两者有着相同的路径。这些贸易的利润巨大，以至于能够显著地促使毒品组织变得富有而强大。如果仅仅将这些贸易看成是非法毒品贸易带来的问题，那么就无法有效地削弱这些有害组织。

我们需要有更多的国际合作来执行针对恐怖主义的联合国决议。要做到这点，我们需要在法律发展、数据搜集，以及在分析那些促进犯罪与恐怖主义的关系网络方面有更多的合作。单独的一个国家无法对付那些危险的非国家行为者，这些国家与

---

① Vanda Felbab-Brown, Shooting Up: Counterinsurgency and the War on Drugs, Washington, D.C.: Brookings Institution, 2009, 84.

那些非国家行为者并不是对等的对手。另外,政府需要各种部门来打击这些行为者,而不仅限于传统的武装力量和执法机关。但很多国家的诚信与能力已经受到了腐败的侵害,他们无力抵制非法贸易。腐败在许多发展中国家尤为严重,特别是在非洲和中东地区,那里有着殖民国家所确定的明确的边界线,那里缺乏内在的诚信,也缺乏市民对国家机构高于宗教和种族的忠诚。许多国家的领导人将自己的个人利益或集团利益放在了民众的一般利益之上。

甚至更强大的国家也不能应对非国家行为者和促进其运行的关系网络所带来的挑战。国家能动员力量去平息一场叛乱,但却不能打击那些深入其他国家的腐败、犯罪和恐怖主义。

国际社会需要一个整体的方法而非大量的策略。一个全社会的方法(A whole-of-society approach)势在必行。但这需要全球社会的回应,包括多国组织的参与,国际与本地的企业和消费者的参与,宗教社会和世俗市民社会的参与,新闻记者与国际在线传媒(其已取代了许多印刷新闻)的参与,研究人员与教育机构的参与。如果没有政府以外的各种社会群体的参与和合作,并最终形成战略合作伙伴的话,那么就不可能抵抗犯罪、腐败与恐怖主义的侵蚀。

(阮重骏 译)

The Relationship of Crime, Corruption and Terrorism

Louise Shelley①

The interaction of crime, corruption and terrorism, I have named "dirty entanglements" drawing an analogy to the quantum physics term of "entanglements."② Once the three elements interact, they have consequences far from their initial point of interaction. This is a problem that is contributing to the enormous instability in the world today. It is part of the reason that 2015 is the most unstable year since World War II with large numbers of illegal migrants, displaced peoples and a wide arc of instability that stretches from West Africa, through North Africa, to the Middle East and on to Pakistan and possibly further into Central Asia. Therefore, the consequences of dirty entanglements in these regions are being experienced far from their initial point of interaction and we are looking at global problems we must all help address.

Fortunately, we are all part of the United Nations Community that is taking an increasingly active role in combating transnational crime and its relationship to terrorism. Transnational crime can exist without terrorism but terrorism cannot exist without crime and

---

① Louise Shelley, University Professor and Omer I. and Nancy Hirst Endowed Chair, Director, Terrorism, Transnational Crime and Corruption Center, School of Policy Government and International Affairs, George Mason University.

② Louise Shelley, Dirty Entanglements: Corruption, Crime and Terrorism (Cambridge: Cambridge University Press, 2014).

transnational crime. Corruption has always been key to the perpetration of organized crime. Therefore, it is now key to the commission of both transnational crime and corruption as was identified in UN Security Council Resolution 2195.[①]

Transnational crime has grown enormously in the past two decades. Its growth is now so significant that it cannot be ignored any longer. In 2004, the UN Security Council cited transnational crime 4 times, in Resolutions and Declarations, in2014, the comparable number is over 30. This represents a growth of 8 times in the past ten years and most of the mentions now are in the form of Resolutions which carry much more weight than a Declaration.[②] The growth is not sudden but every year the attention to this problem has increased. This represents a dramatic shift in the priorities of the United Nations on what constitutes a threat to security. China as a member of the Security Council plays a crucial role in the adoption of this framework.

This attention is warranted because globalization, free trade, technology and the loosening of financial regulations have combined to produce some of the most powerful and efficient crime networks in world history. Transnational crime is increasingly seen as a security threat in many countries and regions of both the developed and developing world.[③] Its impact may be greatest in the developing world where there is less societal and governmental capacity to counter the threat.

Transnational crime poses challenges: to political security, the economic system and the well being of the state and its citizens. Transnational crime is a threat posed by non-state actors who stand distinct or have merged or strongly influenced the state. According to many, it is an asymmetric threat because the harm that these groups cause is disproportionate to their size or resources. Their increasing contacts with terrorists increases the security challenges.

The biggest transnational crime networks operate on multiple continents, have multi-billion-dollar annual turnovers and can threaten whole nation-states and even regions. These networks often operate in the developed, the developing world and in conflict regions. They function across continents linking suppliers, and consumers and financial centers.

---

① http://www.un.org/en/sc/documents/resolutions/2014.shtml, December 19, 2014.

② Ugi Zvekic, "Reinforcing Multilateral Approaches to Transnational OrganizedCrime by Strengthening Local Ownership and Accountability," Global Initiative Against Transnational Organized Crime, 2015, 3.

③ http://www.globalinitiative.net/programs/towards-a-global-strategy/; Strategy to Combat Transnational Organized Crime, https://www.whitehouse.gov/.../transnational-crime/strategy.

Some Modern criminals manage globalized supply chains that are technologically advanced and highly efficient. They, particularly exploit, countries where they can operate effectively—those with good transport, communications and infrastructure. Many crime groups also have legitimate business interests. Therefore, they hide the illicit activity inside of the legal. They often outsource and subcontract, just like commercial firms.

Clever criminals acting across borders are extremely difficult to prosecute. They profit from gaps in enforcement and regulation, and conceal their illegal acts in complex supply chains. The United Nations provides a framework to define the problem but it is up to individual countries to provide mechanisms to ensure that they can counter this growing problem effectively. The absence of harmonized legislation among countries is exploited by the criminals.

Absence of Definition of Corruption

Despite years of attempts, the United Nations has not been able to define the concept of corruption. There has been no international convention adopted on the topic. Different international bodies have developed different definitions some of which are narrower and some of which are broader and are not confined exclusively to government personnel. Because transnational crime intersects so frequently with the business world, it seems important not to limit the definition in ways that circumscribe our analysis. The World Bank definition of corruption is "the abuse of public office for private gain." But this is too narrow, as it does not include private actors who behave in corrupt ways. The Asian Development Bank definition of corruption includes that of private individuals.① This is the definition that I think is more appropriate as it allows us to see bank officials, who laundered money for the drug cartels and different terrorist groups to be seen as corrupt.

Corruption is a complex phenomenon operating at the local, national, and global levels.② Its impact is different in each arena, but in every environment in which corruption operates, it is central to the rise and the perpetuation of crime, terrorism, and other social ills. Corruption can be considered an incubator for the growth of organized crime,

---

① Asian Development Bank, Anticorruption: Our Framework and Strategies, 1998, http://www.adb.org/documents/anticorruption-policy.

② Robert Klitgaard, Controlling Corruption (Berkeley: University of California Press, 1988).

violence,[①] and terrorism.The reverse is also true.Crime incubates corruption,as does instability.All of this is self-reinforcing and complex to combat.

How does the United Nations define transnational crime?

The United Nations defines transnational organized crime as any activity by a group of three or more,who work together over time with the aim of committing one or more serious crimes,in order to obtain,directly or indirectly,a financial or other material benefit.This definition has been in place since 2001 when the UN adopted the Convention on Transnational Organized Crime.[②]

A serious crime represents any crime that carries a maximum punishment of four or more years in prison. Human trafficking and drug trafficking are two examples of serious organized crimes although the penalties for drug trafficking are often much greater than for human trafficking.

A structured group, meanwhile, is a group that is not randomly formed to commit a sudden crime, but rather has some sort of defined configuration. Some organized crime groups are highly structured,with ritualistic indoctrination ceremonies such as the Mafia in Sicily.[③] Others are more fluid and flexible,but still have defined leaders and subordinates.

There are four conditions that determine whether organized crime is characterized as transnational:

1)When it is committed in more than one state for example,drugs that get grown in one country,processed in another,and trafficked to a third place.

2)When it is committed in one state but a substantial part of its preparation,planning, direction,financing or control occurs in another state an example of this is the rhino poaching in South Africa,being led by crime networks across the border in Mozambique with the horn shipped to Vietnam.

3)When it is committed in one state but involves an organized criminal group that engages in criminal activities in more than one state an example of this is the Italian mafia,or

---

① Martha Elena Badel Rueda,Costos de la corrupción en Colombia,República de Colombia Departamento Nacional de Planeación Unidad de Análisis Macroeconómico,Documento 111(May 24,1999),62.

② http://www.unodc.org/unodc/en/treaties/CTOC/index.html.

③ Jane and Peter Schneider,Reversible Destiny:Mafia,Antimafia,and the Struggle in Palermo Berkeley and Los Angeles:University of California Press.2003.

Chinese Triads, which are multi-national crime networks, operating around the globe.

4) When it is committed in one state but has substantial effects in another state an example of this is cigarette counterfeiting, which has had a negative impact on legitimate cigarette companies and on the health of citizens. It also serves as an important funding source for terrorism in many regions of the world.

Although we have a common definition of the problem, we have difficulty addressing it because the laws allowing us to counteract the phenomenon are state-based, yet the criminals are operating globally. If an online network of Nigerian scammers defrauds French, Australian and American credit-card holders, where does the crime occur? And who has the motivation, not to mention the jurisdiction, to prosecute? In the physical world it can be just as complex: Thus the criminals can disguise the source of their ill-gotten goods and middlemen can plead ignorance.

Accelerating the globalization of crime has been the end of the Cold War and the collapse of the Soviet Union. The end of the Cold War and the end of the superpower conflicts, resulted in the breakdown of effective borders across many regions of the world. It also supplanted the large-scale super power conflict with many smaller regional conflicts. These conflicts have contributed to the rise of transnational crime as criminal activity has been used to support the conflicts. Crime has provided the funds to buy arms and maintain military forces. Large-scale immigration away from these conflict regions has also contributed to the rise of human smuggling and trafficking in the last decade.

This "dark side" of globalization creates enormous challenges for nation states around the world-no modern nation is free of this threat. Transnational crime networks operate successfully around the world because they can: 1) Manipulate loose regulations in the global financial and trade systems to move money and goods; 2) Take advantage of gaps in legal systems and legislation, and the complexity of policing crime across multiple borders; 3) Exploit distrust and lack of connectivity among governments; 4) Exploit the infrastructure of key regions that have excellent transport, communications and financial services; 5) Conceal their illegal acts in complex supply chains; 6) Use cyberspace to their advantage.

How large is the problem of Transnational Organized Crime?

Already in the 1980s, narcotics trade represented at least 2% of the world economy, according to UN research, equal to global trade in steel and textiles.[①] The problem has grown since then as many more regions of the world have become producers of drugs and markets for these drugs. But as will be discussed subsequently, transnational criminals and terrorists have diversified into a far broader range of activities than just the drug trade.

The negative consequences of this large economic activity of transnational criminals are not evenly distributed. There is greater impact on conflict regions and states with less rule of law and state capacity to counter the problem. The consequences of this illicit trade are significant as it undermines the sustainability of the planet, it can harm consumers through counterfeit pharmaceuticals and food and undermines development.

The convergence of the drug trade with other forms of illicit trade creates special problems for China. As an official report has reported in June, African drug suspects have acted as agents for Pakistani drug lords.[②] The research that our research center, TraCCC, has undertaken has independently shown the same phenomenon as we are studying the illicit wildlife trade in Africa in ivory and its links to the drug trade. Yet our research reveals that this is a dirty entanglement as it is the link of transnational crime with terrorism, as some of these Pakistani drug lords are linked to terrorist activity, facilitated by corruption. Therefore, the drug traffickers are being enriched by the very rich profitable trade in ivory giving them increased capacity to operate in the drug arena.

Afghanistan has had the most criminalized economy in the world as a result of transnational criminals, corrupt officials and terrorist groups all engaging in illicit activity. At some points in the past decade, at least 50 percent of Afghanistan's economy was dependent on criminal proceeds from the drug trade, illicit timber trade as well as extortion of commodities moving along trade routes.[③]

Investments are not made effectively when transnational crime groups control so much of the economy. In Central America, one of the most violent regions in the world, the World Bank estimates that economic losses to the economy from the criminal violence may be almost 8 percent.[④]

Because transnational organized crime and terrorist groups use corruption so significantly

---

① United Nations International Drug Control Programme, World Drug Report (Oxford: Oxford University Press, 1997).

② Zhang Yan, "Police Face Hard Fight over Drugs", China Daily USA, June 25, 2015, usa.chinadaily.com/cn/china/2015-06/25/content_21097666.htm.

③ Shelley, 238-44.

④ Central American Unit, World Bank, Crime and Violence in Central America, Vol.II, 2010, 28.

to operate, corruption increases in the countries where these groups are based as well as operate. Although the problem of corruption is most pronounced in the developing world, it is not problematic only there. Corruption in developed countries, particularly in their financial markets, provides the possibility of the laundering of illicit capital which allows transnational crime groups to continue to operate.①

The cooperation between criminals and terrorists in all regions of the world means that this is a problem we all share. Therefore, we need to work together on strategies and not just legal frameworks.

How is the global community fighting Transnational Organized Crime and Terrorism?

UN Resolutions on Transnational Crime

In 1988 the United Nations adopted the United Nations Convention Against Illicit Traffic in Narcotic Drugs and Psychotropic Substances (Known as the Vienna Convention) to help countries around the world collaborate to fight narcotics trafficking.② This focused on only one aspect of transnational crime which was too limited.

Therefore, in 2001, the United Nations adopted the Convention on Transnational Organized Crime of which most countries in the world are now signatories. The adoption of the Convention was the culmination of twenty-five years of work by the United Nations in this area. When the term, transnational crime: was first adopted by the United Nations twenty-five years ago it included 18 important politically and economically motivated cross-border crimes, such as terrorism, hijacking and traditional organized crime activities.③

In recent years, more focus has been paid by the UN to the ever-more important elements of transnational crime—drugs, human smuggling and trafficking and the illicit international trade in weapons, culminating in the adoption not only of the Convention on Transnational Organized Crime, but also the companion protocols on Smuggling of Migrants and Trafficking in Persons and Illicit Manufacturing and Trafficking in Firearms.④ The UN's definition is comprehensive, addressing the issue of size, duration, and the transnational nature of criminal groups. This definition accommodates a wide range of criminal actors and

---

① J.C.Sharman, The Money Laundry Regulating: Criminal Finance in the Global Economy (Ithaca: Cornell University Press, 2011).

② https://www.unodc.org/unodc/en/treaties/illicit-trafficking.html.

③ http://www.unodc.org/unodc/en/treaties/CTOC/index.html.

④ http://www.unodc.org/unodc/en/treaties/CAC/index.html.

structures, and allows for different crime organization structures that may be far removed from that of the traditional hierarchical mafia organization or that of the ethnically based traditional crime groups.

The convention criminalizes participation in organized crime groups. It criminalizes laundering of criminal money. It criminalizes corruption linked to transnational crime. It supports governments enacting measures to confiscate the proceeds of crime. It advocates that countries work together to address transnational organized crime.

The UN conventions created a framework for countries to measure, share data about and fight transnational organized crime and terrorism. The Convention also criminalized the proceeds of organized crime globally. This can be applied to the smuggling of narcotics, people, weapons, WMD and wildlife parts, such as ivory and rhino horn and other commodities.

UN Resolutions on Terrorism

In December 2014, the UN Security Council unanimously adopted Resolution 2195, sponsored by Chad, that focuses on the relationship between terrorism and transnational crime and the illicit trade activities that help perpetuate conflict and undermine the world order.① This resolution is now a force for change within the UN structure and in many countries. As the global community shifts to address this new priority, it is imperative to understand the dynamics of illicit trade and its range of consequences.

The Resolution stated that many if not most terrorist groups are dependent on transnational criminal activity. Terrorism, transnational crime, and corruption are linked. The combined presence of terrorism, violent extremism, and transnational crime may worsen conflicts and may perpetuate them. Terrorism depends on diverse forms of criminal activity. The international community has seen this in Afghanistan, the Balkans and now in Iraq and Syria. But it is also a serious problem in Africa, hence the important role of Chad in sponsoring this Resolution.

UN Security Council resolution 2195, identified the diverse forms of illicit trade that support terrorism: Trafficking of arms, persons, drugs, artefacts; illicit trade in natural resources: gold, precious metals, stones, minerals, wildlife, charcoal and oil; kidnapping for ransom; extortion, bank robbery, etc.②

① http://www.un.org/en/sc/documents/resolutions/2014.shtml, December 19, 2014.

② Ibid.

Therefore, the global trade in a commodity may help fund terrorism and instability in another region. Examples of this are examples are antiquities from Iraq sold in Turkey and Europe help fund ISIS. Trade in wildlife parts, such as ivory, sold in the United States and Asia funds political instability and terrorism in Africa. Heroin sold in Russia and Europe funds terrorism in Afghanistan.

In February of this year, the UN Security Council passed resolution 2199, which obliged member states to focus not only on the crimes that generate funds for the terrorist group—ISIS—but particularly on the trade and the trade-based money laundering that supports the militants calling themselves the Islamic State of Iraq and Syria, or ISIS.① Centrality of trade in Iraq represents a historical continuity. The first recorded ancient documents are clay tablets out of Mesopotamia, many of which were concerned with trade. Even Hammurabi's Code made reference to the trade in fenced or stolen goods.② Therefore, illicit trade is countered as long as we have documented records of law.

ISIS

The January 2015 Resolution is a reflection of the fact that ISIS functions as a business. We need to move away from the limited concept of terrorist financing and move to a concept of the "business of terrorism".

ISIS is the most typical example of terrorists acting like business people.

Terrorists, if they are survive they, like legitimate business people, need a product mix—professional services— to engage in cost-benefit analyses, tax strategies, monitor supply chains and seek strategic alliances, competitive advantage, targets of opportunity, and innovate and use of modern technology. Yet as businessmen, you can work against them as you would business competitors.

Indeed, these days ISIS in many ways resembles a legitimate business. It has diverse revenue sources, seeks and develops new profit lines, and focuses on its products and its competitive advantage. ISIS was smuggling oil in Syria before they entered Iraq. The lure of the oil fields might have been one of the incentives to expand their operations. ISIS functions like a transnational business. It has a diversified business model—obtaining money from

---

① "Security Council Approves Resolution Targeting Sources of Funding for ISIL", http://www.un.org/apps/news/story.asp? NewsID=50067#.VdUyFqa6Ve8.

② http://www.commonlaw.com/Hammurabi.html.

oil, kidnapping, bank robbery, trafficking in antiquities, extortion as well as other crimes. It has a worldwide recruitment strategy drawing fighters from the US, Europe, Asia and other parts of the Middle East. ISIS has a professional media strategy to communicate its message and to recruit personnel and supporters. Although it functions as a business, ideology plays a role in its operations. Ideology allows it to pay its fighters less than market salaries for combatants in the regions.①

Enormous attention has been paid to the revenues generated by ISIS's acquisition of oil fields and its sale of oil to and through neighboring countries. But money was also generated from the usual terrorist businesses—smuggling, kidnapping, extortion and robberies. Still more comes from the sale of counterfeit cigarettes, pharmaceuticals, cell phones, antiquities and foreign passports. Smuggling in some of these commodities into Turkey from Syria has risen dramatically. It is now estimated that fuel smuggling has tripled, cigarette smuggling has increased and cell phone smuggling has risen five fold since the rise of ISIS.② Smuggled antiquities are being taxed at rates of 20 to 50 percent by ISIS depending on the region of the country and the type of antiquity.③ Foreign fighters sell their passports for thousands of dollars in Turkey before entering Syria where the proceeds help fund them and ISIS.④ These forms of illicit trade are particularly attractive to terrorists because there is less market saturation, less regulation, reduced competition and limited law enforcement focus than other forms of highly policed crime, such as arms and narcotics trafficking.

ISIS have obtained modular mini-refineries, which are low cost, low capacity and mobile. These mobile refineries have been targeted in the bombing campaigns but many more remain.

ISIS leaders are rational business actors, too. They seek the best professional services, engage in cost-benefit analysis, and use advanced technology to recruit personnel globally. ISIS focuses on crimes with low risk and high reward. Their highly sophisticated recruitment through the Internet ensures that they get individuals with the skills that they need. They re-

① Jacob N. Shapiro and Danielle F. Jung, "The Terrorist Bureaucracy: Inside the Files of the Islamic State in Iraq," Boston Globe, December 14, 2014, https://www.bostonglobe.com/ideas/2014/12/14/the-terrorist-bureaucracy-inside-files-islamic-state-iraq/QtRMOARRYows0D18faA2FP/story.html.

② http://blog.oup.com/2014/11/corruption-smuggling-turkey-government/.

③ http://www.nytimes.com/2014/09/03/opinion/isis-antiquities-sideline.html.

④ Craig Cohen and Josiane Gabel, Global Flashpoints 2015: Crisis and Opportunity (Washington, D.C.: Center For Strategic and International Studies, 2015), 22.

cruit many individuals with criminal pasts as these are "disposable people" under Islam and also have the criminal skills needed to keep ISIS functioning.

The Interaction of Crime, Terrorism and Corruption

The UN Resolution 2195 stated that corruption is also part of the interaction of crime and terrorism. This is the same conclusion that I reached in my recent book *Dirty Entanglements: Corruption, Crime and Terrorism.*① Confining analysis of the interactions to just a crime-terror connection is an oversimplification of the threats that we face today.

The addition of terrorism to the already destabilizing phenomena of crime and corruption can often have unforeseen and chaotic consequences for the dynamics of the problem that can compound the impact of each element in unpredictable ways. This is analogous to what is known in physics as the *gravitational three-body problem*: "While the two-body problem is integrable and its solutions completely understood ...solutions of the three-body problem may be of an arbitrary complexity and are very far from being completely understood." The interactions of the three components are occurring with greater frequency in many regions of the world including both developed and developing nations. Global support networks span continents incorporating criminals, terrorists and corrupt officials. Yet these support networks may have different combinations along their length. Therefore, at one locale, terrorists may work with criminals, and at another locale, the criminals may facilitate transit of the goods supporting the terrorist organization by working with corrupt officials.②

The scholarly research has discussed the problem of criminal—terrorist interactions in the following ways: actors and activities, formation of hybrid organizations, blending of criminal and terrorist activities, and the milieu of convergence and transformation. But I do not believe that these models are the correct way to approach the problem. None of them incorporate the phenomenon of corruption. They, therefore, oversimplify the interactions. Moreover, they fail to address the problem of the global reach where these interactions attain their potency. Therefore, if a model is developed to quantify an oversimplified problem, it will yield spurious results.

The interaction of terrorist and criminal organizations is a rather rare phenomenon. Interactions, if they occur, are more often of members of different organizations rather than the

---

① Shelley.

② Shelley.

whole organization itself. Or, a terrorist activity may outsource a task to a criminal organization or a facilitator who may serve a variety of illicit actors.

Interactions between criminals and terrorists often occur at the individual level rather than the whole organization, although; a leader may sanction the interaction such as in the Shamil Basayev case prosecuted in the United States. In this case, a Los Angeles investigation of a funding cell established by Basayev, the mastermind of the attack on the school in Beslan in the North Caucasus, Russia revealed the criminal funding sources in the U.S. for the Chechen terrorist group. In this case, Basayev's emissary arrived in Hollywood and participated in large-scale criminal fraud with members of Armenian organized crime to buy SUVs, declare them stolen, collect insurance and then ship the cars out of the country to the Caucasus.[①] This case is not atypical—it does not represent a collaboration of a criminal and terrorist organization. Instead it is one representative of a terrorist group cooperating with a criminal organization. The criminals may not have been aware that they were collaborating with a terrorist.

Illustrating the different elements of the case from Los Angeles to the North Caucasus of Russia reveal different relationships of the criminals and terrorists along the lengthy route. See the map of the route for the funding of the Beslan attack illustrated below. At many points there were interactions of only two of the three elements of the dirty entanglement.

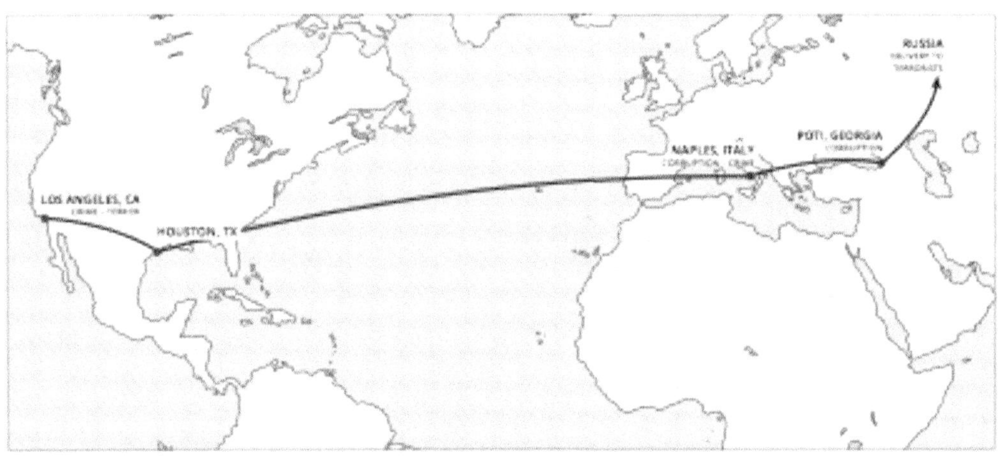

Funding from Los Angeles to the North Caucasus for terrorist group in Chechnya

① Ibid., 135-7.

The Los Angeles case reveals that crime-terror relationships in weak and conflict regions are often supported by networks located in the most developed societies.These networks in the most developed societies provide funding and sometimes logistical support.In other cases,Diaspora communities may provide direct support to terrorist groups either willingly or they may be coerced into this through criminal violence.①

In other situations,it is not a whole organization of criminals or terrorists that are collaborating but facilitators serving both communities.Illustrative of this is the situation with the Division of Motor Vehicles in Northern Virginia prior to 9/11.Corruption in this bureau allowed illegal migrants smuggled from Latin America to obtain drivers' licenses but it also allowed the 9/11 hijackers to obtain their driver permits.② The facilitators can be much more significant figures than petty bureaucrats issuing drivers' licenses.They can be a large-scale supplier of arms or they can manage significant transport networks for both criminals and terrorists.③

Interactions of criminals,corrupt officials,and terrorists have been identified in diverse environments globally,but some locales are more conducive to these relationships.In Latin America, a particularly ominous hub is the tri-border area of Argentina, Brazil and Paraguay where diverse criminal and terrorist groups operate and interact.Interactions occur here because there is a very high level of corruption,a multi-border jurisdiction which is hard to police and important diaspora communities.

The interactions of criminals and terrorists are more likely to occur in:diaspora communities,prisons, megacities, ports, multi-border regions, free-trade zones, and conflict zones. The centrality of these environments are explained by the mobility or impersonality associated with a particular locale,the complexity of some borders,or the enhanced likelihood of the presence of criminals,terrorists,and corrupt officials in one location,such as in prisons or at ports.

The most important consideration that would prevent or hinder relations between organized crime and terrorists is to restrict the opportunities for interaction.Separating criminals and terrorists in prison is key in restricting associations. These interactions can be

---

① Ibid.,137-9.

② Ibid.,32.

③ Doug Farah,"Fixers,Super Fixers,and Shadow Facilitators:How Networks Connect", in Convergence:Illicit Networks and National Security in the Age of Globalization eds.Michael Miklaucic and Jacqueline Brewer(Washington,D.C.:Center for Complex Operations,2013),75- 96.

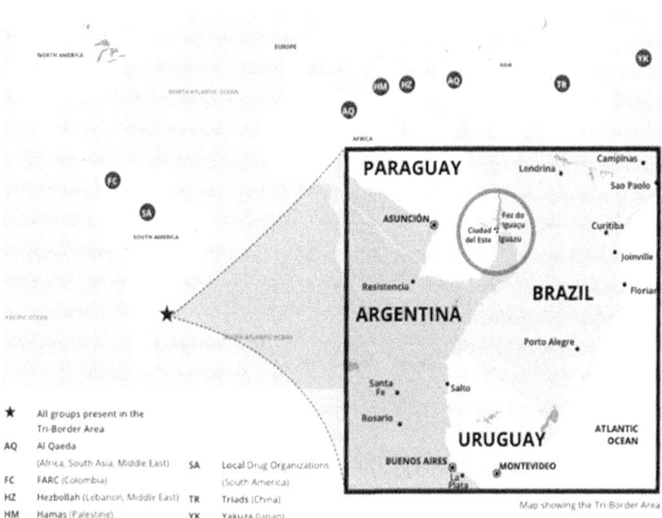

Map showing the Tri-Border Area

done consciously as a result of failing to develop strategies towards inmates as occurred in Bucca prison in Iraq after the invasion when terrorists and former Saddam Hussein officials were incarcerated together leading to the formation of ISIS.① In Europe, these interactions occur inadvertently because terrorists are often apprehended for petty crimes and then are placed in prison with ordinary criminals. When confined with the criminals, the terrorists use the opportunity to recruit these marginalized and alienated people to their cause.②

Also important is that criminals and terrorists often interact over financial transactions. Therefore, it is important to identify the types of businesses in which they may interact and try to disrupt these. For example, Italian law enforcement once pointed out to the Cosa Nostra that their Albanian business partners were not ordinary criminals but members of a terrorist group. The Cosa Nostra that derives extensive revenues from state contracts, therefore, broke off this business relationship, as they did not want to associate with terrorists who undermine the state.③ These interactions were not in their business interests.

There are two primary weaknesses in the crime-terror relationship. Terrorists who have engaged in criminal activity for a very long time become corrupted and less ideological. There-

① http://www.independent.co.uk/news/world/middle-east/camp-bucca-the-us-prison-that-became-the-birthplace-of-isis-9838905.html.

② Shelley, 140.

③ Ibid., 153.

fore, it is then possible to just target them as criminals without having to address the ideological dimension.

Crime and Terrorism in the Developed World

Major urban centers in the developed world have been targets of terrorist attacks. This has been seen with 9/11 in the United States, the United Kingdom, Madrid, Spain subway bombings,[①] Tokyo, Japan by the Aum Shinrikyo group[②] and most recently the Charlie Hebdo attack in Paris.

Crime and corruption played a critical role in every of the previously mentioned attacks. From drug trafficking to credit card fraud, sales of counterfeits, terror groups have exploited black markets to advance their causes, blurring the line between criminal and political activity. Often the investigators fail to examine the crime and corruption behind these attacks, but they are present.

As I discuss in my book, *Dirty Entanglements: Corruption, Crime and Terrorism*, criminal facilitators helped the 9/11 hijackers obtain the visas they needed to stay in the United States. Corruption at the Bureau of Motor Vehicles office in the Washington, DC suburbs allowed the hijackers to obtain the drivers licenses that allowed them to board the planes they hijacked. In Madrid, the terrorists met in prison. All had criminal pasts. Those behind the Madrid subway bombing had to generate their own funds. The Madrid cell received initial funding from al-Qaeda, but this provided only start-up costs and was not sufficient to fund an attack.[③] Instead, it had to develop its own criminal capabilities by using the drug profits of the ringleader, Ahmidan.[④] The Madrid attackers purchased illicit explosives to deploy in the subways. Investigations in the Charlie Hebdo case and kosher supermarket attack in Paris reveal that one of the Kouachi brothers, the attackers of the cartoonists, had been previously named in the sale of counterfeit sneakers and he was also implicated in the sale of

---

① Shelley, 29-63.

② David E. Kaplan and Andrew Marshall, The Cult at the End of the World: The Terrifying Story of the Aum Doomsday Cult, from the Subways of Tokyo to the Nuclear Arsenals of Russia (New York: Crown Books, 1996).

③ Javier Jordán, "The Madrid Attacks: Results of Investigations Two Years Later", Terrorism Monitor 4, no.5 (March 9, 2006), http://www.jamestown.org/programs/gta/single/? tx_ttnews[tt_news] = 696&tx_ttnews[backPid] = 181&no_cache = 1. Category: Terrorism Monitor, Europe.

④ Elaine Sciolino, "Complex Web of Madrid Plot Still Entangled", New York Times, April 12, 2004.

smuggled cigarettes.[1] He had met his fellow terrorist who perpetrated the attack on the supermarket in prison.[2] Corruption in prisons allows terrorists the possibility to operate.

Developed countries figure in important ways in supporting terrorism. As the Los Angeles case discussed earlier, a criminal-terrorist car theft ring provided critical funding for a Chechen terrorist cell in Southern Russia. Salesof cigarettes in Detroit, Michigan that have been smuggled from North Carolina with low tax rates on cigarettes provide funding for a terrorist group.[3]

Many foreign fighters being recruited now in Europe have criminal records. Some of them have been engaged in petty crime whereas others have committed more serious crimes. It has also been hypothesized that many of the foreign fighters support their travel to join ISIS by engaging in petty illicit trade.

Crime and Terrorism in the Developing World

The impact of crime and terrorism is particularly pronounced in the developing world. Corruption on borders and in governments allow the criminals and terrorists the space in which to operate. Trade in both licit and illicit goods may follow the same routes reducing the likelihood of detection.

More developed countries have the capacity to observe and analyze the convergence of criminal activity, trade routes and of the illicit activity of non-state actors. But the limited capacity in the developing world allows these linkages to continue undeterred.

Transnational crime and conflict destabilizes regions allowing groups to operate in the chaotic environment. In fact, this environment may be so conducive to their illicit activity that there is often no incentive to settle conflicts.

Close links may exist between politicized organized crime group, terrorists and insurgents who all have no interest in a well functioning state. This leads to a continuing degradation of the political environment. Without any disincentives to stop, groups can decay into predation and excessive violence. Illustrative of this is the case of ISIS. Yet it is also visible in Africa

---

① Centre d'Analyse du Terrorisme, "Financement du Terrorisme La Contrabande et la contrefaçon de cigarettes", March 2015, http://www.cat-int.org/website/wp-content/uploads/2014/11/Focus-CAT-TF-Cigarette-Mars-2015.pdf.

② Rukmini Callimachi and Jim Yardley, "From Amateur to Ruthless Jihadist in France Chérif and Saïd Kouachi's Path to Paris Attack at Charlie Hebdo", http://www.nytimes.com/2015/01/18/world/europe/paris-terrorism-brothers-said-cherif-kouachi-charlie-hebdo.html.

③ Centre d'Analyse du Terrorisme, "Financement du Terrorisme La Contrabande et la contrefaçon de cigarettes".

where the convergence of different forms of illicit trade such as wildlife, arms, people and cigarettes destabilizes the continent. Yet this instability and crime have consequences far beyond the point of original interaction.

Terrorist and Crime Groups as Service Providers

In corrupt environments, the state does not provide for the needs of citizens. In the absence of the state, nonstate actors step in. These nonstate actors can be nongovernmental and multinational organizations, or they can be illicit nonstate actors, terrorists, and transnational groups that offer services to citizens to advance *their objectives*, which are not just the welfare of the citizens. Therefore, by supplanting the absent state, the illicit actors make major inroads with populations who otherwise might be repelled by their violence.①

Crime groups' provision of services ensures that they remain embedded in their communities. Citizens will not cooperate with law enforcement to rid their communities of the criminal organizations because they are indebted to them for vital services.

When governments do not deliver on basic social services, extremist and terrorist groups can gain much support from the populace through their publicized anticorruption campaigns. Illustrative of this is the Taliban in Afghanistan. The "Taliban/insurgents derive both financial and political capital from the opium economy."② In Yemen, corruption and its affiliated problems results in an absence of public services, the appropriation of natural resource wealth by a few, and the failure to deliver disaster relief. The current instability and acute violence in Yemen is a consequence of this. These are prime elements of the recruiting message of AQAP. As one commentator reported, "to date, AQAP continues to display an impressive talent for assimilating broadly popular grievances into a single narrative in which jihad remains the only solution to the country's multiple crises."③ Similarly, such as the Abu Sayyaf Group (ASG), they advance their political agendas by exploiting citizen repulsion at pervasive corruption and focusing on service delivery to people, in the form of

---

① Justin Magouirk, "Nefarious Helping Hand: Anti-Corruption Campaigns, Social Service Provision and Terrorism", Terorrism and Political Violence, Vol.20, no.3, 2008, 356-75.

② UNODC, Addiction, Crime and Insurgency, 2009, 141 https://www.unodc.org/documents/data-and-analysis/Afghanistan/Afghan_Opium_Trade_2009_web.pdf.

③ Gabriel Koehler-Derrick, ed., A False Foundation? AQAP, Tribes and Ungoverned Spaces in Yemen (West Point, NY: Combating Terrorism Center at West Point, September 2011), 41, http://www.ctc.usma.edu/posts/a-false-foundation-aqap-tribes-and-ungoverned-spaces-in-yemen.

schools, public transport, garbage collection, medical care, and so on.①

Terrorists provide benefits for different reasons than criminals. Social service delivery not only curries favor in the communities where they operate but also helps inculcate the ideology that is at the basis of the terrorist group. In Basque Spain, the ETA developed and sustained support structures among youth, women, and trade unions.② The LTTE in Sri Lanka invested in nongovernmental organization activities.③ AQAP prioritizes charity work to recruit supporters.④

The FARC in Colombia, at its height, became a major provider of public services, including vocational schools, health clinics, and public works, and provided for infrastructure through road paving. Fifteen hundred Colombians surveyed in the late 1990s reported a high usage rate of FARC services.⑤

Conclusion

Diverse and complex relationships characterize the interaction of crime, terrorism, and corruption. These relationships have allowed illicit trade and transnational crime to assume an ever-larger share of the world's global economy and to become a major political force in many countries and regions. Terrorists could not recruit collaborators, develop their organizations, or maintain a broad support network if it were not for the pervasive corruption that undermines quality of life and is repellent to many innocent civilians.

Therefore, the international community needs to focus more on the problems of corruption to limit transnational crime and terrorism. It is too often ignored as a central element of the problem. The importance that China is attaching to anti-corruption activity is illustrative of the recognition of the corrosive impact of the problem.

We need to curtail and control the illicit trade that contributes to the growth of terrorism. Much attention has been paid to the paid to the drug trade. New large funding sources now

① Erica Chenoweth and Jessica C. Teets, "To Bribe or to Bomb: Do Corruption and Terrorism Go Together?", in Corruption, Global Security, and World Order, ed. Robert I. Rotberg (Washington, DC: Brookings Institution Press, 2009), 171.

② B. Tejerina, "Protest Cycle, Political Violence and Social Movements in the Basque Country", Nations and Nationalism 7, no.1 (2001): 51-52.

③ Pierre Emmanuel Ly, "The Charitable Activities of Terrorist Groups", Public Choice 131 (2007): 181.

④ Peter Knoope, "AQAP: A Local Problem, a Global Concern", August 20, 2013, http://icct.nl/publications/icct-commentaries/aqap-a-local-problem-a-global-concern? dm_i = 1ADT, 1SH80, 8J4SN9, 6E9R2, 1.

⑤ Vanda Felbab-Brown, Shooting Up: Counterinsurgency and the War on Drugs (Washington, D.C.: Brookings Institution, 2009), 84.

include human smuggling, trafficking of wildlife products like elephant ivory and antiquities. Yet financial support also comes from trade in small items—counterfeit clothing and sports shoes, smuggled cigarettes and other criminal acts that are small and do not command law enforcement attention. This is particularly true in Western Europe and the United States.

We need to stop stovepiping our responses to transnational crime and terrorism and to address these related problems in an integrated way. We also need to address the convergence of different forms of illicit activity rather than focusing on a single form of illicit activity. For China, to counter the international drug trade into China from Africa, it must also target the illicit wildlife trade that follows the same routes. Because the profits of this trade are so large that they enrich and strengthen the drug organizations significantly. By viewing this only as a problem of illicit drug trade, it is not possible to significantly weaken these harmful organizations.

There needs to be much greater international collaboration in implementing the UN Resolutions on Terrorism. To do this, there needs to be much more cooperation in developing laws, collecting data and analyzing the networks that facilitate crime and terrorism.

States alone cannot deal with threatening nonstate actors, who are not their symmetric opponents. Moreover, diverse elements of government are needed to counter these actors than just traditional military forces or law enforcement. But many states' integrity and capacity have been compromised by corruption; they are not capable of opposing illicit actors. Corruption is particularly acute in many states in the developing world, particularly in Africa and the Middle East, that have had their boundaries defined by colonial powers and lack any inherent integrity or citizen loyalty to state institutions that transcend the clan or the tribe. Many have leaders who have placed their personal interests or those of their clan ahead of the general interests of their citizens.

Yet even stronger states are often not equipped to counter the challenges of nonstate actors and the network structures that facilitate their operations. States may mobilize to counter an insurgency, but they cannot counter the corruption, crime, and terrorism that have penetrated other states.

Rather than a grand strategy, the international community needs a wholistic approach. *A whole-of-society approach is needed.* But this requires a response from the global community, consisting of the participation of multilateral organizations, international and local business, consumers, religious and secular civil society, journalists and international online communications (which have replaced much print journalism), researchers, and educational institutions. Without the participation and cooperation of different communities outside of government forming strategic partnerships, it will prove impossible to counter the corrosive impact of crime, corruption and terrorism.

正在增长的恐怖主义:认识其原因,达到有效预防和成功防御

埃米利奥·C.维亚诺(Emilio C.Viano)①

一、如今的策略及干预措施

当今世界所面临的最大挑战之一就是,如何去开展和部署一个有效的策略来打击正在持续增长的恐怖主义。一个好的策略必须同时包括两个方面:防护方面和预防方面。防护方面要求能进行成功的防卫以避免恐怖袭击,而预防方面要求能够去除那些为恐怖主义的产生提供条件、证明恐怖主义合理性并促进其成长的根本因素。②

现在,针对恐怖主义的大多数干预措施都属于保护性措施。③ 这些措施主要是通过军事、警务和情报方面的干预措施来试图去破坏恐怖组织,阻止其运作,拆除其训练设施,并击杀或逮捕其组织的领导人。制裁是另一种常用手段,一般由联

① 埃米利奥·C.维亚诺(Emilio C.Viano),国际犯罪学会主席。

② Jackson,Brian A.,Groups,Networks or Movements:A Command-and-Control Approach to Classifying Terrorist Organizations and Its Applications to Al Qaeda,Studies in Conflict and Terrorism 29(2006):241-62.

③ Wisner,Ben,Assessment of Capability and Vulnerability,in Greg Bankoff,George Frerks,and Dorothea Hillhorst,Mapping Vulnerability:Disaster,Development and People,(2004),183-93.London:Earthscan.

合国或是一些强大的国家作出，这些国家将特定的恐怖组织成员作为打击目标，并力求制止其他的人或国家为恐怖组织及恐怖活动提供支持和帮助。联合国反恐部门正致力于构建国家之间以及像欧盟这样的区域组织之间的国际合作①，以期能够冻结恐怖组织资产，更牢固地控制边境区域，并提高情报机关和警察部门的国际合作。② 另一个联合国机构——不扩散委员会，以及联合国的其他一些双边项目或国际项目③，也在致力于加强成员国的干预力度，尤其是在避免恐怖分子获得强力武器和毁灭性材料方面。[④,⑤]毫无疑问，对各种邪恶组织施压并给其运作带来困难，或是帮助构建国际合作来打击恐怖主义，像这样的活动是很有价值的。但是我们也必须承认，从长远来看，所有这些项目在持续且有效地减少全球恐怖主义威胁上，都不是非常成功。事实上，要想有效地镇压和战胜恐怖主义，关键是要发展并实施一些更为有效的措施。这些措施必须能够解决造成政治极端主义、意识形态极端主义和宗教极端主义的根本原因，并能够彻底改变那些支持、帮助并公然为像“基地”组织、ISIS 这样的恐怖组织进行辩护的社会、经济和政治的现实条件。⑥

二、一种流行病学方法

流行病学的方法是众多打击恐怖主义策略中的一种与众不同的方式，该方法把恐怖主义当作埃博拉疫情（一种由病毒或是突变的疾病导致的具有致命性和传染性

① Bures, Oldrich and Stephanie Ahern, The European Model of Building Regional Cooperation Against Terrorism, in David Cortright and George A.Lopez, Uniting Against Terror: Cooperative Non Military Responses to the Global Terorist Threat, Cambridge MA: MIT Press, 2007, 187-236.

② Cortright, David, George A.Lopez, Alistair Millar, and Linda Gerber-Stellingwerf, Global Cooperation Against Terrorism: Evaluating the United Nations Counter-Terrorism Committee, in David Cortright and George A.Lopez, Uniting Against Terror: Cooperative Non Military Responses to the Global Terorist Threat, Cambridge MA: MIT Press, 2007, 23-50.

③ WMD Commission, World at Risk: The Report of the Commission on the Prevention of WMD Proliferation and Terrorism. New York: Vintage, 2008.

④ Millar, Alistair and Jason Ipe, Cutting the Deadly Nexus: Preventing the Spread of Weapons of Mass Destruction to Terrorists, in David Cortright and George A. Lopez, Uniting Against Terror: Cooperative Non Military Responses to the Global Terorist Threat, Cambridge MA: MIT Press 2007, 123-156.

⑤ Mowatt-Larsen, Rolf, Al Qaeda Weapons of Mass Destruction Threat: Hype or Reality? Belfer Center for Science and International Affairs, Kennedy School, Harvard University February 1, 2010.

⑥ Barkun, Michael. Chasing Phantoms: Reality, Imagination and Homeland Security Since 9/11. (Chapel Hill NC: University of North Carolina Press, 2011)

的感染)来进行治疗。[①] 在此情形下,我们的第一要务是要控制传染病的蔓延。[②] 第二,对有被感染风险的人实施保护也是必不可少的。第三,必须要处理那些为该传染病的产生和传播提供帮助的潜在情景和条件。[③]

该模式可以适用于恐怖主义的保护性干预措施之中,比如在一般区域中对人们的活动进行限制,而在更为严重的疫区要进行严格的限制;阻止意识形态通过不同的方式进行传播;拉拢那些更为温和的"沉默的多数人",并努力让他们通过和平的方式来表达政治观点和寻求改变。

在预防方面,必不可少的是,将各种不同类型的纷争,比如经济纠纷、政治纠纷、军事纠纷,以一种公平的方式快速地解决,从而避免其进一步演变为武装冲突。同时,我们必须尽快解决那些作为交战理由的根本原因。[④] 在这些根本原因中,被边缘化和被排斥是最重要的原因,其存在于许多移民群体中,并造成了许多负面的影响。战胜并治愈这种"疾病",不仅需要许多年的时间,还需要大家的通力合作,认识到这一点也是十分重要的。[⑤]

三、科菲·安南的"五 D"原则

2005 年,在一次关于民主、恐怖主义和安全的峰会上,时任联合国秘书长的科菲·安南提出了打击恐怖主义的总体方法,并在预防和保护两个方面进行了梳理。这包含于我们所称的"五 D"原则(the "five Ds")中:

1. 劝说那些对政府或社会不满的组织不要选择恐怖主义作为实现目标的策略;
2. 剥夺恐怖分子发动袭击的手段;
3. 阻止任何国家支持恐怖分子;
4. 增强各国防范恐怖主义的能力;
5. 在反恐斗争中保卫人权。

一年后,科菲·安南又再次重申了其观点,他呼吁"我们要强化恐怖主义是不可

---

① Stares, Paul and Monica Yacoubian, "Terrorism as a Virus", The Washington Post, 23 August, 2005.

② Waugh, William L., Jr., Terrorism and the All-Hazards Model, Washington DC: FEMA, 2004.

③ Posner, Richard, Catastrophe: Risk and Response, New York: Oxford University Press, 2004.

④ Barkun, Michael. Chasing Phantoms: Reality, Imagination and Homeland Security Since 9/11. Chapel Hill NC: University of North Carolina Press, 2011.

⑤ Croft, Stuart and Cerwyn Moore, The Evolution of Threat Narratives in the Age of Terror: Understanding Terrorist Threats in Britain, International Affairs 86(2010): 821-35.

原谅且不被接受的这一观念，同时还要致力于消除恐怖主义所赖以生存的条件”。[①] 美国白宫于 2006 年发布了打击恐怖主义的国家战略，该战略指出，“打击恐怖主义不仅仅是一场军备之争，更是一场观念之争”。其也强调，我们需要创建一个排斥暴力极端主义的全球环境，发展自由以及人格尊严，并做更多努力来促使争端的和平解决，以及法治程度的提升。[②] 这些声明已经被奥巴马政府所确认并得到了扩充。[③]

我们也需要对恐怖活动的“需求”方面施以影响，尤其是鉴于数千年轻男性和女性离开自己的国家，包括一些欧洲国家，去加入 ISIS。我们必须要找到一个新的方法制止其新成员的加入，切断其资金支持，阻止其意识形态的正当化，阻止其歪曲事实，并且破坏其政治上的友好关系。

四、本文的目标

本文探知并说明了：令近年来的一些重大恐怖活动得以开始、发展和显示自己权威的各种因素；被恐怖分子有效利用，以试图证明其存在、运行和极端行为的合理性的那些宗教方面的不满、政治方面的怨愤和军事方面的指责；为恐怖主义提供支撑的社会现状和经济现状；恐怖主义与原教旨主义之间的联系；以及利用网络和社交媒体而被恐怖组织完善和使用的那些生存策略和招募策略，其中包括了对自杀式袭击者的招募。关于女性成员的招募以及她们加入恐怖组织的动机，本文也进行了详细的调查研究。

最后，本文还提供了一些预防和有效打击恐怖主义的创新型策略以供大家参考。

五、广义的反恐战争

21 世纪的首个十年里，由布什政府以及其随后的政治人物一起作出的“反恐战

---

① U.N.General Assembly, Uniting Against Terrorism: Recommendations for a Global Counter-terrorism Strategy, A/60/825, New York, 27 April 2006, par.7.

② White House, National Strategy for Combatting Terrorism.Washington DC: Government Printing Office, September, 7, 2006.

③ National Academies, Promoting Individual Privacy in the Struggle Against Terrorism: A Framework for Program Assessment(Washington DC: National Academies Press, 2008).

争”总声明已经导致了一个不好的后果，即把各种恐怖主义全归类在了一种广义的分类之下，并对它们一概而论。① 结果，有效策略的开展变得困难且混乱。②

恐怖组织可以生存在不同的政治、经济、社会、文化、宗教的环境下。③

不顾其本质区别，而使用所谓的“一刀切”的方法，并不能给我们带来一个明确的、有针对性的、标准的反恐政策和方法。④ 举例来说，“基地”组织与哈马斯之间就有着本质的区别，前者更注重全球性任务，而后者则很明确要求优先考虑当地的工作。当然，他们也具有一定的共同点，如意识形态。但这些区别十分重要，它们可以指导我们如何处理不同的恐怖活动。⑤ 打个比方，对于那些由于其自己以为的历史错误，而妄想利用恐怖行动来满足诉求的恐怖组织，我们可以通过一个当地的政治方案来解决，而对另一些拥有大量全球性任务的恐怖组织，则很难有一个有效且令人满意的解决措施。

当布什政府强调那些资助恐怖活动的国家是其干预措施的重点，并将那些诸如入侵伊拉克、推翻萨达姆政权、处决萨达姆的行动正当化时，像是拥有大量分支的“基地”组织以及 ISIS 这样的有实力的恐怖组织，却表现得像是不受国家控制或是超越了国家的控制一样。⑥ 即使本·拉登接受了许多政府的支持，比如苏丹的支持，尤其是阿富汗的支持，但是其真正的恐怖网络结构和配置都是独立于某一确定的国家，尤其是在阿富汗塔利班组织被推翻之后，其独立性就更加明显了。当奥萨马·本·拉登隐藏起来以躲避美国和其他国家的侦查时，“基地”组织开始变得四分五裂，而在其死亡以后，这个现象则被进一步地加剧，后来该组织遍布于几十个国家，且主要集中于中东和北非地区。⑦ 这些组织虽然可能有共同的意识形态和统一的战略目标，但是他们的运作却是独立的，他们有自己的资金来源、自己的招募机制和训练新兵的方式。他们能够自己决定袭击的对象、地点和时间，他们也会自己策划袭击方式。

---

① Frewer, Lynn J., Truth, Transparency and Social Context: Implications for Social Amplification of Risk, in Nick Pidgeon, Roger E. Kasperson and Paul Slovic (editors), The Social Amplification of Risk, 123-37, Cambridge, UK: Cambridge University Press, 2003.

② Fussey, Pete, Observing Potentiality in the Global City: Surveillance and Counterterrorism, in International Criminal Justice Review 17, September, 2007, 171-92.

③ Cortright, David and George A. Lopez, Strategic Counter-Terrorism, in David Cortright and George A. Lopez, Uniting Against Terror: Cooperative Non Military Responses to the Global Terrorist Threat, Cambridge MA: MIT Press, 2007, 1-22.

④ Mueller, John, Overblown: How Politicians and the Terrorism Industry Inflate National Security Threats and Why We Believe Them, New York: Free Press, 2006.

⑤ Nacos, Brigitte L., Yaeli Bloch-Elton, and Robert Y. Shapiro, Prevention of Terrorism in Post 9/11 America: News Coverage, Public Perceptions, and the Politics of Homeland Security, Terrorism and Political Violence, 20, January-March, 2008, 1-25.

⑥ Bergen, Peter, The Longest War: The Enduring Conflict Between America and al-Qaeda, New York, NY: Free Press, 2011.

⑦ Bergen, Peter, Manhunt: The Ten-Year Search for Bin Laden from 9/11 to Abbottabad, New York, NY: Crown, 2012.

这在ISIS也是一样的,ISIS是一个明显的跨国组织,他们高效地利用了全球化这一工具来进行信息传播、成员招募、组织经营、财富积累以及业务的开展。ISIS已经证明,他们很善于使用网络、社交软件,他们也能熟练地运用像YouTube这样的全球性网站来发布视频,他们还擅长于进行国际旅行以及突破诸如欧盟国家之间的边境区域。他们通过这些方式传递信息以便与其他成员沟通,并在全球各个地区,尤其是中东地区,计划和实施恐怖行动。

此外,这种离心式的组织形态在最近一段时间呈现指数的增长。自称"伊斯兰圣战者"的恐怖分子所带来的威胁已经变得更具灵活性和扩散性。不论是自主创立的还是国家扶植的,大量与"基地"组织和ISIS没有关系或者关系不密切的恐怖组织正在欧洲和其他地方兴起。恐怖组织的分裂带来了大量的"独狼式"恐怖分子。这些恐怖分子与已知的恐怖组织或是国家都没有任何联系。他们是巨大的威胁,因为他们的恐怖行为有很强的不可预测性、独立性和随机性。①

六、自给自足的"独狼式"恐怖主义

一些人认为,由于消灭了奥萨马·本·拉登和其他的恐怖组织领导人,恐怖组织中的层级制度遭到了破坏,这导致恐怖主义变得越来越分散。许多自给自足的、以家为基地的恐怖组织开始在欧洲、中东和其他地区出现。这些恐怖组织实施了:2004年3月的西班牙马德里阿托查火车站炸弹袭击,2005年7月的伦敦地铁爆炸案②,以及2010年3月的莫斯科地铁系统投弹事件。虽然伦敦爆炸案的投弹者中有些人与巴基斯坦的"基地"组织成员存在一定的联系,但是这些案件的实施者却都是当地的居民。据有关报道,虽然马德里的投弹者想仿效的是奥萨马·本·拉登,但是他并没有与"基地"组织取得任何切实的联系。

在其他一些知名的恐怖袭击中也有相同的情况,比如,发生在2009年的胡德堡枪击案。该案中,美国陆军少校、精神病学家——纳达尔·马里克·哈桑射杀13人并致超过30人受伤。枪击事件后数天,就有媒体报道披露称,反恐怖特别工作组早已知悉了哈桑与也门的阿訇·安瓦尔·奥拉基(该人被视为一个安全威胁而受到美

① Sageman, Marc, Leaderless Jihad: Terror Networks in the 21st Century, Philadelphia PA: University of Pennsylvania Press, 2008.

② JFO McAllister et alii, Hate Around the Corner: In a Stunnng Twist Investigators Blame the London Attacks on Four Homegrown Suicide Bombers and Look for Global Links to Al Qaeda, Time, July 25, 2005.

国国家安全局的监视，其最终被美国无人机所射杀）之间的一系列电子邮件，而且，哈桑的同事也一直知道，最近几年，他正变得越来越激进。可有趣的是，当受害者家人以及受伤士兵向美国政府施压，希望能够将这起事件定义为一起恐怖袭击并且把哈桑定义为一名恐怖分子时，五角大楼却拒绝了他们的请求。其给出的解释是，在军事司法系统下，指控哈桑是一名恐怖分子是不可能的，因为这么做将会使得军事检察官难以支持对哈桑的有罪判决。①

类似地，在 2015 年 7 月，一名持枪者在田纳西州的两处军事设施中实施了扫射，杀死了两名美国海军陆战队士兵，并造成了另外两名服役人员和一名警官的重伤。枪击者最终被击毙。经确认，该名枪击嫌犯叫穆罕默德·尤瑟夫·阿卜杜拉泽茨，现年 24 岁。他出生于科威特，于 1996 年来到美国。报道称，执法机关没有发现阿卜杜拉泽茨与恐怖分子有任何联系的可能以及联系意向。FBI 也没有意识到他会成为一个威胁。② 美国发生的这些案例表明，自我产生激进意识的人以及所谓的“独狼”(lone wolf)已经开始出现，他们虽然没有恐怖分子那么专业，但是他们具有同等的致命性。这使得我们识别是否是恐怖分子变得更加困难，同时也加大了打击恐怖主义的难度。③ 虽然有人会说，这些自主创立的组织的成员并没有获得如同“基地”组织成员和 ISIS 成员那样的训练程度，也没有他们那样的纪律性，但是从另一方面来看，他们却更有能力去计划和实施恐怖袭击，因为他们与任何恐怖网络都不存在联系，因此我们很难通过监察恐怖主义网络及其代理人之间的对话来发现他们。如果展开袭击的时间以及地点都是无法预测的话，那么对我们来说，要想阻止其发生就是相当困难的。④ 毫无疑问，自 2001 年以来，我们在对抗“基地”组织方面已经取得了巨大的进步。据报道，我们已经击毙了数千“基地”组织成员，而其绝大部分领导人，包括奥萨马·本·拉登，也都已经被消灭。执法机关和情报机构之间国际合作的增强使得我们能够更有效地预防恐怖袭击的发生。但同时，一些令人不安的问题也正在悄然增长。美国以及当地政府武装所使用的抓捕、监禁、讯问的方式存在很大的质疑和争议。关于阿布格莱布监狱内囚犯被虐待、羞辱、折磨甚至是被杀害的照片；[⑤,⑥]关

① Arizona Daily Star, “Terror act or workplace violence? Hasan trial raises sensitive issue”, August 11, 2013; http://tucson. com/news/national/terror-act-or-workplace-violence-hasan-trial-raises-sensitive-issue/article _ be513c51 - a35d-5b4f-b3a0-13654f019ea6.html.

② CBS/AP, Four Marines killed in attacks on Chattanooga military facilities, July 16, 2015; http://www.cbsnews.com/news/report-police-officer-shot near-tennessee-army-recruiting-center.

③ Whitlock, Craig, Terrorists Proving Harder to Profile, Washington Post, March 12, 2007.

④ Sageman, Marc, The Reality of Grass Roots Terrorism, Foreign Affairs 87, July-August, 2008, 163-65.

⑤ Bergen, Peter, The Longest War: The Enduring Conflict Between America and al-Qaeda, New York, NY: Free Press, 2011.

⑥ Greenberg, Karen J. and Joshua L. Datel, The Torture Papers: The Road to Abu Ghraib, New York: Cambridge University Press, 2005.

于巴格拉姆空军基地中人满为患、囚犯被虐待以及囚犯大量死亡的照片;关于关塔那摩军事监狱中严苛的监禁条件、讯问方式、折磨手段(水刑)、隔离条件的照片①;在CIA 的秘密拘留所以及欧洲和其他国家的讯问中心内发生的相似的骇人听闻的事件报告;对嫌疑人,甚至有些是被冤枉的人,采用非法绑架和示众的方式,这种种证据与事实,使得这些实施了折磨与杀害行为,如今还频繁地使用无人机对恐怖主义领导人及其追随者进行超越司法之外的暗杀活动的国家,它们与恐怖主义无异②,也使得美国以及西方世界的道德品质在所谓的"反恐战争"中染上了污点。[③,④]

七、恐怖主义的财务问题

在打击恐怖主义的财务领域上,我们已经取得了很大的进步,尤其是在冻结与恐怖主义有关的资产方面。⑤ 资助恐怖主义的那些资金流,在很长一段时间内一直持续地运作着,其通过不同的形式来获取资金并进行资金的运输。[⑥,⑦,⑧,⑨,⑩,⑪,⑫,⑬,⑭,⑮,⑯]尤其是当资金流通过各种形式来到"基地"组织时。

① Warrick, Joby, and Dan Eggen, Hill Briefed on Waterboarding in 2002, Washington Post, 9 December, 2007.

② Bergen, Peter, Drone Wars: Transforming Conflict, Law, and Policy, New York, NY: Cambridge University Press, 2014. (Co-editor with Daniel Rothenberg)

③ Wagner, Abraham, Meeting the Terrorist Challenge: Coping with Failures of Leadership and Intelligece, New York: Harper Collins, 2007.

④ Weinmann, Gabriel and Conrad Winn, The Theatre of Terror: The Mass Media and International Terrorism, New York: Longman, 1993.

⑤ Gardner, Kathryn L., Terrorism Defanged: The Financial Action Task Force and International Efforts to Capture Terrorist Finances, in David Cortright and George A. Lopez, Uniting Against Terror: Cooperative Non Military Responses to the Global Terorist Threat, Cambridge MA: MIT Press, 2007, 157-186.

⑥ Interpol, General Secretariat, The Hawala Alternative Remittance System and its Role in Money Laundering, Lyon, January, 2000.

⑦ U.S. Department of Justice, Benevolence International Foundation Director Indicted for Racketeering Conspiracy: Providing Material Support to Al Qaeda and Other Violent Groups, Press Release, October 9, 2002.

⑧ Levitt, Matthew, Combating Terrorism Financing, Despite the Saudis, PolicyWatch, November 1, 2002.

⑨ U.S. Treasury, Shutting Down the Terrorist Financial Network, Office of Public Affairs press release, December 4, 2001.

⑩ U.S. Treasury, U.S. Designated Five Charities Funding Hamas and Six Senior Hamas Leaders as Terrorist Entities, Treasury Department Press Release, August 22, 2003.

⑪ U.S. Treasury, Treasury Designates Director, Branches of Charity Bankrolling Al Qaeda Network, Treasury Department Press Release, August 3, 2006.

⑫ U.S. versus Holy Land Foundation for Relief and Development etalii, 04-CR-240, Indictment(ND TX 2004).

⑬ National Commission on Terrorist Attacks against the United States, Staff Report, Monograph on Terrorism Financing, August, 2004.

⑭ Collier, Robert, Michigan Based Charity Finds Itself Caught in the Middle, San Francisco Chronicle, June 17, 2004.

⑮ U.S. versus Baz Mohammed et al., S1403-CR 486(DC), indictment(SD NY 2005).

⑯ U.S. versus Medina-Castellanos etalii, o5-CR-155, indictment(ED NC 2005).

但是,对这一领域的干预并没有像人们所期望的那样有效地打压恐怖主义的活动。其中主要的原因是,一些恐怖行动的组织与实施并不需要高昂的经费。除了像是发生在纽约、华盛顿以及宾夕法尼亚的"9·11"恐怖袭击这样的大规模恐怖袭击①,那些小型的恐怖行为或者"独狼式"的袭击都不需要大量的资金,这些袭击可以很轻松地通过自筹经费来实施。自主创立的恐怖组织,其运营费用十分低廉。据估计,马德里阿托查火车站炸弹袭击的总费用不超过 10000 美元。② 就 ISIS 而言,有报道称,其资金情况要比这些组织好得多。2015 年 5 月,《纽约时报》③就曾基于兰德公司的信息刊登出了这样一个报道,该报道称,ISIS 有着十分强大的资金支持,自从 2014 年 6 月攻陷摩苏尔以后,其已获得大约 8.75 亿美元。虽然专家学者也赞同 ISIS 是一个十分富有的组织,但是他们并不认为恐怖组织有着稳定的财政收入。

依据兰德公司分析员的分析,尽管我们希望通过空袭以及降低油价来破坏 ISIS 的资金支持,但其目前所拥有的收益和资产都远高于其所需的开销。兰德公司的统计结果显示,ISIS 拥有多种收益来源。虽然其最初的资金主要来自石油行业,但是现在已有报告指出,如今石油收益只占其总收益的很小一部分。2014 年,ISIS 的主要收益来自:在伊拉克进行的敲诈勒索和征税行为(大约有 6 亿美元),从伊拉克国有银行中窃取的钱款(大约 5 亿美元)、石油收益(大约 1 亿美元)以及绑架赎金收益(大约 2000 万美元)。

根据《纽约时报》的报道,通过降低运营成本、保持收益的多样性,如今 ISIS 的开销主要用于支付成员的薪水。每个月,ISIS 都要向其成员支付 300 万到 1000 万美元的薪水。许多专家同意,ISIS 非常富有。通过提供各种资金源④,一些国家,在叙利亚发挥着深层而又隐蔽的作用,他们向反叛者提供资金,而在这些反叛者中就包括了早期的 ISIS。根据《纽约时报》的报道⑤,富有的海湾人民,不论其是否有政府意识,都会为在叙利亚的恐怖主义者提供资金支持。毫无疑问,这使得如今的情况变得更加复杂,美国在该区域中的一些强力的同盟可能会一边与美国合作进行打击 ISIS 的

---

① National Commission on Terrorist Attacks against the United States, The 9/11 Commission Report: Final Report. New York: Norton, 2004.

② U.N., Security Council, Fifth Report of the Analytic Support and Sanctions Monitoring Team Appointed Pursuant to Resolution 1526(2004) and 1617(2005) Concerning Al-Qaida and the Taliban and Associated Individuals and Entities, S/2006/750, New York, 20 September 2006, paragraphs 59 and 61.

③ New York Times, Sarah Almukhtar, ISIS Finances Are Strong, 19 May, 2015.

④ New York Times, Ben Hubbard, Wealthy Gulf Nations Are Criticized for Tepid Response to Syrian Refugee Crisis, September 5, 2015.

⑤ 同上。

轰炸行动,而同时在另一边,他们希望削弱和消灭什叶派以及伊朗在该地区的影响,并把该地区控制权掌握在海湾国家手中,所以他们就将ISIS看成是一个用来达成这一目的的武装组织,而向其提供资金和支持。自从ISIS通过走私来自伊拉克或库尔德斯坦的石油,尤其是穿越土耳其进行走私石油活动,从而获得相当可观的收益以后,有人开始质疑,为什么一些有能力的行为主体不能够阻断非法石油的流通以及ISIS的资金流,比如库尔德人,他们被认为是对抗ISIS的最高效的本地士兵;再比如土耳其人,他们虽然可能正支持着温和的叛乱组织以试图推翻叙利亚政权,但他们同时也控制着那些从伊拉克北部运来的石油和那些购买石油的土耳其公司;甚至是以美国为首的联盟,他们能够更加有效地对ISIS控制下的油田和相关设施,比如管道,进行轰炸。

八、新　兵

同样重要甚至可能更为重要的是,已知的恐怖组织,尤其是ISIS,都依赖于大量训练有素的步兵。包括年轻男女在内,ISIS的新兵在各个时期都有巨大的增长,2003年美国入侵伊拉克后的情况就是一个典型例子,但是,当ISIS在叙利亚和伊拉克中出现、开展活动并获取领地收益之后,这个问题就变得尤其严重。根据美国情报专家的分析[①],自2011年以来,有来自超过100个国家的将近3万名外国士兵来到了伊拉克和叙利亚。一年以前,他们就曾估计过,大约有来自80个国家的1.5万名士兵奔赴伊拉克和叙利亚。这表明在过去的12个月里就有一倍数量的新兵加入了恐怖组织,这也突出表现了国际社会在紧缩边界区、分享情报以及实施反恐法律上所做的努力并没有成功减少加入恐怖组织的新兵数量。

情报机关和执法机关的官员表示,在那些已经参与或试图参与伊拉克冲突或者叙利亚冲突的人里面,美国人的数量从一年前的100人上升到了现在的250多人。[②]早在ISIS出现以前,美国以及其他地区的人就已经开始奔赴中东地区以加入到各种恐怖组织之中。[③,④]

---

① New York Times, Eric Schmitt and SominiSengupta, Thousands Enter Syria to Join ISIS Despite Global Efforts, September 26, 2015.

② Berger, J.M., Jihad Joe: Americans Who Go to War in the Name of Islam. (Washington DC: Potomac Books, 2011)

③ Kaplan, David E.etalii, Hundreds of Americans have Followed the Path to Jihad, U.S.News & World Report, June 10, 2002.

④ Williams, Lance. Bin Laden's Bay Area Recruiter, San Francisco Chronicle, November 21, 2001.

尽管五角大楼报告称，联合打击行动已经击毙了至少1万名ISIS成员，但是恐怖组织却一直在持续地扩充自己的军队，其每个月可以招募到大约1000名战士。在几个月以前，美国政府就公开了对超过25000名ISIS新兵的评估报告，其中有至少4500人来自西方国家。由于中东地区的国家边界有着很强的可渗透性，所以美国官员强调，这些数字只是根据同盟国对本国市民出行的报告以及各国给出的情报所推算出的一个初步的估计，并不能精确地反映现实情况。①

我们需要记住，如今还存在着一个网络效应（network effect），即朋友和家人会带来更多的朋友和家人。

还有一点也十分重要，据报道称，自从2014年ISIS宣称伊拉克和叙利亚是自己领域后，数以百计的西方反恐志愿者，包括许多美国人，已经慢慢地进入到了伊拉克和叙利亚地区。志愿者的到来在当地激起了各种不同的反应：虽然库尔德人很感谢这些为作为少数派的宗教信徒提供保护的民兵组织，但是一些库尔德战士更希望美国能提供给他们枪支和重型武器。

可是，美国和其他国家的志愿者的涌入看起来不会很快结束。一些主要由退伍老兵组成的新兴组织也已经开始出现，他们希望能够为那些愿意冒着生命危险而参与外国战斗的人们提供一个更有组织性的框架体系。和ISIS积极利用自己的网上业务进行恐怖活动的招募一样，库尔德派，如伊拉克的“自由斗士”以及叙利亚的“国民保卫联盟”，如今也在加强其网上招募成员的能力。除了军事方面，外国士兵穿越前线加入到库尔德或是其他武装组织的现象还表明，ISIS的兴起速度以及西方政府对此的回应使得大众产生了一个错误的认知，即这是一场发生在正邪之间、现代与落后之间的史诗般的斗争。②

九、女性的招募

众所周知且需要重点关注的是，如今ISIS一直致力于在西欧以及其他西方国家建立起一个强大的女性招募系统。这并不新奇，因为“基地”组织和其他组织也都曾

① New York Times, Eric Schmitt and SominiSengupta, Thousands Enter Syria to Join ISIS Despite Global Efforts, September 26, 2015.

② The Guardian, FazelHawramy and Raya Jalabi, U.S.Civilians and Veterans Leave Home for ISIS Fight with Help from Social Media, 18 April, 2015.

进行过尝试。[①,②,③,④,⑤]隐写术(Steganography)也曾被拿来使用。[⑥] 如今进入叙利亚和伊拉克的外国人潮之所以受到了极大的注目,不仅因为其规模之大,还因为其中包含了许多女性。很多文章都有写到:许多男性为参与冲突而前往冲突地区;这些人总是活跃于社交媒体上,与其支持者及对手分享他们的每日经历。但是,很少有文章了解那些加入 ISIS 的女性以及她们在支持 ISIS 建设中所作出的努力。[⑦] 一些国家十分担心,被 ISIS 所招募的人在回归家园后会成为一个严重的威胁。对这些国家来说,不论加入 ISIS 的是男性还是女性,他们都应该被给予高度的重视。2015 年年初,西方移居者的数量估计有 3500 人,其中女性为 600 人。

一些女性是陪同她们的丈夫或者伙伴而来到中东或其他交战区的。有文件曾记录过西方人带着整个家庭进入到 ISIS 控制区的情况,这其中就包括了他们的妻子和孩子。与 ISIS 的男性成员有联系或者与他们有婚姻关系,一直是女性来到 ISIS 控制区域的重要原因。同样地,也有女性来到交战区是为了和她们的丈夫以及伙伴在一起。

也有一些女性是依照自己的意愿来到 ISIS 的控制地区的,她们的到来与其丈夫或是伙伴无关。这一群体已经受到了媒体、政府和大众的高度关注,尤其是那些还是未成年或非常年轻并且从小成长于西方文化以及教育系统当中的女性。我们主要关注的有以下几点:这些年轻女性可能是通过一个组织有序的,集雇佣、运输与接待为一体的系统而被走私到 ISIS 所控制的区域中的;她们可能被虐待、侮辱以及被强迫与 ISIS 成员结婚或是成为他们的性奴;她们可能会被多次抛弃或变得贫穷,尤其是在她们丈夫或伙伴阵亡以后;她们可能会被雇佣或强迫参加战斗,尤其是被用来作为自杀式炸弹袭击的实施者;她们也有可能会在某一天回到自己的祖国,然后受到激励和训练来实施恐怖袭击或为此提供帮助。

---

① Paz, Reuven, editor, Who Wants to Email Al Qaeda? Project for the Research of Islamist Movements(PRISM).vol. 2, no.2, 2005.

② Usher, Sebastian, Jihad Magazine for Women on the Web, BBC News, August 24, 2004.

③ Phillips, John, Women's Magazine Offers Tips to Terrorists, Washington Times, January 17, 2005.

④ Whine, Michael, Islamist Organizations on the Internet, International Policy Institute for Counter Terrorism, April, 2005.

⑤ O'Neil, Sean and Yaakov Lappin, Britain's Online Imam Declares War as He Calls Young to Jihad: Omar BakriMohammed, Banned from Many British Mosques, Is Issuing a Call to Arms to a Committed Audience, Times Online, January 17, 2005.

⑥ Kessler, Gary C., An Overview of Steganography for the Computer Forensics Examiner, Forensic Science Communications, 6, no.3, July, 2004.

⑦ Jacques, Karen and Paul J.Taylor, Male and Female Suicide Bombers: Different Sexes, Different Reasons, Studies on Conflict and Terrorism 31:4(2008), 304-26.

十、自杀式炸弹袭击:“悲惨的”恐怖主义

国际恐怖主义威胁,其性质在最近已经发生了剧烈的变化。虽然自 1987 年达到峰值后,国际恐怖袭击的数量已经开始下降,但是其造成的伤亡人数却在上升。随着“基地”组织、ISIS 以及其他组织的兴起,新型的恐怖行动,即自杀式炸弹袭击,开始出现。法哈德·霍斯罗哈瓦尔[①]对两种“殉道者”(martyr)进行了区分:那些来自发展中国家,被拒绝给予现代生活必需品的人;以及少数居住于西方世界中的中产移民群体,他们主要来自中东和马格里布,能够轻松适应多种文化,但是在西方世界他们仍然受到了严重的种族歧视。

自杀式炸弹袭击可以被描述成一种集体事故或是“悲惨的”恐怖主义。[②] 这导致了每起事件的死亡人数的显著增长。死亡人数的增长开始于 20 世纪 90 年代,当时发生了许多臭名昭著的事件,比如,1996 年对沙特阿拉伯霍巴塔的袭击;1998 年对内罗毕和达累斯萨拉姆的美国大使馆的炸弹袭击;2001 年 9 月 11 日发生在纽约、华盛顿以及宾夕法尼亚的震惊世界的“9·11”恐怖袭击;2004 年发生在马德里阿托查火车站的爆炸案;2008 年的孟买恐怖袭击;2009 年的美国胡德堡枪击案;2011 年的孟买炸弹袭击;2015 年田纳西州枪击案;以及发生在伊拉克、阿富汗、也门、巴勒斯坦、尼日利亚以及一些非洲国家的一连串自杀式炸弹袭击,其中 2015 年 10 月发生在土耳其的自杀式炸弹袭击造成了 97 人死亡大约 200 人受伤,政府将这起事件归咎于 ISIS;还有库尔德人所表达出的对当地政府、该区域的其他国家以及世界上的其他一些国家的不满。自杀式炸弹袭击的增长,意味着当代恐怖主义已经进入了一个可怕而又恐怖的新局面。[③] 这势必会带来一个剧烈的改变,即恐怖主义已不再像先前一样仅仅采取适度的暴力来获取人们对其事业的关注,也不再仅仅为了取得改变或达成协商谈判的目的而通过恐怖行为来向政府及公众施压。[④]

与其说,自杀式炸弹袭击给不论是男性还是女性的恐怖分子提供了掌控他人以

---

① Khosrokhavar, Farhad, Suicide Bombers: Allah's New Martyrs, London: Pluto Press, 2005.

② Asad, Talal, On Suicide Bombing, New York: Columbia University Press, 2006.

③ Ungar, Sheldon, Moral Panics versus the Risk Society: The Implications of the Changing Sites of Social Anxiety, British Journal of Sociology 52, June, 2001, 271-91.

④ Taarnby, Michael, Profiling Islamic Suicide Terrorists. A Research Report for the Danish Ministry of Justice, November, 2003.

及自己生命的力量，不如说给他们提供了掌控他人以及自己死亡的力量。① 拥有力量以及控制一切的感觉②，使恐怖分子深刻地感受到了自己的能力、力量和自我价值。③ 对于女性自杀式炸弹袭击者来说，这种行为让她们能够从压抑中获得解放，也容许她们体现出自己对在其他强势群体的控制和支配下所受到的政治迫害的愤怒④，和对性别歧视的愤恨。⑤

事实上，女性有很强的杀伤力，她们被认为是最好的自杀式炸弹袭击者⑥，因为她们渴望证明自己有实施这种行为的能力，而且她们意识到除此之外，她们没有办法发现自我。⑦ 车臣妇女之所以能够获得极大的尊重与认可也是因为这个原因。⑧

向那些压迫她们的人，展示自己的愤怒与憎恨，以打破压迫她们的枷锁、打破女性低下的社会地位对她们的禁锢、打破日常的屈辱，这对女性来说是十分光荣的。⑨ 许多案例里面，自杀式炸弹袭击为女性的个人问题或者家庭问题提供了一个解决之道。⑩ 女性实施自杀式炸弹袭击，以一种光荣的方式摆脱如今其所处的进退两难的局面。⑪ 导致这种局面的情况有：由于各种原因而不能获得一个体面的婚姻，同时其家族又不想或是不能继续供养、保护和支持她；或者她一直在遭受虐待、殴打、奴役，而没有其他男性来保护她，她无法避免那些将自己意愿强加于她身上的好斗的男性对她自己的伤害；或者她已经失去了最为重要的贞洁；或者其还没有结婚就已经怀有身孕。其中，最后的两种情况对其家族来说是一种极大的羞耻，甚至足以被

---

① Eager, Paige W., From Freedom Fighters to Terrorists: Women and Political Violence. (Aldershot UK: Ashgate, 2008)

② Bloom, Mia, Dying to Kill: The Allure of the Suicide Bomber, New York: Columbia University Press, 2007.

③ Reuter, C., My Life is a Weapon: A Modern History of Suicide Bombings, Princeton NJ: Princeton University Press, 2004.

④ Elster, Jon, Motivations and Beliefs in Suicide Missions, in Diego Gambetta (editor), Making Sense of Suicide Missions, Oxford UK: Oxford University Press, 2005.

⑤ Berko, Anat, The Moral Infrastructure of Chief Perpetrators of Suicidal Terrorism: Cognitive and Functionalist Perspectives. Unpublished dissertation, Bar Ilan University, Israel, 2002.

⑥ Brown, Katherine, Blinded by the Explosion? Security and Resistance in Muslim Women's Suicide Terrorism, in Laura Sjoberg and Caron Gentry (editors), Women in Global Terrorism. (Athens GA: University of Georgia Press, 2011)

⑦ Naaman, Dorit, Brides of Palestine, Angels of Death: Media, Gender and Performance in the Case of the Palestinian Female Suicide Bombers, Signs: Journal of Women in Law and Society 32:4(2007), 933-55.

⑧ Speckhard, Anna and KhaptaAkhmedova, Black Widows: The Chechen Female Suicide Terrorism in Yoram Schweitzer (editor), Female Suicide Bombers: Dying for Equality, (2006), 63-80. Tel Aviv: Jaffee Center for Strategic Studies, Tel Aviv University.

⑨ Gerda Lindner, Evelyn, Women and Terrorism: The Lessons of Humiliation. New Routes: A Journal for Peace Research and Action on Women and Peace, 6:3(2001): 10-12.

⑩ Gambetta, Diego, Making Sense of Suicide Missions, Oxford UK: Oxford University Press, 2005.

⑪ Pape, R., Dying to Win: The Strategic Logic of Suicide Terrorism, New York: Random House, 2005.

施以死刑。[①] 这就像是在与恶魔讨价还价一样：当这些女性发现自己可以通过这种被认可的方式来毁灭自己以解决其所面临的问题时，那些把她们送上死亡之路的人可能反会以她们为荣，但她们不能仅仅因为个人原因而自杀。[②]

十一、千禧一代(The Millenials)与全球性“飞散”(Global“Splash”)

如今的恐怖分子与以往的差异在于，他们很多都是千禧一代，他们大都接受着极端主义误读。[③] 对于千禧一代来说，他们的计划和目标就是绝不受制于谈判。而且，在如今这个可以即时地进行全球通信的时代，恐怖分子的目标在于实现全球的飞散，尤其是通过极端暴力的手段。最明显的例子就是，ISIS 实施了那些骇人听闻的死刑之后，还将其拍摄成为录像，通过网络和社交媒体发往世界各地。[④] 很明显，恐怖分子的目的就是想要令世人感到极度的震惊和恐惧，由于除了库尔德自由斗士之外，要想再寻找到其他愿意与 ISIS 对抗并与之为战的士兵是十分困难的，甚至可以说是难以实现的，所以恐怖分子的这个目的很容易就能达到。伊拉克陆军显然没有对抗 ISIS 的能力，当 ISIS 进攻的时候，他们大都选择逃之夭夭，这不仅使得 ISIS 拥有了大量的领地，也使得 ISIS 获得了大量的装备、武器、军火、建筑、军用载货车、装甲车和大量的现金。这就像是在比赛场上一样，对于对手的恐惧会导致进攻与防守策略的全面崩溃，并最终带来战败的耻辱。[⑤] 同样地，虽然在武器数量以及武器火力上处于劣势，但阿富汗塔利班组织在与阿富汗陆军的对抗中也明显占据着上风，占领昆都士就是最好的证据。似乎只有依靠美国空军的支援，只有在昆都士遭受到猛烈的空袭而成为废弃之地后，阿富汗陆军才能有机会重新占领这块地方。同样的模式也发生在了叙利亚城市卡巴尼中，该城市被 ISIS 所占领后，为了将其驱逐，叙利亚只能借助

① Tzoreff, Mira, The Palestinian Shahida: National Patriotism, Islamic Feminism, or Social Crisis in Yoram Schweitzer (editor), Female Suicide Bombers: Dying for Equality, (2006), 13-24. Tel Aviv: Jaffee Center for Strategic Studies, Tel Aviv University.

② Berko, Anat, The Smarter Bomb: Women and Children as Suicide Bombers. (Lanham MD: Rowman and Littlefield, 2012)

③ Juergensmeyer, Mark, Terror in the Mind of God: The Global Rise of Religious Violence, Berkeley CA: University of California Press, 2003.

④ Sageman, Marc, Understanding Terror Networks, Philadelphia PA: University of Pennsylvania Press, 2004.

⑤ Gray, Colin S., Thinking Asymmetrically in Times of Terror, Parameters: U.S. Army War College Quarterly, Spring, 2003, 5-14.

于美国猛烈的空袭。①

十二、虔诚的成员

如今,恐怖主义的一个重要特点就是拥有虔诚的成员,这在中东地区尤为明显。从这个角度看,这是一场宗教派系之间的斗争,也是一场正邪之间的较量。这为对叛教者、异教徒和无信仰者实施极端残酷的行为提供了正当性。没有任何的限制和战争法能够保护那些不接受或者不认同这些"正确"信仰或意识形态的人。② 数千年来,这样的观点和解释已经为各种残杀、大屠杀以及大规模破坏行为提供了正当性。而对于哪些信仰能够被正式定义为一种宗教信仰,目前却并没有任何的限制。当强势者通过武力来强迫其他人积极追随某一种意识形态时,即使这些被强制者并不愿意宣誓遵从这种意识形态,也不愿意为之奉献,这种宗教信仰还是能够得以产生。不论是在古代史还是在近代史中,都充斥着大量的例证,在各个大洲,甚至是各个国家,也都发生过这样的悲剧。这些以狂热的宗教信仰以及意识形态信念为动机的恐怖分子,较少受到道德准则以及法律原则的限制,而且他们有更加充足的心理准备,也更加愿意牺牲自己的生命来实现他们数千年来的目标。他们愿意牺牲的原因是,他们期待他们的神能够赐给他们荣耀、救赎以及无可言喻的回报。这些宗教极端组织,通过篡改和剽窃那些著名且公认的宗教符号、神圣的经文及话语等,来获取公众的支持。③

十三、如同政治行动一般的恐怖主义

为了能够准确了解并妥善解决恐怖主义的问题,我们必须理解它的政治本质,但这是十分困难的。那些遭受到恐怖活动伤害的人,例如遭受"9·11"恐怖袭击的美国人,对他们来说,试图为恐怖主义的起源找到一个理性解释,尤其是承认那些支持

---

① Cronin, Audrey Kurt, Counterterrorism Will Not Work Against ISIS. Washington DC: Carnegie Council for Ethics in International Affairs, 2014; https://www.youtube.com/watch? v=3xDdnAoMTHY.

② Lincoln, Bruce, Holy Terrors: Thinking about Religion after September 11. (Chicago IL: University of Chicago Press, 2003)

③ Gray, Helen T., Contradictory to the Faith: American Muslims Say Terrorists Aren't Following Religious Teachings, Kansas City Star, January 28, 1995.

和参加恐怖活动的人已经遭受了政治不公，是对他们的深深的冒犯。试图去解释恐怖分子开展恐怖袭击和造成大量的破坏与死亡的原因，似乎能够为他们的犯罪行为提供辩护并得到和解。但是，我们必须对恐怖行为的辩护理由进行区分，判断哪些是不可接受的，而哪些又是对理解恐怖分子实施恐怖行为有帮助的，这样我们就能在以后发生类似的情况时提前进行预防。

为了有效预防、打击恐怖主义，我们必须认识并理解一些核心问题，这些问题为恐怖主义的产生提供了适宜的环境，同时这些问题也正在被恐怖组织领导人巧妙地利用着。①

"基地"组织、ISIS还是其他恐怖组织，这些组织的发起者和领导人会借助宗教背景来粉饰他们的宣言和理由。宗教原因是其进行恐怖活动的主要原因之一。② 但是如今对最为活跃的恐怖组织来说，其领导人却好像与这一观点背道而驰。

这些恐怖组织的行动目的中有很大的政治成分。恐怖主义的目的更多的是为了促进或提出特殊的政治目的和政治事项。毫无疑问，宗教与政治的混合为其带来了强大的动力。这导致了相互对抗的结果。

十四、抵制西方的恐怖主义

那些活跃于今日的主要的恐怖组织，其政治任务是要表现出对西方社会的力量、影响力、统治力和控制力的激烈反抗。③ 为了给"基地"组织、ISIS和其他组织的恐怖行为提供依据，从本·拉登到ISIS领导人阿布·巴克尔·巴格达迪，他们提出的理想目标都是，从西方的征服、侵占和虐待下解放社会，并取代那些以腐败和专制而闻名的政府。直到如今，这些理想目标仍然在起作用，它们依靠着那些所谓的"规则"来实施控制。这些恐怖组织的最终梦想是，废除第一次世界大战后，西方势力强加给奥斯曼帝国的国境线，并重建一个所谓的"阿拉伯帝国"，将其建成一个唯一的神圣的超级大国。而其最为紧迫的短期目标有：推翻在中东地区的美国同盟或接受美国救济的政府；解除他国对伊拉克、阿富汗和巴勒斯坦的占领；将外国军队和异教徒部

---

① Sageman, Marc, Understanding Terror Networks. (Philadelphia PA: University of Pennsylvania Press, 2004)

② Saniotis, Arthur, Re-Enchanting Terrorism: Jihadists as "Liminal Beings" Studies in Conflict and Terrorism 28, November, 2005, 533-45.

③ Cronin, Audrey Kurt, Transnational Terrorism and Security, in Grave New World: Security Challenges in the 21st Century, Michael E.Brown, editor, 279-304. (Washington DC: Georgetown University Press, 2003)

队驱逐出沙特阿拉伯和其他国家。①

十五、外国对于中东地区和恐怖主义的干涉

毫无疑问,除了占领巴勒斯坦,2003 年美国对伊拉克的入侵给了世界上的许多人以充分的理由加入到反美主义的怒火中。② 这是一剂能够将各种因素融合在一起的催化剂,从大众普遍的不满到对贫困以及遭受排挤的现实感到的不平,它将这些因素全转变成了对西方的憎恨、拒绝以及愤怒。阿拉伯地区的近代史则说明,入侵行动发生在阿拉伯世界的复杂性。20 世纪 80 年代,苏联对阿富汗的入侵遭到了强烈抵抗,这直接导致了"基地"组织的出现。③

当时,许多外国士兵涌入阿富汗以助其对抗苏联政权,这些外国战士在那里获得了美国政府所提供的大量资金、训练、武器和情报。美国鼓励并训练这些组织来参加对抗苏联的战斗。一些阿拉伯国家,在遭受入侵的刺激之后,就开始领导和团结那些虔诚的宗教追随者来与这些异教徒和苏联军队交战。他们为宗教提供支持并将其传播到世界各地,还提供资金为宗教建造场所,出版相关材料,训练、输送工作人员并支付薪水。据报道称,"基地"组织的最初资金就来自于社会名流们。④ 这是一个由"无意识的"政策所导致的,给美国以及西方世界带来巨大危害后果的典型例子。⑤

毫无疑问,在过去的 50 年里,美国不断地进行着军事扩张,并试图利用政治、军事以及经济来控制拥有丰富石油储备的波斯湾以及中亚地区,而且还妄图阻止俄罗斯以及中国获取这些昂贵且有战略价值的资源。⑥ 美国填补了英国在 20 世纪 70 年代从苏伊士运河东部撤出后和 1997 年向中国归还香港以后所留下的真空地带。美国最初之所以会这么做,一部分是来自于 20 世纪 70 年代的石油危机所导致的急迫感以及脆弱感,另一部分是来自其国内的压力,在 1967 年以色列占领并逐步吞并巴勒斯坦领地之后,人们希望美国给出解释,为什么要给予以色列强力的支持。但在 1991 年海湾战争之后,美国类似的活动开始急剧增加,尤其是在 2001 年 9 月 11 日以

---

① De Wijk, Rob, The Limits of Military Power, Washington Quarterly 25:1(2002), Winter, 86.

② Fukuyama, Francis, After Neo-Conservatism, New York Times Magazine, 19 February, 2006, 62.

③ Mitchell, James K., Urban Vulnerability to Terrorism as Hazard, in Susan L. Cutter, Douglas B. Richardson and Thomas J. Wilbanks, The Geographical Dimensions of Terrorism. 17-26. (New York: Routledge, 2003)

④ Simpson, Glenn R., List of Early Al Qaeda Donors Points to Elite Saudis, Charities, Wall Street Journal, March, 2003.

⑤ Lief, Louise et alii, The War Will Reshape the Arab World in Unpredictable Ways, U.S.News & World Report, January 28, 1991, p.26.

⑥ Boot, Max, The Savage Wars of Peace: Small Wars and the Rise of American Power. (New York: Basic Books, 2003)

后。美国在该区域的许多国家中都建立了军事基地。美国军队数量在中东地区的突然增加，激起了当地人们对其深深的憎恨、愤怒和敌对情绪。[①] 这导致并助长了政治极端主义的产生，也为恐怖主义和恐怖袭击的产生提供了前提条件。[②]

除了建立军事设施之外，另一个使矛盾激化的因素是美国承认的同盟国们所实施的具有压迫性和专制特征的政治体制。美国几乎是盲目且不加疑问地认可了以色列对其所占土地的占领政策和土地吞并行为，这也造成了一般民众对美国在该地区所实施的政策的厌恶。[③] 美国作为一个拥护民主和人权，积极干预他国对人权和民主的保护，并在一个国家或是区域中主张保护人权和民主的国家，其公信力正在遭到损害。这个破坏美国公信力的消极因素就是，美国在该地域的同盟们都是些残暴、独裁、压迫人民的政体的这一事实，其中沙特阿拉伯就是最明显的一个例子。他们习惯于对政治自由进行镇压，也不会适当地向市民提供一些社会必需品。其对待外国劳工的方式，容易使我们想起奴隶制度或至少是契约仆役制度。民主在这里根本不可能存在，甚至要受到镇压；人权也常常遭到侵犯；不同意见将被扼杀。支持与维护这些专制主义者和腐败政权并不能令法治得到人们的尊崇，美国所维护的局面反而增加了产生恐怖主义的可能性。[④]

美国军队数量的剧烈增长、区域内的交战次数的剧烈增长，以及美国支持的非民主政府数量的剧烈增长，这一切导致了大量的愤怒与敌意的产生，而这些愤怒与敌意又进一步刺激了反抗和叛乱的发生。[⑤]

有人可能会不同意这个推论。他们认为，仅仅从美国拥有基本无人可匹敌的力量这一点出发，我们就可以推断出不论美国如何作为，都将导致相同的敌对后果。如此强大而又不可阻挡的巨兽，其本身就会产生出一个几乎是自然生成的排斥反应，并引发反击和敌意。也有人提出，如今的恐怖主义，尤其是ISIS，是对美国所领导和支持的国际秩序和体制的一种排斥形式。[⑥] 我们也可以从另一个角度来看待这个问

---

① McNamara，Thomas E.，Unilateral and Multilateral Strategies Against State Sponsors of Terror：A Case Study of Libya，1979-2003，in David Cortright and George A.Lopez，Uniting Against Terror：Cooperative Non Military Responses to the Global Terorist Threat，(Cambridge MA：MIT Press，2007)，83-122.

② Anghie，Anthony，Imperialism，Sovereignty and the Making of International Law.(Cambridge UK：Cambridge University Press，2004)

③ Telhami，Shibley，The World Through Arab Eyes.(New York：Basic Books，2013)

④ Rosand，Eric and Alistair Millar，Strengthening International Law and Global Implementation，in David Cortright and George A.Lopez，Uniting Against Terror：Cooperative Non Military Responses to the Global Terorist Threat，Cambridge MA：MIT Press，2007，51-82.

⑤ Cronin，Audrey Kurt，Rethinking Sovereignty：American Strategy in the Age of Terrorism，Survival 44：2(2002)：119-139.

⑥ Cronin，Audrey Kurt，Behind the Curve：Globalization and International Terrorism，International Security 27：3，(2002-2003)，Winter，30-58.

题。美国通过滥用和误用自己压倒性的力量,以支持和强迫大家接受一个不公平的体系,这个体系会造成大多数人的损失,而只对少数人有利,也只受到少数人的欢迎。①

全球化之所以尤为受到憎恶和排斥,有以下几个原因:它是一个为美国以及西方的跨国公司对世界其他国家进行系统性开发提供便利的机制;它是文化同化的一种方式,它会以进步的名义来消除地区间的传统价值观和生活方式;它也是一个将西方的定义以及价值观,例如女性地位以及宗教自由,强加给人的工具,它蔑视和拒绝数世纪来所形成的古老而又根本的宗教教义和文化信条。

美国特殊论也是导致激烈争论的根源。美国欺凌弱小,它声称自己扮演着世界警察的角色,可以强制他国执行国际机构和国际法院制定的法律和作出的决定,但是当法律和决定作用到它自己身上时,它就开始不承认或者不服从这些由国际机构或国际法院所制定的法律或作出的决定了。美国要求,当其军队在国外进行任务时,尤其是在中东执勤时,可以免于当地法以及国际法的规制,并且当其军人或是承包商违反法律或公众普遍认可的刑法准则时,只能受到轻微的刑罚或免于受罚。这使得美国被认为是一个"口是心非"的国家。据说美国印第安人就常这样说它,他们曾经因为外来定居者的背叛以及美军对这些人的支持而学到了这个深刻的教训。大家普遍认为,这种行为方式是专横的、傲慢的、轻视他人的,这促使其他的人感到无力和屈辱,并为自身的软弱感到愤怒。因此,这些人才会致力于通过恐怖行为这种非对称的方式来寻求正义。

十六、加入 ISIS 的动机和理由,尤其对女性来说

接下来,我们要讨论一个十分值得思考的问题,即为什么女性,当然也包括男性,尤其是那些在西方出生、成长、接受教育的年轻人,愿意放弃自己的家庭、朋友、生活方式、价值观以及成为一个大家所认为的拥有世界上最好条件的人的机会,而前往 ISIS 的领土去加入恐怖组织。② 2011 年 3 月由"基地"组织发行的杂志——《神圣女性》("Al Shamikha")清楚地证明了,即使对于最保守的恐怖组织来说,女性仍旧是他们的未来。和激进有各种不同的表现形式一样,女性加入恐怖组织的理由也是因人

---

① Mani, Rama, The Root Causes of Terrorism and Conflict Prevention, in Jane Boulder and Thomas G. Weiss (editors), Terrorism and the UN: Before and After September 11, Bloomington IN: Indiana University Press, 2004, 230-231.

② Bloom, Mia, Bombshell: Women and Terrorism. (Philadelphia PA: University of Pennsylvania Press, 2011)

而异的。①

驱使男女前往 ISIS 领地或是其他恐怖组织的动因是他们所感受到的严重不公，他们认为自己在遭受虐待，而西方的外交政策又着重体现并支持了他们的看法。为了解决这些问题，他们想出了一个对策：就是建立一个严格遵照并严格执行教法的社会。他们对这一理想社会怀有共同的愿景，他们希望能在 ISIS 的控制区域内建立这么一个社会。甚至，一些女性相信，前往 ISIS 是她们的宗教义务。她们相信，移居至恐怖组织区域能使她们更加接近自己的神，更重要的是，这能够确保她们死后能够上至天国。而同时，在尘世中，恐怖组织带给她们一种强烈的归属感以及深厚的姐妹情谊，这是毫无人情味的浅薄的西方世界所不能给予她们的。对于 ISIS 的士兵怀着浪漫的想法，希望通过婚姻与这些 ISIS"雄狮"们分享光荣的冒险经历，是吸引妇女前往 ISIS 的另一个动因。

十七、总　结

正如上文所说，如果恐怖主义更可能是一个政治现象而非宗教现象的话，那么我们就必须从政治观念、政治现实和政治问题方面着手来预防和打击恐怖主义。② 例如，认真处理那些助长激进主义并将其合理化的不满情绪，这是对抗恐怖主义同时避免其产生和进一步发展的基本措施，也是必经步骤。采用一些政治手段和方法来回应这一社会群体所感到的深切的不幸与贫穷，或许能有效地说服那些为了释放怨气而考虑采取恐怖行为或者已经实施了恐怖行为的人，使他们更愿意通过政治协商来解决问题，而不是诉诸武装对抗。虽然这些策略并不总是能获得成功，但它能减少暴力的发生并将冲突转化成一些更容易处理的形式。③

虽然恐怖主义的千年目标确实远远超出了政治范畴，而且基本上没有商量的余地，但是在极端的激进分子和其可能的支持者之间制造裂痕和阻隔，在某些时候还是有可能的，也是可以完成的。致力于处理那些合理的怨愤，并同时为政治上的差异寻

① Brown, Katherine, Utopian Visions in Jihadi Gender Politics, Presented at SymposionDürnstein: Glücksbilder. Die Wirklichkeit der Utopien, 19.-21.2.2015, http://www.symposionduernstein.at.

② Feste, Karen A., Terminate Terrorism: Framing, Gaming, and Negotiating Conflicts. (Boulder CO: Paradigm Publishers, 2010)

③ Cortright, David and George A.Lopez, Strategies and Policy Challenges for Winning the Fight Against Terrorism, in David Cortright and George A.Lopez, Uniting Against Terror: Cooperative Non Military Responses to the Global Terorist Threat (Cambridge MA: MIT Press, 2007), 237-274.

求一个中间地带,这些努力不能也不应该被理解为是试图去向极端主义者妥协。我们更应该说,这是一个能够减少政治压迫、政治对立以及政治上的种族歧视的有效工具,最重要的是,它能降低极端主义者以及暴力手段对那些恐怖主义支持者的诱惑力和吸引力。

大体上,一个非常有可能取得成功的反恐政治策略必须包含以下方面:为那些对宗教极端分子怀有同情或提供支持的人提供更好的安排;以一种可信的、稳定的方式提供给他们一个替代选项。这场"更好的交易"的核心是承诺、保证并实现民主体系,这能有效地促使一个真正的切实的政治参与的产生,它允许人们参与到所有对其生活和生计有影响的决定之中。民众表达意愿的自由,是自由、秩序和安全的最佳保障,也是打击恐怖主义专制的最佳良方。①

(阮重骏 译)

① Cortright, David and George A.Lopez, Uniting Against Terror: Cooperative Non Military Responses to the Global Terrorist Threat. (Cambridge MA: MIT Press, 2007)

Growing Terrorism: Recognizing its Causes for Effective Prevention and Successful Defense

Emilio C.Viano①

1. Today's Strategies and Interventions

One of the major challenges facing the world today is how to develop and deploy an effective strategy against growing terrorism. A good strategy must include both a protective dimension to successfully defend against terrorist attacks and a preventive dimension to eliminate the root factors that give origin, justify or facilitate the growth of terrorism.②

The majority of interventions against terrorism today are protective.③ They support mostly military, police, and intelligence interventions to try to undermine terrorist groups; prevent their operations; dismantle their training facilities; and kill or apprehend their leaders. Another tool often used are sanctions, imposed by the United Nations or by powerful countries that target specific members of terrorist organizations and aim at deterring others, including certain countries, from supporting and facilitating terrorist organizations and activities. The counter-terrorism arm of the United Nations is working at building international cooperation

---

① Emilio C.Viano, President, International Society of Criminology.

② Jackson, Brian A., Groups, Networks or Movements: A Command-and-Control Approach to Classifying Terrorist Organizations and Its Applications to Al Qaeda, Studies in Conflict and Terrorism 29(2006): 241–62.

③ Wisner, Ben, Assessment of Capability and Vulnerability, in Greg Bankoff, George Frerks, and Dorothea Hillhorst, Mapping Vulnerability: Disaster, Development and People, (2004), 183–93. London: Earthscan.

among countries and within regional organizations like the European Union,[①] to freeze the assets of reputed terrorist organizations; control more tightly their frontiers; and improve intelligence and police cooperation at the international level.[②] Another United Nations body, the Non Proliferation Committee and different bilateral and international programs[③] are also working with member states to intervene more forcefully especially to keep powerful weapons and destructive materials away from terrorists. [④, ⑤] There is no doubt that these activities are valuable. For example, they put pressure on and make operating difficult for various malevolent groups and help build international coordination against terrorism. However, it must be admitted that all these programs are not very successful on the long run in diminishing in a major and durable way the worldwide terrorist menace. In reality, to effectively put down and vanquish terrorism hinges very much on developing and implementing measures that address the root causes of political, ideological or religious extremism and that substantially change the social, economic, and political realities that support, succor, and apparently justify terrorist groups like Al Qaed, ISIS and similar.[⑥]

2. An Epidemiological Approach

A different approach for developing a strategy against terrorism is an epidemiological one, that is, to treat it as if it is an epidemic of "Ebola", a spreading lethal infection caused by a virus or a mutating disease.[⑦] In such case, the first priority is to keep the contagion under control.[⑧] Then, it is essential that people at risk of being affected be protected from

---

① Bures, Oldrich and Stephanie Ahern, The European Model of Building Regional Cooperation Against Terrorism, in David Cortright and George A. Lopez, Uniting Against Terror: Cooperative Non Military Responses to the Global Terorist Threat (Cambridge MA: MIT Press, 2007), 187–236.

② Cortright, David, George A. Lopez, Alistair Millar, and Linda Gerber-Stellingwerf, Global Cooperation Against Terrorism: Evaluating the United Nations Counter-Terrorism Committee, in David Cortright and George A. Lopez, Uniting Against Terror: Cooperative Non Military Responses to the Global Terorist Threat (Cambridge MA: MIT Press, 2007), 23–50.

③ WMD Commission, World at Risk: The Report of the Commission on the Prevention of WMD Proliferation and Terrorism. New York: Vintage, 2008.

④ Millar, Alistair and Jason Ipe, Cutting the Deadly Nexus: Preventing the Spread of Weapons of Mass Destruction to Terrorists, in David Cortright and George A. Lopez, Uniting Against Terror: Cooperative Non Military Responses to the Global Terorist Threat (Cambridge MA: MIT Press 2007), 123–156.

⑤ Mowatt-Larsen, Rolf, Al Qaeda Weapons of Mass Destruction Threat: Hype or Reality? Belfer Center for Science and International Affairs, Kennedy School, Harvard University February 1, 2010.

⑥ Barkun, Michael. Chasing Phantoms: Reality, Imagination and Homeland Security Since 9/11. (Chapel Hill NC: University of North Carolina Press, 2011)

⑦ Stares, Paul and Monica Yacoubian, "Terrorism as a Virus", The Washington Post, 23 August, 2005.

⑧ Waugh, William L., Jr., Terrorism and the All-Hazards Model, Washington DC: FEMA, 2004.

it. Thirdly, one must correct the underlying situations and conditions that favored its beginning and then its spreading.①

Adapting this model to terrorism, protective interventions consist, for example, of restricting the movement of people in general but especially in the more affected areas; stopping in many different ways the diffusion of ideologies; and rallying the "silent majority," that is the more moderate people, to support peaceful ways to express political opinions and seek change.

On the prevention side, it is essential that various types of disputes, be they economic, political, military, be solved in an equitable way and quickly before they escalate into armed conflict. Also the root causes that are the seed of militancy must be addressed.② Among them, a crucial one is the marginalization and exclusion that operate in such a negative way in the diaspora communities. It is important to underline that defeating this "disease" and cure it will require many years and a concerted effort.③

3. The "Five Ds" of Kofi Annan

In 2005 then U.N. Secretary General Kofi Annan at a summit on Democracy, Terrorism and Security presented his overall approach to fight against terrorism, combing prevention and protection. It contained what he called the "five Ds":

1. Dissuading disaffected groups from going down the terrorism path;
2. Denying terrorists the means to carry out their attacks;
3. Deterring states from supporting and giving refuge to terrorists;
4. Developing state capacity to prevent the beginning and development of terrorism; and finally,
5. Defending human rights in the fight against terrorism.

The following year, Kofi Annan repeated his appeal to "reinforce the inexcusability and unacceptability of terrorism while working to address the conditions that terrorists

---

① Posner, Richard, Catastrophe: Risk and Response. (New York: Oxford University Press, 2004)

② Barkun, Michael. Chasing Phantoms: Reality, Imagination and Homeland Security Since 9/11. (Chapel Hill NC: University of North Carolina Press, 2011)

③ Croft, Stuart and Cerwyn Moore, The Evolution of Threat Narratives in the Age of Terror: Understanding Terrorist Threats in Britain, International Affairs 86(2010): 821-35.

exploit".[1]The National Strategy for Combatting Terrorism, released by the White House in 2006, states that the combat against terrorism is not just a battle of arms but also a "battle of ideas." It also stresses the need for the "creation of a global environment inhospitable to violent extremists"; calls for the advancement of freedom and human dignity and for more efforts for the peaceful resolution of disputes and the advancement of the rule of law.[2] These statements have been confirmed and expanded by the Obama administration as well.[3]

There is also a need to impact the "demand" side of terrorist movements, especially in light of thousands of young men and women leaving their countries, even in Europe, to join ISIS. Creative ways to stop the departure of recruits; financial backing; ideological justifications; the wrong narrative; and political amity must be found.

4. Objectives of this Chapter

This chapter ascertains and specifies the factors that have made it possible for recent well known terrorist movements to begin, develop and assert themselves; the religious, political and military complaints that terrorist groups use so effectively to attempt to justify their existence, operations, and excesses; the social and economic realities that give them support; the links between terrorism and fundamentalist religion; and the survival and recruiting strategies, including of suicide bombers, that these terrorist organizations develop and use so well through the Internet and the social media. The recruitment of women and their motivation to join are examined in detail

At the end, the chapter presents some innovative strategic choices to prevent terrorism and effectively combat it.

5. The Generalized War on Terrorism

The general declaration of "war on terrorism" by the Bush administration and subsequent political figures in the first decade of the 21st century has had the negative consequence of

---

① U.N. General Assembly, Uniting Against Terrorism: Recommendations for a Global Counter-terrorism Strategy, A/60/825, New York, 27 April 2006, par.7.

② White House, National Strategy for Combatting Terrorism. Washington DC: Government Printing Office, September, 7, 2006.

③ National Academies, Promoting Individual Privacy in the Struggle Against Terrorism: A Framework for Program Assessment. (Washington DC: National Academies Press, 2008)

lumping together into one generalized classification various types of terrorism.① Consequently developing an effective strategy has been difficult and muddled.②

Terrorist organizations operate in different political, economic, social, cultural and religious environments.③

Disregarding those substantial differences by using the famed "one size fits all" approach does not lead to a clear, focused and well calibrated anti-terrorism policy and methodology.④ For example, there is a substantial difference between Al Qaeda and Hamas, the first having more of a global agenda while the second definitely has local priorities. They have of course points in common, like their ideological roots. These distinctions are important in guiding how to approach different movements.⑤ For example, some groups use terror to pursue demands based on perceived historical wrongs for which there may be a local political solution while others have a more global agenda that is much more difficult to effectively and satisfactorily address.

While the Bush administration underlined very much state sponsored terror as the major focus of its interventions, thus justifying for example the invasion of Iraq and the overthrow and the eventual execution of Saddam Hussein, powerful terrorist groups like Al Qaeda in its various incarnations and ISIS act without and beyond state control.⑥ Even though Bin Laden received considerable state support, for example in Sudan and especially in Afghanistan, the true configuration and constitution of his network was always independent of a particular state and became even more so after the overthrow of the Taliban in Afghanistan. When Osama Bin Laden became very much a recluse trying to avoid detection by the Americans and others and especially after his death, Al Qaeda became even more fragmented and

---

① Frewer, Lynn J., Truth, Transparency and Social Context: Implications for Social Amplification of Risk, in Nick Pidgeon, Roger E. Kasperson and Paul Slovic (editors), The Social Amplification of Risk, 123–37. (Cambridge, UK: Cambridge University Press, 2003)

② Fussey, Pete, Observing Potentiality in the Global City: Surveillance and Counterterrorism, in International Criminal Justice Review 17, September, 2007, 171–92.

③ Cortright, David and George A. Lopez, Strategic Counter-Terrorism, in David Cortright and George A. Lopez, Uniting Against Terror: Cooperative Non Military Responses to the Global Terrorist Threat (Cambridge MA: MIT Press, 2007), 1–22.

④ Mueller, John, Overblown: How Politicians and the Terrorism Industry Inflate National Security Threats and Why We Believe Them. (New York: Free Press, 2006)

⑤ Nacos, Brigitte L., Yaeli Bloch-Elton, and Robert Y. Shapiro, Prevention of Terrorism in Post 9/11 America: News Coverage, Public Perceptions, and the Politics of Homeland Security, Terrorism and Political Violence, 20, January-March, 2008, 1–25.

⑥ Bergen, Peter, The Longest War: The Enduring Conflict Between America and al-Qaeda. (New York, NY: Free Press, 2011)

decentralized with cells scattered in dozens of countries largely in the Middle East and South Asia.① The various cells may embrace an ideology and follow a strategy in common but they operate autonomously. They have their own funding sources and their own mechanisms for recruiting and training new followers. They decided whom, where, and when to strike a target and how to do it.

The same is true with ISIS, for example, that is clearly a transnational organization that very effectively uses the tools of globalization to diffuse its message, recruit, operate, raise money and carry out its operations. ISIS has proven quite adept at using the Internet, social media, videos posted on worldwide sites like YouTube, international travel and open borders, like those within the European Union, to send out its message, communicate with its members, and plan and execute its operations in various parts of the world but especially in the Middle East.

Furthermore, this centrifugal dynamic has grown exponentially in very recent times. The threat posed by the terrorist so called "jihadists" has become much more flexible and diffuse. Different groups, from those self-started to homegrown ones, with very limited or no connection at all with Al Qaeda and ISIS have sprung up in Europe and elsewhere. The fragmentation of the movement reaches its maximum level with the "lone wolf" terrorist operating without any links to a known movement or state and who represents a formidable level of danger because of the unexpected, unaffiliated and random appearance of the actual terrorist act.②

6. Do It Yourself and Lone Wolf Terrorism

In the opinion of some, because of the elimination of Osama Bin Laden and other terrorist leaders, which destroyed the hierarchy of their organizations, terrorism has become increasingly scattered about. Many "do it yourself" and "home based" groups have appeared in Europe, the Middle East and other continents. Examples of their activities are the bombing of the Atocha train station in Madrid, Spain in March 2004; of the underground in London

---

① Bergen, Peter, Manhunt : The Ten-Year Search for Bin Laden from 9/11 to Abbottabad. (New York, NY: Crown, 2012)

② Sageman, Marc, Leaderless Jihad: Terror Networks in the 21st Century. (Philadelphia PA: University of Pennsylvania Press, 2008)

in July 2005;[①] and of the Moscow metro system in March 2010.Local people carried them out, even though some of the London bombers had links with members of Al Qaeda in Pakistan.The bombers in Madrid reportedly were trying to emulate Osama Bin Laden.However, they did not have any actual operational links to Al Qaeda.

The same dynamics apply to other well known terrorist attacks like, for example, the 2009 Fort Hood shooting when Nidal Malik Hasan, a U.S.Army major and psychiatrist, fatally shot 13 people and injured more than 30 others. Days after the shooting, reports in the media revealed that a Joint Terrorism Task Force had been aware of a series of e-mails between Hasan and the Yemen-based imam Anwar al-Awlaki, who had been monitored by the U.S.National Security Agency as a security threat and was eventually killed by a U.S.drone attack, and that Hasan's colleagues had been aware of his increasing radicalization for several years.Interestingly, when the families of the dead and injured soldiers pressured the government to declare the event an act of terrorism and to try Hasan as such, the Pentagon rejected their demand stating that charging Hasan with terrorism was not possible within the military justice system and that such action could harm the military prosecutors' ability to sustain a guilty verdict against Hasan.[②]

Similarly, in July 2015, a gunman unleashed a barrage of gunfire at two military facilities in Tennessee, killing four Marines and wounding two other service members and a police officer.The shooter also was killed.The shooting suspect was identified as 24-year-old Mohammod Youssuf Abdulazeez. He was born in Kuwait and came to the United States in 1996. Reportedly, Abdulazeez was not on any law enforcement radar concerning possible terror links or aspirations.The FBI was not aware of him as being any kind of a threat.[③] These examples in the United States exemplify the advent of the self-radicalized and "lone wolf", less professional but equally deadly, terrorist. This increases considerably the difficulty of identifying and oppose threats posed by terrorists.[④] On the one hand one can argue that these self-starter groups are less trained and less disciplined than Al Qaeda or I-

---

① JFO McAllister et alii, Hate Around the Corner: In a Stunnng Twist Investigators Blame the London Attacks on Four Homegrown Suicide Bombers and Look for Global Links to Al Qaeda, Time, July 25, 2005.

② Arizona Daily Star, "Terror act or workplace violence? Hasan trial raises sensitive issue", August 11, 2013; http://tucson. com/news/national/terror-act-or-workplace-violence-hasan-trial-raises-sensitive-issue/article _ be513c51 - a35d-5b4f-b3a0-13654f019ea6.html.

③ CBS/AP, Four Marines killed in attacks on Chattanooga military facilities, July 16, 2015; http://www. cbsnews. com/news/report-police-officer-shot near-tennessee-army-recruiting-center.

④ Whitlock, Craig, Terrorists Proving Harder to Profile, Washington Post, March 12, 2007.

SIS operatives who have undergone training. On the other hand, they are better able to plan and carry out their terrorist attacks because they are not connected to any network and thus extremely difficult to identify through surveillance of communications with known terrorist networks and their agents. If, when and where they will carry out an attack is totally unpredictable and therefore very difficult, if not impossible, to foil.① There is no question that considerable progress has been made against Al Qaeda since 2001. Reportedly, thousands of its members have been killed and its leadership, including Osama Bin Laden, has been decimated. The increased international cooperation of law enforcement and in the intelligence community have allowed for the more effective prevention of terrorist attacks. However, many disquieting questions have been raised at the same time about problematic and controversial methods of capture, imprisonment and interrogation used by U.S. and local governmental forces. The photographs of prisoners' mistreatment, degradation, torture and even killings at the Abu Ghraib prison; [②,③] of overcrowding, mistreatment and death at Bagram Air Force base; of the harsh conditions of confinement, interrogation, torture ("water boarding") and isolation at the Cuantanamo military prison;④ reports of similar gruesome events at CIA's secret detention and interrogation centers in various European and other countries; illegal kidnappings and "renditions" of people at times wrongly suspected of ties with terrorism to countries known for practicing torture and killings, and now the frequent use of drones for extra-judicial assassinations of reputed terrorist leaders and their followers⑤ have tarnished the moral standing of the U.S. and of the West in the so-called "war on terrorism". [⑥,⑦]

7. Financial Aspects of Terrorism

An area where there has been considerable progress is in the financial area, especially in

① Sageman, Marc, The Reality of Grass Roots Terrorism, Foreign Affairs 87, July-August, 2008, 163-65.

② Bergen, Peter, The Longest War: The Enduring Conflict Between America and al-Qaeda. (New York, NY: Free Press, 2011)

③ Greenberg, Karen J. and Joshua L. Datel, The Torture Papers: The Road to Abu Ghraib. (New York: Cambridge University Press, 2005)

④ Warrick, Joby, and Dan Eggen, Hill Briefed on Waterboarding in 2002, Washington Post, 9 December, 2007.

⑤ Bergen, Peter, Drone Wars: Transforming Conflict, Law, and Policy. (New York, NY: Cambridge University Press, 2014) (Co-editor with Daniel Rothenberg)

⑥ Wagner, Abraham, Meeting the Terrorist Challenge: Coping with Failures of Leadership and Intelligece. (New York: Harper Collins, 2007)

⑦ Weinmann, Gabriel and Conrad Winn, The Theatre of Terror: The Mass Media and International Terrorism. (New York: Longman, 1993)

freezing terrorist-related financial assets.[①] The flow of money to finance terrorism has long been in operation, taking advantage of various forms to raise and transmit money. [②,③,④,⑤,⑥,⑦,⑧,⑨,⑩,⑪,⑫] This especially when it comes to Al Qaeda in its various forms. However, intervention in this area is not as effective in stamping out acts of terrorism, as one would anticipate. The main reason is that such acts can be quite inexpensive to organize and carry out. Except for massive attacks like the 9/11 events in New York, Washington DC and Pennsylvania,[⑬] smaller terrorist actions and "lone wolf" attacks require modest sums of money and can easily be self-financed. The overall cost of operations conducted by self-starter groups can be quite low. It is estimated that the Madrid Atocha station bombing cost less than $10,000.[⑭] When it comes to ISIS, its financial situation is reportedly quite stronger. A report published in May 2015 by the New York Times[⑮], based on information from the RAND Corporation, claims that ISIS's finances are strong and have brought in around $875 million since the fall of Mosul in June 2014. While experts widely agree that ISIS is wealthy, they do not all agree that the terror group is financially stable.

---

① Gardner, Kathryn L., Terrorism Defanged: The Financial Action Task Force and International Efforts to Capture Terrorist Finances, in David Cortright and George A. Lopez, Uniting Against Terror: Cooperative Non Military Responses to the Global Terorist Threat, (Cambridge MA: MIT Press, 2007), 157-186.

② Interpol, General Secretariat, The Hawala Alternative Remittance System and its Role in Money Laundering, Lyon, January, 2000.

③ U.S. Department of Justice, Benevolence International Foundation Director Indicted for Racketeering Conspiracy: Providing Material Support to Al Qaeda and Other Violent Groups, Press Release, October 9, 2002.

④ Levitt, Matthew, Combating Terrorism Financing, Despite the Saudis, PolicyWatch, November 1, 2002.

⑤ U.S. Treasury, Shutting Down the Terrorist Financial Network, Office of Public Affairs press release, December 4, 2001.

⑥ U.S. Treasury, U.S. Designated Five Charities Funding Hamas and Six Senior Hamas Leaders as Terrorist Entities, Treasury Department Press Release, August 22, 2003.

⑦ U.S. Treasury, Treasury Designates Director, Branches of Charity Bankrolling Al Qaeda Network, Treasury Department Press Release, August 3, 2006.

⑧ U.S. versus Holy Land Foundation for Relief and Development et alii, 04-CR-240, Indictment (ND TX 2004).

⑨ National Commission on Terrorist Attacks against the United States, Staff Report, Monograph on Terrorism Financing, August, 2004.

⑩ Collier, Robert, Michigan Based Charity Finds Itself Caught in the Middle, San Francisco Chronicle, June 17, 2004.

⑪ U.S. versus Baz Mohammed et al., S1403-CR 486 (DC), indictment (SD NY 2005).

⑫ U.S. versus Medina-Castellanos et alii, o5-CR-155, indictment (ED NC 2005).

⑬ National Commission on Terrorist Attacks against the United States, The 9/11 Commission Report: Final Report. New York: Norton, 2004.

⑭ U.N., Security Council, Fifth Report of the Analytic Support and Sanctions Monitoring Team Appointed Pursuant to Resolution 1526 (2004) and 1617 (2005) Concerning AlQaida and the Taliban and Associated Individuals and Entities, S/2006/750, New York, 20 September 2006, paragraphs 59 and 61.

⑮ New York Times, Sarah Almukhtar, ISIS Finances Are Strong, 19 May, 2015.

The ISIS has revenue and assets that are more than enough to cover its current expenses despite expectations that airstrikes and falling oil prices would hurt the group's finances, according to analysts at RAND.The statistics from RAND show that ISIS has a diverse revenue stream.Though its financial strength was initially based on oil, the report states that oil now only makes up a fraction of its revenue.In 2014, ISIS's major revenue came from extortion and taxation in Iraq (around $600 million), money stolen from state-owned banks in Iraq (around $500 million), oil (around $100 million) and ransom from kidnappings (around $20 million).

By keeping its operating costs low and diversifying its income sources, the largest portion of spending by ISIS is going toward salaries, the NYT reported. ISIS spends between $3 million and $10 million every month on salaries. Many experts agree that ISIS is quite wealthy. According to various sources①, some countries have played deep and shadowy roles in Syria, bankrolling rebels, including at least initially, ISIS. According to the Times②, wealthy Gulf citizens — with or without their governments' knowledge — have helped fund the rise of Syria's terrorists. There is no question that this seriously complicates the situation if some of the supposedly strongest allies of the U.S. in the region, participating at times in the bombing campaign coordinated by the U.S. against ISIS, are at the same time supporting and funding ISIS as an armed group with the objective of debilitating and eliminating the Shiites' and Iran's influence in the region and give Gulf Countries the control of the region. Moreover, since a considerable amount of revenues for ISIS stem from the smuggling of oil from Iraq/Kurdistan especially through Turkey, some question why this illegal flow of oil and of revenues for ISIS is not being stopped by various actors that could do something about it: the Kurds who are generally considered the most effective local fighters against ISIS; the Turks who supposedly support moderate insurgents to force regime change in Syria and who control the ports from which oil can be shipped from northern Iraq or the businesses buying the oil in Turkey; and even the U.S.-led coalition that could bomb more effectively oil fields and related infrastructure, like pipelines, controlled by ISIS.

---

① New York Times, Ben Hubbard, Wealthy Gulf Nations Are Criticized for Tepid Response to Syrian Refugee Crisis, September 5, 2015.

② Ibid.

8. The Flow of Recruits

Equally if not more importantly, known terrorist organizations, and especially ISIS, can count on considerable numbers of trained foot soldiers. The flow of recruits, including young men and women, has substantially increased at various times, for example after the American invasion of Iraq in 2003, but especially now with the presence, activities and territorial gains of ISIS in Syria and Iraq. According to American intelligence analysts① nearly 30,000 foreign fighters have traveled to Iraq and Syria from more than 100 countries since 2011. A year ago, the same officials estimated that flow to be about 15,000 combatants from 80 countries. This represents a doubling of volunteers in just the past 12 months and is stark evidence that an international effort to tighten borders, share intelligence and enforce anti-terrorism laws is not diminishing the ranks of new militant fighters.

Among those who have entered or tried to enter the conflict in Iraq or Syria are more than 250 Americans, up from about 100 a year ago, according to intelligence and law enforcement officials.② It must be noted that Americans and others have been joining various terrorist groups in the Middle East for a long time prior to the appearance of ISIS. [③, ④]

Despite Pentagon reports that coalition strikes have killed about 10,000 ISIS fighters, the group continues to replenish its ranks, drawing an average of about 1,000 fighters a month. The U. S. government several months ago publicly assessed the flow at "more than 25,000," including at least 4,500 from the West. Given the region's porous borders, American officials emphasize that these figures are rough estimates, not precise head counts, based on allies' reports on citizens' travel and other intelligence, which vary by country.⑤

It must be kept in mind that by now there is also a "network effect", that is friends and family are bringing along other friends and family.

It is important to note that hundreds of Western volunteers, including many Americans, reportedly have trickled into Iraq and Syria since ISIS declared its caliphate in 2014. Their arrival has provoked mixed reactions on the ground.

---

① New York Times, Eric Schmitt and Somini Sengupta, Thousands Enter Syria to Join ISIS Despite Global Efforts, September 26, 2015.

② Berger, J.M., Jihad Joe: Americans Who Go to War in the Name of Islam. (Washington DC: Potomac Books, 2011)

③ Kaplan, David E. et alii, Hundreds of Americans have Followed the Path to Jihad, U.S. News & World Report, June 10, 2002.

④ Williams, Lance. Bin Laden's Bay Area Recruiter, San Francisco Chronicle, November 21, 2001.

⑤ New York Times, Eric Schmitt and Somini Sengupta, Thousands Enter Syria to Join ISIS Despite Global Efforts, September 26, 2015.

But the influx of American and other volunteers does not look set to end any time soon. Several new groups, predominantly of military veterans, have emerged, hoping to provide a more organized framework for those willing to risk their lives in a foreign war. Just as the ISIS has exploited its aggressive online presence to recruit foreign terrorists, Kurdish factions the "Peshmerga" in Iraq and the YPG in Syria are now expanding their online recruitment efforts. Beside the military aspect, foreign fighters joining Kurds or other armed groups over the front line reveals the extent to which the rise of ISIS and the western governments' response to it has forged the general perceptions that an epic struggle is ongoing between the forces of good and evil, modernity and backwardness.①

9. Female Recruitment

It is well known and it is very important to note that currently ISIS has been on a very strong female recruitment drive in Western Europe and other "Western" countries. This is not new since Al Qaeda, and other groups also attempted it. [②, ③, ④, ⑤, ⑥] Steganography has also been used.⑦ The current flow of foreigners to Syria and Iraq is remarkable not only for its scale, but also for its inclusion of many women. Much has been written about the male who migrate to engage in the conflict there; these people are prolific on social media and share details of their day-to-day experiences with supporters and opponents alike. Less, however, is known about the women who travel to join ISIS and support its state-building efforts.⑧ The flow of both men and women is a concern for Western governments, who fear that these individuals could pose a serious threat on returning home. In early 2015, the number of Western migrants overall is estimated at 3,500, with as many as 600 of these being

---

① The Guardian, Fazel Hawramy and Raya Jalabi, U.S. Civilians and Veterans Leave Home for ISIS Fight with Help from Social Media, 18 April, 2015.

② Paz, Reuven, editor, Who Wants to Email Al Qaeda? Project for the Research of Islamist Movements (PRISM). vol. 2, no.2, 2005.

③ Usher, Sebastian, Jihad Magazine for Women on the Web, BBC News, August 24, 2004.

④ Phillips, John, Women's Magazine Offers Tips to Terrorists, Washington Times, January 17, 2005.

⑤ Whine, Michael, Islamist Organizations on the Internet, International Policy Institute for Counter Terrorism, April, 2005.

⑥ O'Neil, Sean and Yaakov Lappin, Britain's Online Imam Declares War as He Calls Young to Jihad: Omar Bakri Mohammed, Banned from Many British Mosques, Is Issuing a Call to Arms to a Committed Audience, Times Online, January 17, 2005.

⑦ Kessler, Gary C., An Overview of Steganography for the Computer Forensics Examiner, Forensic Science Communications, 6, no.3, July, 2004.

⑧ Jacques, Karen and Paul J. Taylor, Male and Female Suicide Bombers: Different Sexes, Different Reasons?, Studies on Conflict and Terrorism 31:4(2008), 304–26.

women.

Some of these women accompany their husbands or partners to the war zones in the Middle East or elsewhere. There are documented cases of western people bringing entire families with them to ISIS-controlled territory, including young children and wives. Association with or marriage to a male member of ISIS remains a strong reason for women to travel to ISIS-held territory. Similarly, there are women who travel to join their husbands or partners inside the war zone.

Then, there are those who travel to ISIS controlled territory on their own, independently of a husband or partner. This group has received the most attention on the part of the media, governments and the public especially when the women are minors, very young and raised in a Western culture and system of education. The major concerns are that these young women may be trafficked through a well organized system of recruitment, travel and handling until they reach ISIS controlled territory; that they may be mistreated, abused, forcefully married to ISIS members or used as sex slaves; that at times may be abandoned and become destitute, especially if their partner or husband is killed in action; that they may be recruited or forced to join the fight, especially as suicide bombers; and that they may one day return to their Western homeland motivated and trained to carry out or support terrorist attacks.

10. Suicide Bombings: "Catastrophic" Terrorism

The nature of the menace of international terrorism has changed considerably in recent times. While the number of international terrorist attacks has diminished since its peak in 1987, at the same time, the number of casualties has been increasing. With the rise of Al Qaeda, ISIS and other terrorist movements a new type of terrorist act hasappeared, the suicide bomber. Farhad Khosrokhavar① distinguishes between two types of "martyr": those from the developing world, who are excluded from what modernity has to offer; and the minority who live at the heart of the Western world, a mainly middle-class diaspora from the Middle East and the Maghreb who are at ease with several cultural codes, but whose experience of the West is still marked by racism and discrimination.

Suicide bombing can be described as mass casualty or "catastrophic" terrorism.② This

① Khosrokhavar, Farhad, Suicide Bombers: Allah's New Martyrs. (London: Pluto Press, 2005)

② Asad, Talal, On Suicide Bombing. (New York: Columbia University Press, 2006)

reflects that fact that the number of casualties per incident has been growing quite noticeably. The number of casualties began to increase in the 1990s when high notoriety incidents took place like the attack against the Khobar Towers in Saudi Arabia in 1996; the bombings of the U.S. embassies in Nairobi and Dar-es-Salaam in 1998; obviously with the attacks on 9/11/2001 in New York, Washington DC and Pennsylvania; the Atocha train station bombing in Madrid in 2004; the London underground attack in 2005; the Mumbai attacks in 2008; the Fort Hood shooting in the U.S. in 2009; the Mumbai bombings in 2011; the 2015 shooting in Tennessee; and the continuous suicide bombings going on in Iraq, Afghanistan, Yemen, Palestine, Nigeria and other African countries, and Turkey in October 2015 with 97 dead and almost 200 injured, the government blaming ISIS; the Kurds accusing the government and many other countries in the region and across the world. The increase in suicide bombings represents a scary and fearsome new dimension in contemporary terrorism.[①] It certainly signifies a drastic change from previous terrorist acts that used just the right amount of violence to attract attention to their cause; put pressure on the population in general and the government in particular with the final goal of achieving change and negotiate a solution.[②]

The action of suicide bombing provides the terrorist, both male and female, not the power to control life but rather to control death, that of others and their own.[③] That feeling of power and control[④] gives the terrorists a profound awareness of their capacity, agency and self worth[⑤]. For female suicide bombers, the act frees them from their inhibitions and gives them permission to externalize their anger at their political oppression[⑥] in situations where they are under the domination or control of another, more powerful group and also gender oppression.[⑦]

---

① Ungar, Sheldon, Moral Panics versus the Risk Society: The Implications of the Changing Sites of Social Anxiety, British Journal of Sociology 52, June, 2001, 271-91.

② Taarnby, Michael, Profiling Islamic Suicide Terrorists. A Research Report for the Danish Ministry of Justice, November, 2003.

③ Eager, Paige W., From Freedom Fighters to Terrorists: Women and Political Violence. (Aldershot UK: Ashgate, 2008)

④ Bloom, Mia, Dying to Kill: The Allure of the Suicide Bomber. (New York: Columbia University Press, 2007)

⑤ Reuter, C., My Life is a Weapon: A Modern History of Suicide Bombings. (Princeton NJ: Princeton University Press, 2004)

⑥ Elster, Jon, Motivations and Beliefs in Suicide Missions, in Diego Gambetta (editor), Making Sense of Suicide Missions. (Oxford UK: Oxford University Press, 2005)

⑦ Berko, Anat, The Moral Infrastructure of Chief Perpetrators of Suicidal Terrorism: Cognitive and Functionalist Perspectives. Unpublished dissertation, Bar Ilan University, Israel, 2002.

Actually, women are especially lethal and are recognized as the best suicide bombers① because of the necessity to tangibly prove that they have the capacity to act and, often, because of the realization that there is no way out of the condition in which they find themselves.② Chechen women have been especially respected and acknowledged because of this.③

It is a honorable way for a woman to manifest her rage and hatred toward her oppressors, and to break the chain of oppression and of the low social status of being female, and of the daily humiliations④⑤. In many cases a suicide bombing provides a solution for her personal or family problems.⑥ Women are pressed to carry out the bombing as a honorable way out of the particular dilemma she is experiencing.⑦ It maybe that she has no decent marriage prospects for a variety of reasons and the family cannot or does not want to continue feeding, protecting and supporting her; or that she is being mistreated, beaten, enslaved or has no male to protect her from aggressive males who are imposing their will on her; or that she has lost her virginity; or that she is pregnant out of wedlock, the last two situations a source of great dishonor to her family and worth a death sentence.⑧ It is a classical bargain with the devil: those who send her to her death supposedly honor her while she found a solution for her problem by annihilating herself in an approved way, suicide solely for personal reasons and to leave this world being strictly forbidden.⑨

---

① Brown, Katherine, Blinded by the Explosion? Security and Resistance in Muslim Women's Suicide Terrorism, in Laura Sjoberg and Caron Gentry (editors), Women in Global Terrorism. (Athens GA: University of Georgia Press, 2011)

② Naaman, Dorit, Brides of Palestine, Angels of Death: Media, Gender and Performance in the Case of the Palestinian Female Suicide Bombers, Signs: Journal of Women in Law and Society 32:4(2007), 933-55.

③ Speckhard, Anna and Khapta Akhmedova, Black Widows: The Chechen Female Suicide Terrorism in Yoram Schweitzer (editor), Female Suicide Bombers: Dying for Equality, (2006), 63-80. Tel Aviv: Jaffee Center for Strategic Studies, Tel Aviv University.

④ Gerda Lindner, Evelyn, Women and Terrorism: The Lessons of Humiliation. New Routes: A Journal for Peace Research and Action on Women and Peace, 6:3(2001): 10-12.

⑤ Berko, Anat and Edna Eretz, Gender, Palestinian Women and Terrorism: Women's Liberation or Oppression?, Studies in Conflict and Terrorism, 30:6(2007): 493-519.

⑥ Gambetta, Diego, Making Sense of Suicide Missions. (Oxford UK: Oxford University Press, 2005)

⑦ Pape, R., Dying to Win: The Strategic Logic of Suicide Terrorism. (New York: Random House, 2005)

⑧ Tzoreff, Mira, The Palestinian Shahida: National Patriotism, Islamic Feminism, or Social Crisis in Yoram Schweitzer (editor), Female Suicide Bombers: Dying for Equality, (2006), 13-24. Tel Aviv: Jaffee Center for Strategic Studies, Tel Aviv University.

⑨ Berko, Anat, The Smarter Bomb: Women and Children as Suicide Bombers. (Lanham MD: Rowman and Littlefield, 2012)

11. The Millenials and Global "Splash"

What is different is that today's terrorists are millenials, that is are inspired by extremist interpretation.① Millenial plans and objectives are not subject to negotiation. Moreover, in this age of instant communications around the world, terrorists aim at achieving a global splash, especially through extreme violence. This is evident in the gruesome executions carried out by ISIS and filmed for diffusion worldwide through the Internet and the social media.② The intent to shock and terrorize to an extreme level is obvious and it is normally achieved, to the point that it has been difficult, if not impossible, to find fighters willing to confront and battle ISIS, with the reported exception of the Kurd Peshmerga. The Iraqi army has been apparently incapable of confronting ISIS and took flight when ISIS was advancing, leaving to ISIS not only vast expanses of territory but abundant equipment, arms and ordnance, buildings, military trucks and armored cars, and even cash. Just like in sports, fear of the opponent can make both offensive and defensive strategies crumble and lead to ignominious defeat.③ Similarly, the Taliban in Afghanistan have apparently the upper hand over the Afghan army as shown in their conquest of Kunduz, even though the Taliban were outnumbered and outgunned. It is only with massive support from the America Air Force that the Afghani army seems to have a chance to re-conquer what is left of Kunduz after heavy bombardment. A similar pattern took place in the Syrian city of Khobani eventually conquered by ISIS that was dislodged from it only after heavy American bombardment.④

12. The Religious Component

An important dimension is the religious component of today's terrorism, especially in the Middle East. This perspective translate the struggle between factions as a fight between good versus evil. This justifies acts of extreme cruelty inflicted on those considered apostate, heretics or infidels. There are no limits or law of war that can shield those who do not accept or

---

① Juergensmeyer, Mark, Terror in the Mind of God: The Global Rise of Religious Violence. (Berkeley CA: University of California Press, 2003)

② Sageman, Marc, Understanding Terror Networks. (Philadelphia PA: University of Pennsylvania Press, 2004)

③ Gray, Colin S., Thinking Asymmetrically in Times of Terror, Parameters: U.S. Army War College Quarterly, Spring, 2003, 5-14.

④ Cronin, Audrey Kurt, Counterterrorism Will Not Work Against ISIS. Washington DC: Carnegie Council for Ethics in International Affairs, 2014; https://www.youtube.com/watch? v=3xDdnAoMTHY.

subscribe to the true faith or ideology.① This perspective and interpretation has justified blood baths, wholesale massacres and destruction throughout the millennia. It is not limited to what can be officially identified as a religion. It can also happen when the zealous pursuit of a particular ideology is imposed by force over others perceived not to share it with the same commitment and dedication. History, ancient and recent, provides ample examples of these tragic events in all continents and basically all countries. While the terrorists who are motivated by fanatical religious or ideological beliefs feel less limited by moral or legal tenets, they are also more ready and willing to sacrifice their own lives for millennial objectives. By dying for the cause, they expect glory, salvation and untold rewards by their God. These religious extremist groups are able to generate popular support by manipulating and hijacking widely known and accepted religious symbols, sacred texts, language, and so on.②

13. Terrorism as a political act

To understand correctly and properly address terrorism, we must comprehend its political nature.

This is difficult to do. For people scarred by egregious terrorist acts, like Americans impacted by 9/11, attempting to offer a rational explanation of the roots of terrorism and particularly recognizing the political grievances of people supporting and participating in terrorist activities can appear to be deeply offensive. Trying to explain why terrorists did attack and inflict vast damage and loss of life may seem to be an accommodation or an apology for their criminal acts. However, we must distinguish justifying terrorist acts, which would be unacceptable versus comprehending why they took place so that we can prevent such situations in the future.

To effectively combat and prevent terrorism we must identify and understand the central issues that create the propitious background for generating terrorism which are cunningly exploited by terrorist leaders.③

---

① Lincoln, Bruce, Holy Terrors: Thinking about Religion after September 11. (Chicago IL: University of Chicago Press, 2003)

② Gray, Helen T., Contradictory to the Faith: American Muslims Say Terrorists Aren't Following Religious Teachings, Kansas City Star, January 28, 1995.

③ Sageman, Marc, Understanding Terror Networks. (Philadelphia PA: University of Pennsylvania Press, 2004)

The founders and leaders of AI Qaeda, ISIS and other terrorist groups have dressed up their manifestoes and justifications within a religious context. Religion is one of the main causes of terrorist activities.① The leaders of today's most active terrorist movements appear to endorse that view.

The plan of action of these terrorist movements is also quite political. The aim of terriorism is to promote and bring forward specific political objectives and agendas. There is no question that the mix of religion and politics generates a very strong motivational dynamics. The outcome is a two-tier confrontation.

14. Terrorism as Rejection of the West

The political order of business for the major terrorist movements active today is the expression ofa rabid recoil against Western power, influence, domination and control.②From Bin Laden to the ISIS leader Abu Bakr al-Baghdadi, the ideal objective presented as the justification for the horrors of Al Qaeda, ISIS and others is to liberate societies from Western conquest, occupation and abuse and to supplant governments known for their corruption and despotism that now control several countries with the so called"rule". Their ultimate dream is to abolish national borders imposed by Western powers on the Ottoman empire after its defeat in World War One and to reestablish the"Caliphate", a sole theocratic Muslim super-state. [③,④] The most urgent and quick goal is to overthrow governments that are allies and clients of the United States in the Middle East; end the occupation of Iraq, Afghanistan and Palestine; and remove foreign and infidel troops from Saudi Arabia and from other countries.⑤

15. Foreign Interventions in the Middle East and Terrorism

Beside the Palestinian occupation, there is no question that the U.S. invasion of Iraq in

---

① Saniotis, Arthur, Re-Enchanting Terrorism: Jihadists as "Liminal Beings", Studies in Conflict and Terrorism 28, November, 2005, 533-45.

② Cronin, Audrey Kurt, Transnational Terrorism and Security, in Grave New World: Security Challenges in the 21st Century, Michael E. Brown, editor, 279-304. (Washington DC: Georgetown University Press, 2003)

③ Besson, Sylvain, La Conquete de l'Occident: Le Projet Secret des Islamistes (The Conquest of the West: The Secret Project of the Islamists). (Paris: De Seuil, 2005)

④ Emerson, Steven, Jihad Incorporated: A Guide to Militant Islam in the U.S. (Amherst NY: Prometheus Books, 2006)

⑤ De Wijk, Rob, The Limits of Military Power, Washington Quarterly 25: 1 (2002), Winter, 86.

2003 gave ample reason to much of the world to join in a fury of anti-Americanism.① It was the catalyst for a fusion of various elements, from generalized dissatisfaction to feelings of injustice to the realities of poverty and exclusion, into a cauldron of hate, rejection and rage against the West. The complexity of what is taking place in the Arab world is demonstrated by the recent history of the region. The Soviet invasion of Afghanistan in the 1980s generated strong resistance and led to the eventual emergence of Al Qaeda.②

The foreign fighters who flocked to Afghanistan to help overthrow the Soviet regime there received considerable financial support, training, arms and intelligence from the United States. The United States encouraged and nurtured several groups to enter the combat against the Soviet Union there. Several Arab states, that support and spread their religion throughout the world financing the construction, publication of materials, and training, sending and paying the salaries, were galvanized to marshal and rally pious followers of religion to combat against the "infidel" and the Soviet Union army. Al Qaeda was reportedly initially financed by the elite.③ This is a classic example of a policy with "unintended" and very damaging consequences for the U.S. and the West.④

There is no question that in the last 50 years, the United States has been constantly augmenting its military footprint and has tried to exercise political, military and economic control over the oil-rich Persian Gulf and Central Asia, also to deprive Russia and China of easy access to those valuable and strategic resources.⑤ The U.S. filled the vacuum created by the withdrawal of Britain from east of the Suez Canal in the 1970s and its surrender of Hong Kong to China in 1997. This was justified initially by the feeling of urgency and vulnerability caused by the oil crisis in the 1970s and also by internal pressures in the U.S. to demonstrate a strong support for Israel after its 1967 occupation and gradual but steady annexation of the Palestinian territories. This pattern increased considerably after the Gulf War of 1991 and, of course, particularly after 9/11/2001. The United States built military bases in many countries. This growth of the American military presence in the Middle East

---

① Fukuyama, Francis, After Neo-Conservatism, New York Times Magazine, 19 February, 2006, 62.

② Mitchell, James K., Urban Vulnerability to Terrorism as Hazard, in Susan L. Cutter, Douglas B. Richardson and Thomas J. Wilbanks, The Geographical Dimensions of Terrorism. 17-26. (New York: Routledge, 2003)

③ Simpson, Glenn R., List of Early Al Qaeda Donors Points to Elite Saudis, Charities, Wall Street Journal, March, 2003.

④ Lief, Louise et alii, The War Will Reshape the Arab World in Unpredictable Ways, U.S. News & World Report, January 28, 1991, p.26

⑤ Boot, Max, The Savage Wars of Peace: Small Wars and the Rise of American Power. (New York: Basic Books, 2003)

was exceptional and extraordinary, inflaming deep animosity and feelings of indignation and hostility.① It bred and nourished political extremism and contributed to creating the very prerequisite for terrorism and terrorist attacks.②

Above and beyond the establishment of military facilities, an aggravating factor has been the alliances established by the United States with oppressive and autocratic regimes. The United States almost blind and unquestioning endorsement of the occupation policies and land annexation of Israel in the occupied territories has also engendered a general loathing toward American policies in the region.③ Another negative element that undermines the credibility of the United States as a country that champions human rights and democracy and intervenes to protect them or to help institute them in a country or region is the fact that all the allies of the U.S. in the region are despotic, autocratic and repressive regimes, with Saudi Arabia being the most visible one. They routinely squash political freedom and do not provide properly for the social necessities of their citizens. The treatment of foreign workers reminds us easily of slavery or at least of indentured servitude. Democracy is inexistent and suppressed; human rights are routinely violated; and dissent is throttled. By propping up and sustaining these absolutist and often corrupt regimes that do not honor the rule of law, the U. S. preserves the situations that increase the likelihood of terrorism.④

The dramatic increase of the U.S. military presence and war activities and its support for undemocratic governments generates an explosive blend of antagonism and resentment that incites defiance and rebellion.⑤

One could argue with reason that, regardless of what the U.S. does, it would generate the same hostile response simply because of the amplitude and range of American power that is basically unrivaled in the world. Such a powerful and unstoppable behemoth in itself pro-

---

① McNamara, Thomas E., Unilateral and Multilateral Strategies Against State Sponsors of Terror: A Case Study of Libya, 1979-2003, in David Cortright and George A. Lopez, Uniting Against Terror: Cooperative Non Military Responses to the Global Terorist Threat, (Cambridge MA: MIT Press, 2007), 83-122.

② Anghie, Anthony, Imperialism, Sovereignty and the Making of International Law. (Cambridge UK: Cambridge University Press, 2004)

③ Telhami, Shibley, The World Through Arab Eyes. (New York: Basic Books, 2013)

④ Rosand, Eric and Alistair Millar, Strengthening International Law and Global Implementation, in David Cortright and George A. Lopez, Uniting Against Terror: Cooperative Non Military Responses to the Global Terorist Threat (Cambridge MA: MIT Press, 2007), 51-82.

⑤ Cronin, Audrey Kurt, Rethinking Sovereignty: American Strategy in the Age of Terrorism, Survival 44: 2 (2002): 119-139.

duces an almost automatic rejection, push back and antagonism. One could say that today's terrorism, especially ISIS, is a form of rejection of the international order and system headed and supported by the United States.①

There is also a perception of a double standard. the United States abuses and misuses its overwhelming power to support and impose an inequitable system that favors and is good for the few but generates a loss of the many.②

Globalization is especially resented and rejected as a mechanism to facilitate the systematic exploitation of the rest of the world by U.S. and Western multinational corporations; as a type of cultural homogenization that is obliterating local and traditional values and ways of life in the name of progress; and as a tool to impose Western definitions and values, for example about the status of women or religious freedom, disparaging and rejecting centuries old fundamental religious and cultural tenets.

American exceptionalism is also a source of deep contention. The United States is seen as a bully that claims for itself the role of world policeman enforcing laws and decisions of international bodies and tribunals that it does not recognize or obey when it comes to itself and its actions. The demand by the United States that its troops be held immune from local or international law while on missions abroad, especially in the Middle East, and the mild or non existent penalties imposed on the military and contractors violating the law of war and universally accepted tenets of criminal law foster this perception of a country that "speaks with a forked tongue" as reportedly the American Indians used to say once they learned hard lessons because of the treachery of the invading settlers and of the U.S. Army supporting them. This way of acting is seen internationally as presumptuousness, condescension and contempt and fosters a sense of powerlessness, humiliation and rage at one's impotence. Hence the commitment to seek justice in asymmetrical ways through terrorist acts.

16. Motivation and Justification to Join ISIS, Especially as Applied to Women

There is considerable discussion on why women, and also men of course, especially those

① Cronin, Audrey Kurt, Behind the Curve: Globalization and International Terrorism, International Security 27: 3, (2002-2003), Winter, 30-58.

② Mani, Rama, The Root Causes of Terrorism and Conflict Prevention, in Jane Boulder and Thomas G. Weiss (editors), Terrorism and the UN: Before and After September 11. (Bloomington IN: Indiana University Press, 2004), 230-231.

young and Western born, raised and educated, migrate to ISIS held territory and join terrorist groups leaving behind family, friends, a way of life, values and opportunities that are deemed to be among the best in the world.① As evidenced by the March 2011 release of Al Qaeda's magazine *Al Shamikha*, it is clear that women are the future of even the most conservative terrorist organizations. As with all forms of radicalization, the reason the women give for travelling are as varied as the women themselves.②

In conclusion, women, and also men, who migrate to the ISIS state or other terrorist movements are motivated by serious grievances because of the perceived mistreatment of themselves underlined and confirmed by the foreign policy of the West. To address these problems, they have a solution: an society founded on the strict interpretation and application of Sharia law. They share in common a vision for their ideal society that they plan to build in the ISIS-held territory. Even more, these women believe that migrating is their religious duty. This migration will take them closer to God and be an important factor in guaranteeing their place in heaven. At the same time, on this earth, it provides them with a strong feeling of belonging and sisterhood, contrasted to the impersonality and superficiality of the West. A romantic view of the ISIS ' Lions" and a strong attraction to sharing a glorious adventure with them through marriage are also a motivator.

17. Conclusion

If terrorism, as it has been said in this work, is first of all and especially a political and not a religious phenomenon, the approach on how to prevent or combat it must address political perceptions, realities and issues as well.③For instance, seriously pursuing the grievances that foster and justify radicalization is a fundamental and indispensable step against terrorism, incipient or well established. Making political means and tools available to respond to a community's profoundly felt distress and neediness may be quite effective in persuading those who may consider resorting to terrorist violence or already have used it to find a solution to their complaints through political and negotiating processes rather than through armed confrontations. Such tactics do not always succeed but can diminish violence

① Bloom, Mia, Bombshell: Women and Terrorism. (Philadelphia PA: University of Pennsylvania Press, 2011)

② Brown, Katherine, Utopian Visions in Jihadi Gender Politics, Presented at Symposion Dürnstein: Glücksbilder. Die Wirklichkeit der Utopien, 19.-21.2.2015. http://www.symposionduernstein.at.

③ Feste, Karen A., Terminate Terrorism: Framing, Gaming, and Negotiating Conflicts. (Boulder CO: Paradigm Publishers, 2010)

and convert conflict into more easily tractable form.①

Even though it is true that millennial objectives are well past the sphere of normal politics and essentially non-negotiable, it is at times possible and doable to cause cracks and exploitable divisions between extremist militants and their likely supporters. Working to resolve legitimate grievances and find a middle ground for political differences does not and should not be understood as an attempt at appeasement of extremists. Rather it is an effective tool to reduce political pressures, antagonisms and strains and, most of all, diminish the allure and desirability of extremist and violent methods among the sympathizers.

In essence, a political game plan against terrorism with a high potential for success involves offering a better arrangement to those who may feel sympathetic or support religious extremists; that is, offer them an alternative in a credible and stable fashion. At the core of this "better bargain" are the promise, commitment and reality of a democratic system that is effective and facilitates a veritable, palpable political involvement of the people in all the decisions that impact the lives and livelihood of the citizens. The freely expressed will of the people is the best assurance and guaranty of freedom, order and security and the best antidote against terrorist despotism.②

---

① Cortright, David and George A. Lopez, Strategies and Policy Challenges for Winning the Fight Against Terrorism, in David Cortright and George A. Lopez, Uniting Against Terror: Cooperative Non Military Responses to the Global Terorist Threat (Cambridge MA: MIT Press, 2007), 237-274.

② Cortright, David and George A. Lopez, Uniting Against Terror: Cooperative Non Military Responses to the Global Terorist Threat. (Cambridge MA: MIT Press, 2007)

二、案例研究

Part Ⅱ　Case Studies

打破冲突、非法贸易条件与犯罪组织或恐怖组织的动态发展所组成的循环圈

埃内斯托 · U.萨沃纳(Ernesto U.Savona)①、
维罗妮卡 · 珀西勒(Veronica Pecile)②

通过对世界不同地方的国家冲突、区域冲突和局部冲突的分析,我们发现冲突、区域中可被利用的违法机会、犯罪组织的出现及其权力的获取之间存在着联系。该联系有两种可能的运作方式:非法贸易条件驱使着冲突,或者,相反地,冲突组织利用这些可用的非法贸易条件来帮助自己进行战斗或者对抗合法政府。这样的例子在以前以及近期都有很多。巴尔干半岛的分裂,既造成了局部冲突也创造了非法贸易(汽油走私)的条件。结果导致处于萌芽期的犯罪组织得以成长,并在一段时间之后发展成为稳定的有组织犯罪集团。索马里政府垮台后,借助了亚丁湾商业航线的条件,索马里海盗开始出现。如今,ISIS 利用伊拉克的非法石油贸易以及其他非法贸易来获取恐怖活动的资金。塞拉利昂的钻石、阿富汗的海洛因导致了社会和经济的动荡并引发了相关的战争。了解这些不同联系背后的驱动力能够帮助我们支配这个循环圈,并帮助我们找到有效的补救措施。我们可以思考以下两种观点:采用法律途径,其意味着起诉犯罪人并宣告他们有罪,和/或采用减少条件的途径,这意味着改变那些推动冲突、违法条件和犯罪组织之间联系的情景(情景预防方法)。本文对该循环圈进行了阐释,提供了相关的例子,并提出了可行的干预措施。

---

① 埃内斯托 · U.萨沃纳(Ernesto U.Savona),跨国犯罪联合研究中心主任,米兰天主教圣心大学犯罪学教授。
② 维罗妮卡 · 珀西勒(Veronica Pecile),米兰天主教圣心大学犯罪学国际博士的博士候选人。

一、引　言

威慑模式，以传统方式打击有组织犯罪和恐怖主义的方法为基础，其效力一直十分低下，然而其直接（社会的、经济的）费用和间接（刑事司法的）费用却很高。考虑到犯罪组织和恐怖组织的叛乱行为与非法贸易的联系日益紧密，而非法贸易已成为犯罪组织和恐怖组织的经济机会，本文主张关注这些条件以减少犯罪与恐怖主义的威胁。了解与非法贸易相关的有组织犯罪和恐怖主义的恶性循环圈能够帮助我们找到瓦解犯罪组织的有效的补救措施。

这一恶性循环圈是冲突、非法贸易条件和犯罪组织之间辩证交互的结果。这三个因素是基于一种循环关系而被捆绑在一起的，这种循环关系有下面两种可能的运作方式：一方面，冲突带来了非法贸易的条件，而该非法贸易条件会被新生的犯罪组织利用；另一方面，非法贸易条件的存在能够引起冲突并促使那些愿意利用这些条件的犯罪组织成长。本研究有以下两重目标：首先，我们希望展示恶性循环圈是如何运作的；其次，我们致力于提出解决方案，来改变那些推动三者间联系的情景，从而打破这一恶性循环圈。

二、恶性循环

冲突、非法贸易条件以及犯罪组织的联系，有两种可能的运作方式。一方面，与非法贸易相关的金融机会能够吸引犯罪组织并最终推动冲突进行。1994 年之后的哥伦比亚似乎就是这个情况，当时古柯的价格受到外因的影响而升高，加速了农村地区的古柯生产，之后这些地区的暴力程度都有了极大的提升。这证明，哥伦比亚内战的恶化是由于非法贸易条件。① 类似的，在撒哈拉以南的非洲地区，石油和钻石是可盗取的资源，其对国内战争的引发起着重要的作用。② 例如，在 1975 年至 2002 年发生的安哥拉内战中，军阀就常常通过开采自然资源，也就是钻石，来为自己的活动提

---

① Angrist, Joshua, and Adriana D.Kugler. "Rural Windfall or a New Resource Curse? Coca, Income, and Civil Conflict in Colombia", The Review of Economics and Statistics XC(2), 2008.

② Basedau, Matthias, and Tim C.Wegenast. "Oil and Diamonds as Causes of Civil War in Sub-Saharan Africa", Colombia Internacional, December, 2009.

供经费。①

这三者的联系也会反向进行,因为冲突会导致法律制度被严重破坏,以至于犯罪组织能够轻易利用那些从国家垮台后留下的空隙中生成的新型非法贸易条件。例如,索马里海盗,其之所以变得如此强大,是因为1991年脆弱的索马里政府的崩溃,之后几十年索马里的逐渐衰弱,以及一个让他们可以利用索马里存在重要航线这一条件的方案的产生。② 另一个典型的案例是,2002年以来阿富汗鸦片生产的急剧增长,当时,冲突弱化了法律制度,并对公共设施和灌溉系统造成了破坏,因此迫使阿富汗开始大量地种植罂粟。然后这些非法所得进一步提升了冲突,从而推动了恶性循环的发展。③

大量的实例显示,恶性循环适用于那些有默认经济目标的犯罪集团。长期的有组织犯罪与恐怖主义并不相同,他们的区别是是否具有意识形态成分。如今国际恐怖主义的演变以及其对组织性的要求,迫使其需要拥有比过去更多的资源来进行新兵的招募,以及恐怖主义战争中的作战人员与作战武器的分配。于是,国际恐怖主义暴动与有组织犯罪的区别变得更加模糊。如果有组织犯罪与恐怖主义仍旧存在概念上以及事实上的区别,那么本文还想去解决恶性循环是否也可适用于恐怖主义的问题。

换句话说,是否有案例证明非法贸易的增加是由于恐怖主义的存在,抑或者非法贸易本身具有产生恐怖主义的可能?

现在,我们的分析将着重于三个案例研究,以此来解释,在给定区域中,来自可被盗资源的非法贸易条件的存在是如何创造或者推动一个藉由该机会而逐渐强大的恐怖组织并进而推动恶性循环的。

三、国际恐怖主义恶性循环的实例

(一)安非他命贸易推动了叙利亚内战

在第一个案例研究中,我们以叙利亚作为研究对象,2011年叙利亚内战爆发,死

① Guidolin, Massimo, and Eliana La Ferrara, "Diamonds Are Forever, Wars Are Not: Is Conflict Bad for Private Firms?" The American Economic Review 97:5(2007):1978-93.

② Dugato, Marco, and Giulia Berlusconi, "Transcrime Research in Brief-01. Maritime Piracy Worldwide", Transcrime Research in Brief 1/2015.

③ Lind, Jo Thori, Karl Ove Moene, and Fredrik Willumsen, "Opium for the Masses? Conflict-Induced Narcotics Production in Afghanistan", Review of Economics and Statistics 96 :5(2013):949-66.doi:10.1162/REST_a_00418.

亡人数超过 100000 人，自此之后，叙利亚成为了安非他命市场的区域领导者。

一方面，该国大多数地区内法律制度的削弱和缺失使得安非他命供给得以产生，而由于政府基础设施的崩溃，也使得潜在生产者能够十分轻松地利用这个赚钱的非法贸易机会，这最终导致叙利亚安非他命的产量一举超越了该贸易的前区域领导者黎巴嫩。[①] 叙利亚生产的安非他命的种类是芬乃他林——苯丙氨乙茶碱的商品名称，这是一种在中东地区十分流行的兴奋剂。[②] 有官方报告称，由于处于中东交叉口的战略要地，叙利亚多年来一直作为将毒品从欧洲流入海湾地区的中转国，但是如今安非他命供应的增长太过剧烈以至于叙利亚一跃成为中东地区安非他命的主要生产者。仅在 2013 年，黎巴嫩当局就在与叙利亚的接壤区域内查获芬乃他林药丸 1230 万颗，而土耳其警方也查获了从叙利亚直销往沙特阿拉伯的药丸 700 万颗。制造芬乃他林的一大便利因素就是，不需要有很高的制造能力，只需要知道基本的化学概念就行，而且该种毒品的制造往往在家中就可以完成，几乎不需要拥有一个完备的实验室。[③]

另一方面，据媒体报道，内战给人民带来的创伤也推动了对安非他命的需求[④]。在一定的区域中，内战会造成毒品需求的增长，这是很常见的现象，安非他命作为兴奋剂能够为战争时期的人们带来欢愉，缓解沮丧。也有证据表明，为了能够继续作战，冲突双方的作战人员都会使用芬乃他林。

安非他命产品的年收入合计达数百万美元，这为叙利亚士兵提供了重要的经费支持，他们可以用安非他命贸易中获得的资金来购买武器。[⑤] 虽然没有证据证明哪边的叙利亚士兵从安非他命贸易中赚得最多，但是来自这一非法活动中的数百万美元确实极大地导致了叙利亚地区的动荡，并在随后又促使了其与 ISIL 势力的接触。2013 年至 2014 年间，在处于内战边缘的叙利亚与伊拉克之间的领土内，恐怖组织正在蔓延，并且其计划进一步扩大自己的领地以便控制整个阿拉伯地区。

从安非他命的案例之中，我们可以得出这样的结论，内战情况下，法律制度的缺乏触发了这个高盈利的非法贸易条件，而之后对该条件的利用又使得这一地区更加

---

① Kalin, Stephen, "Insight: War Turns Syria into Major Amphetamines Producer, Consumer", Reuters, January 12, 2014, http://www.reuters.com/article/2014/01/12/us-syria-crisis-drugs-insight-idUSBREA0B04H20140112.

② Henley, Jon, "Captagon: The Amphetamine Fuelling Syria's Civil War", The Guardian, January 13, 2014, http://www.theguardian.com/world/shortcuts/2014/jan/13/captagon-amphetamine-syria-war-middle-east.

③ Kalin, Stephen, "Insight: War Turns Syria into Major Amphetamines Producer, Consumer", Reuters, January 12, 2014, http://www.reuters.com/article/2014/01/12/us-syria-crisis-drugs-insight-idUSBREA0B04H20140112.

④ Henley, Jon, "Captagon: The Amphetamine Fuelling Syria's Civil War", The Guardian, January 13, 2014, http://www.theguardian.com/world/shortcuts/2014/jan/13/captagon-amphetamine-syria-war-middle-east.

⑤ Kalin, Stephen, "Insight: War Turns Syria into Major Amphetamines Producer, Consumer", Reuters, January 12, 2014, http://www.reuters.com/article/2014/01/12/us-syria-crisis-drugs-insight-idUSBREA0B04H20140112.

动荡，从而为活跃于这一地区的恐怖组织增添了力量。

（二）作为 ISIL 主要资金来源的石油贸易

第二个案例针对的是直接作为恐怖组织资金来源的非法贸易：开采油井以及非法石油交易是 ISIL 资产负债表上重要的收入来源。①

ISIL 是新型恐怖主义的完美体现，领土扩张是其重要的职责。事实上，在其跨出叙利亚和伊拉克而进行发展的最初阶段，ISIL 就是依靠当地资源来进行系统化的区域镇压以此巩固自己的政权。当内战导致叙利亚处于无国家状态时，ISIL 成功地建立了如毛细血管般的系统来进行勒索，进行前政府财产、美国军事装备的买卖，以及最重要的，进行来自恐怖组织自己控制下的油田和精炼厂的石油买卖。② ISIL 所从事的工作，我们可以把它看成是一个真正的基于石油贸易的“战争经济”（war economy），因为存在着一个穿越了整个国家以及边境区域的完善的走私网络，ISIL 的石油可以从伊拉克和土耳其南部向外走私出去。[③，④]

有研究指出，除非能获得其他的领地，否则 ISIL 的统治模式将很快无法支撑。⑤第一，ISIL 的石油贸易可能会供应不足，因为恐怖分子提取和精炼石油的能力十分有限，其基本依靠模块化的精炼厂来进行精炼，而这被认为是十分原始的精炼技术。第二，国际联军的空袭对 ISIL 控制下的石油精炼厂造成了极大的打击。第三，土耳其当局在打击石油走私方面作出了努力，伊拉克政府也决心要查获那些与 ISIL 有联系的石油运载货物。但是，安卡拉政府并没能成功地发挥其严格的边境管控能力来阻挡资源、武器、人口的运输。此外，对交易员、运输员、买家和涉及 ISIL 管理的非法石油贸易航线进行更精确的鉴别也是不可或缺的。⑥

（三）作为尼日利亚动乱征兆的“博科圣地”组织

我们第三个考虑的案例是“博科圣地”组织，其于 2015 年 3 月宣布与 ISIL 联

---

① Levitt，Matthew，“Declaring an Islamic State，Running a Criminal Enterprise”，July，2014，http://www.washingtoninstitute.org/policy-analysis/view/declaring-an-islamic-state-running-a-criminal-enterprise.

② FATF，“Financing of the Terrorist Organisation Islamic State in Iraq and the Levant”，2015，http://www.fatf-gafi.org/topics/methodsandtrends/documents/financing-of-terrorist-organisation-isil.html.

③ Zarate，Juan C.，and Thomas M.Sanderson，“In Iraq and Syria，ISIS Militants Are Flush With Funds”，The New York Times，June 28，2014，http://www.nytimes.com/2014/06/29/opinion/sunday/in-iraq-and-syria-isis-militants-are-flush-with-funds.html.

④ FATF，“Financing of the Terrorist Organisation Islamic State in Iraq and the Levant”，2015，http://www.fatf-gafi.org/topics/methodsandtrends/documents/financing-of-terrorist-organisation-isil.html.

⑤ FATF，“Financing of the Terrorist Organisation Islamic State in Iraq and the Levant”，2015，http://www.fatf-gafi.org/topics/methodsandtrends/documents/financing-of-terrorist-organisation-isil.html.

⑥ FATF，“Financing of the Terrorist Organisation Islamic State in Iraq and the Levant”，2015，http://www.fatf-gafi.org/topics/methodsandtrends/documents/financing-of-terrorist-organisation-isil.html.

盟。① 该组织于2009年在尼日利亚的东南区域暴动，该暴动已经演变为一个更大范围的国家危机，这是尼日尔三角洲南部区域现状的缩影，该区域国民收入的80%都归功于丰富的自然资源，因而这里对尼日利亚犯罪集团和寡头组织都有极大的吸引力。②

“博科圣地”组织的影响力得以传播的根源在于，1999年为结束军事独裁所提出的政策正逐渐地动摇。军事独裁的打破引入了一系列的选举程序，这为犯罪军团竞争领土以及资源的控制权提供了机会。虽然“博科圣地”组织主要在北方活动，但是其地缘政治目标应该从全国范围来理解：废除非洲人口最多的国家的联邦制，消灭南方和北方的领导人以便对本国最富裕的区域进行掠夺。③ 利用薄弱的法律制度，“博科圣地”组织至今为止的恐怖活动的费用都来自于对黑市交易网络的开发，包括一个强大的奴隶市场和一个绑架求赎和敲诈勒索的恐怖体系。④ 他们通过从尼日利亚军队中偷盗或者是向腐败的士兵购买来获取武器。⑤ 选择参加“博科圣地”组织或其他犯罪组织，对尼日利亚的年轻人来说非常有吸引力，因为在普遍失业的情况下，这为他们提供了一个备选方案。⑥

“博科圣地”组织的地缘政治目标是与强烈的意识形态要求相结合的。索科托的神话可以追溯到19世纪，当时其占领了尼日尔河以及乍得湖之间的北方土地。如今这一神话仍旧存在于恐怖分子的想象中。“博科圣地”组织所公布的目标就是通过实行沙里亚法（此为“shari'a”的音译）来恢复这个前殖民地时期的帝国。⑦

在该案例中，就像我们所分析的其他案例一样，薄弱的法律制度以及准国家的失败是导致恐怖组织成功的两个初始条件。这是引发那些与非法贸易和非法活动有关的盈利性条件的必要前提。为了获得力量以及在未来使先前的政策产生动摇，恐怖主义网络会轮流利用这些条件，从而推动这个有害的恶性循环。

---

① NBC News,“Boko Haram Leader Pledges Allegiance to ISIS in New Audio”, NBC News. March 7, 2015, http://www.nbcnews.com/storyline/isis-terror/boko-haram-leader-pledges-allegiance-isis-new-audio-n319256.

② Cholewa, Ewa, and Andrea Romoli,“Non È Boko Haram La Vera Minaccia per La Nigeria”, Limes. Accessed June 10, 2015, http://www.limesonline.com/non-e-boko-haram-la-vera-minaccia-per-la-nigeria/76859.

③ De Volder,“Boko Haram: Prima Secessionisti Poi Terroristi”, Limes 3, Jan, 2015.

④ McCoy, Terrence,“This Is How Boko Haram Funds Its Evil”, The Washington Post, June 6, 2014, http://www.washingtonpost.com/news/morning-mix/wp/2014/06/06/this-is-how-boko-haram-funds-its-evil/.

⑤ De Volder,“Boko Haram: Prima Secessionisti Poi Terroristi”, Limes 3, Jan, 2015.

⑥ Adebayo, Anthony Abayomi,“Implications of ‘Boko Haram’ Terrorism on National Development in Nigeria: A Critical Review”, Mediterranean Journal of Social Sciences 5:16(2014):480.

⑦ De Volder,“Boko Haram: Prima Secessionisti Poi Terroristi”, Limes 3, Jan, 2015.

四、结论:减少军事行动,更多地开展研究与执法

从有组织犯罪的分析和涉及国际恐怖主义的案例之中,我们可以明确地看出,非法贸易是其发展的中心。脆弱的当地政府是其发展的主要促进因素。正因为这可能是恶性循环中的一个原因和/或结果,所以我们应该对此进行思考。破坏犯罪组织和恐怖分子的资源可能是瓦解他们的一个正确方法。我们认为,相较于抑制他们利用这些机会,破坏非法贸易的条件是一条更为有效的打击犯罪和恐怖主义的策略。最近的研究指出,阻断那些为恐怖主义和犯罪提供便利的前提条件,例如贫穷、不平等以及较低的非法活动的机会成本,相较于定罪或采取军事途径更为重要。① 对于饱受战争、犯罪组织与恐怖组织的传播,以及社会经济组织重建的影响的人们,这个策略能显著地降低他们所需承担的费用。② 在这个意义上,我们相信,减少条件的方法是解决犯罪组织与恐怖组织的传播最为有效的长期方法,也是打破冲突、非法贸易条件、犯罪组织与恐怖组织兴起这一恶性循环的唯一选择。联合国安理会于2015年2月通过的2199号决议中,着重考虑了将切断资金流作为打击恐怖主义的工具。该决议采用了减少条件的方法,这是观念上与文化上的一大进步。它将打击的目标定为资源,而不是那些仍然被军队看作是目标的人民。

开展这个方法需要在了解资金流方面(其来路和去向,以及其大小)做更多的研究,同时对该区域的组织运作进行更多的学习,并关注这些组织的收入情况。这种理解应该转化为行动,这意味着我们要关闭和(或)重制那些产生非法贸易的漏洞,并开展情景预防措施来消除那些使非法贸易能够有利可图、有吸引力的因素。

解决非法资金流也是联合国发展议程提出的第16个目标的第四项所规定的任务,该议程到2030年的目标是"显著减少非法资金流与武器流,加强被盗资产的恢复与归还能力,并且打击各种形式的有组织犯罪"。③

这是研究和执法的共同任务。这意味着执法机关要实施更多的应用性研究与创

---

① Khan, Alam, and Mario Arturo Ruiz Estrada, "The Effects of Terrorism on Economic Performance: The Case of Islamic State in Iraq and Syria(ISIS)", Quality & Quantity, May, 2015, 1-17. doi: 10.1007/s11135-015-0226-9.

② Ianchovichina, Elena, "The Economic Impact of the Syrian War and the Spread of ISIS: Who Loses & How Much?" Text, Voices and Views: Middle East and North Africa, December 18, 2014, http://blogs.worldbank.org/arabvoices/economic-impact-syrian-war-and-spread-isis-who-loses-how-much.

③ United Nations, "Open Working Group Proposal for Sustainable Development Goals", 2014, https://sustainabledevelopment.un.org/focussdgs.html.

新型调查。这两组工作都将面临挑战:改变他们的行为习惯,并随之改变他们的专业知识以及训练方式。在以后,这能够减少军事方法与军事成分,并以更加文明的方法进行。这也将为所有人带来利益:减少经济的、社会的以及人类的成本,提高瓦解犯罪组织以及恐怖组织的效力。

（阮重骏 译）

Breaking The Circle of Conflicts, Illicit Trade Opportunities and Criminal/Terrorist Groups Dynamics ①

Ernesto U.Savona②and Veronica Pecile ③

Analysing national, regional and local conflicts in the different parts of the world, what emerges is that there's a link among conflicts, illicit opportunities available in the area, and the emergence or empowerment of criminal groups. This link has two possible directions: opportunities of illicit trade driving conflicts or, the reverse, groups in conflict exploiting the available opportunities of illicit trade to combat themselves or legitimate governments. There are many old and recent examples. The fragmentation of the Balkans has produced local conflicts and created opportunities for illicit trade (gasoline smuggling). As a consequence, embryonic criminal groups raised and became permanent organized criminal groups after some time. Pirates in Somalia emerged when the Somali State failed, exploiting the opportunities of the commercial routes in the Gulf of Aden. Today, ISIS is exploiting the illicit oil trade and other illicit trades in Iraq to fund its terrorist activities. Diamonds in Sierra Leone, heroin in Afghanistan have produced social and economic instability and related

① Paper for the conference on 29 June 2015 at Zhejiang Police College, Hangzhou.

② Director of Transcrime (Joint Research Centre on Transnational Crime) and Professor of Criminology Università Cattolica, MIlan.

③ Ph.D. candidate, International Ph.D. in Criminology at Università Cattolica, Milan.

wars. Understanding the drivers behind these different links could help in governing this circle and addressing effective remedies. Two main perspectives could be considered: the legal approach, which means prosecuting and convicting criminals, and/or the reduction of opportunity approach, which means changing those situations (situational prevention approach) that drive the relations among the three components: conflicts, illicit opportunities and criminal groups. This paper explains this circle providing relevant examples and suggesting possible interventions.

1. Introduction

The deterrence model is at the basis of the traditional approach to the fight against organized crime and terrorism. Its effectiveness has been low, whereas its direct (social and economic) and indirect costs (criminal justice) have been high. Considering that the insurgence of criminal groups and terrorist groups is increasingly linked to illicit trade, which has become an economic opportunity for both, this paper advocates an approach that focuses on these opportunities to reduce the criminal and terrorist threat. Understanding the vicious circle that links organized crime on one side and terrorism on the other with illicit trade could help in finding effective remedies to dismantle their criminal organizations.

The vicious circle is the result of a dialectical interaction of conflicts, illicit trade opportunities, and criminal groups. These three elements are bound together by a circular relationship going in two possible directions: on the one hand, conflicts may cause the emergence of illicit trade opportunities, which are then exploited by newly emerged criminal groups; on the other hand, the presence of illicit trade opportunities can cause conflicts and the rise of criminal groups willing to exploit them. The goal of this study is twofold: firstly, we want to show how this vicious circle works; secondly, we aim at pointing out solutions to change those situations which drive the relations among the three components, thus breaking the vicious circle.

2. The vicious circle

The link of conflicts with illicit trade opportunities and criminal groups works in both possible directions. On the one hand, financial opportunities associated to an illicit trade are attractive to criminal groups and fuel conflicts as a consequence. This seems to be the case for Colombia after 1994, when an exogenous rise in coca prices accelerated its production in rural areas, which then experienced a significant increase in the level of violence. This proved that the Colombian civil war was exacerbated by illicit trade opportunities.① Similarly, oil and diamonds in sub-Saharan Africa are lootable resources playing a crucial role in triggering civil conflicts.② For instance, in the Angolan civil conflict, which took place between 1975 and 2002, warlords used to finance their activities through the exploitation of natural resources, namely diamonds.③

This triadic connection works also in reverse, as conflicts disrupt the rule of law to such an extent that criminal groups can easily exploit new illicit trade opportunities arose in the void left by a failed state. For example, in Somalia pirates became powerful because of the fragility of the Somali state collapsed in 1991 and further weakened in the following decades, a scenario which allowed them to exploit the opportunity offered by the presence of a major ship route.④ Another emblematic case is the dramatic rise in opium production in Afghanistan since 2002, when the conflict brought to a weakening of the rule of law and to the destruction of infrastructure and irrigation, thus persuading Afghans to massively cultivate poppy. Then, these illicit gains further escalated the conflict thereby fueling the vicious circle.⑤

There are plenty of examples showing that this vicious circle applies to criminal organizations having by default an economic goal. For a long time organized crime has been differentiated from terrorism because of its ideological component. Today's evolution of international terrorism and its need of organization requests more than in the past resources for recruitment, and distribution among the members and arms to combat the terrorist war. Consequently, the insurgence of international terrorism is making the distinction with organized crime lighter. Also if a conceptual and factual difference between organized crime and terrorism still exists, the question this paper wants to address is whether this vicious circle is applicable to terrorism.

---

① Angrist, Joshua, and Adriana D. Kugler. "Rural Windfall or a New Resource Curse? Coca, Income, and Civil Conflict in Colombia." The Review of Economics and Statistics XC(2), 2008.

② Basedau, Matthias, and Tim C. Wegenast. "Oil and Diamonds as Causes of Civil War in Sub-Saharan Africa." Colombia Internacional, December, 2009.

③ Guidolin, Massimo, and Eliana La Ferrara. "Diamonds Are Forever, Wars Are Not: Is Conflict Bad for Private Firms?" The American Economic Review 97:5(2007):1978-93.

④ Dugato, Marco, and Giulia Berlusconi. "Transcrime Research in Brief-01. Maritime Piracy Worldwide." Transcrime Research in Brief 1/2015.

⑤ Lind, Jo Thori, Karl Ove Moene, and Fredrik Willumsen. "Opium for the Masses? Conflict-Induced Narcotics Production in Afghanistan." Review of Economics and Statistics 96 :5(2013):949-66.doi:10.1162/REST_a_00418.

In other words, are there cases where an illicit trade rises because of the presence of terrorist groups, or the illicit trade itself has the potential of generating terrorism?

Our analysis will now focus on three case studies illustrating how the emergence of an illicit trade opportunity connected to the presence of a lootable resource in a given region is able to create or boost a terrorist group which then grows stronger thanks to this new chance, thus fueling the vicious circle.

3. Examples of the vicious circle for international terrorism

1) Amphetamine trade fueling the Syrian civil conflict

The first case study analyzed is the Syrian one, which has become a regional leader in the amphetamines market after the outburst of the civil conflict that killed over 100. 000 people since 2011.

On the one hand, the weak or absent rule of law in most of the country creates the supply of amphetamines, since the breakdown of state infrastructure enables potential producers to easily exploit this profitable illicit trade opportunity, to such an extent that Syria has outpaced the production of Lebanon, the former regional leader of this trade.① The type of amphetamine produced in Syria is Captagon, the brand name of Fenethylline, a popular stimulant in the Middle East region.② The official report that this increase in supply has been so dramatic that Syria has turned into the main amphetamine producer of the Middle East region, after being for many years a transit country for drugs passing from Europe to the Gulf because of its strategic location at the crossroads of the Middle East. Only in 2013, the Lebanese authorities seized 12. 3 million Captagon pills at the border with Syria, and Turkish police found 7 million pills directed from Syria to Saudi Arabia. An easing factor for the production of Captagon is the low level of required skills to generate it, as its making only requires basic chemistry notions and scarcely equipped laboratories, which are often home-based.③

---

① Kalin, Stephen. "Insight: War Turns Syria into Major Amphetamines Producer, Consumer." Reuters, January 12, 2014. http://www.reuters.com/article/2014/01/12/us-syria-crisis-drugs-insight-idUSBREA0B04H20140112.

② Henley, Jon. "Captagon: The Amphetamine Fuelling Syria's Civil War." The Guardian, January 13, 2014. http://www.theguardian.com/world/shortcuts/2014/jan/13/captagon-amphetamine-syria-war-middle-east.

③ Kalin, Stephen. "Insight: War Turns Syria into Major Amphetamines Producer, Consumer." Reuters, January 12, 2014. http://www.reuters.com/article/2014/01/12/us-syria-crisis-drugs-insight-idUSBREA0B04H20140112.

On the other hand, media report that the trauma of the civil war suffered by the population fuels the demand of amphetamines, too.① A rise in the demand of drugs associated with the presence of a civil conflict on a given territory is often observable, and amphetamines work as a stimulant boosting euphoria and alleviating the depression suffered by a population in war times. There is also evidence that Captagon is used by combatants of both sides of the conflict in order to keep on fighting.

The annual revenues of amphetamine production amount to several millions of dollars and provide conspicuous funding for Syrian combatants, who then buy weapons with the money gained in this trade.② Although there is no evidence of which side of Syrian fighters earns the most from amphetamine production, millions of dollars coming from this illicit activity significantly contribute to the destabilization of the Syrian territory and its subsequent exposure to the power of ISIL. The terrorist group spread in the territories between Syria and Iraq at the edge of the civil war, between 2013 and 2014, and plans to further expand its territorial control to the whole Arab region.

In the case of amphetamines, we can conclude that the absence of rule of law characterizing a civil war context triggers a profitable illicit trade opportunity, whose exploitation further destabilizes a region fuelling the power of a terrorist group active on the territory.

2) Oil trade as ISIL's primary source of funding

The second case deals with illicit trade of a resource directly enriching a terrorist group: the exploitation of oil wells and oil trafficking as a key source of income in ISIL's balance sheet.③

ISIL perfectly embodies the category of new terrorism and its territorial expansion is a critical aspect of its power. In fact, in the initial phase of its development across Syria and Iraq ISIL consolidated its presence through a systematic territorial oppression based on the exploitation of local resources. In the context of statelessness determined by the Syrian civil war, ISIL succeeded in establishing a capillary system of extortions, sale of ex-governmental

① Henley, Jon. "Captagon: The Amphetamine Fuelling Syria's Civil War." The Guardian, January 13, 2014. http://www.theguardian.com/world/shortcuts/2014/jan/13/captagon-amphetamine-syria-war-middle-east.

② Kalin, Stephen. "Insight: War Turns Syria into Major Amphetamines Producer, Consumer." Reuters, January 12, 2014. http://www.reuters.com/article/2014/01/12/us-syria-crisis-drugs-insight-idUSBREA0B04H20140112.

③ Levitt, Matthew. "Declaring an Islamic State, Running a Criminal Enterprise", July, 2014. http://www.washingtoninstitute.org/policy-analysis/view/declaring-an-islamic-state-running-a-criminal-enterprise.

properties and US military equipment and, most importantly, sale of oil coming from oilfields and refineries controlled by the terrorist organization itself.① ISIL engaged in what we can consider as a real "war economy" based on oil trade, which is then smuggled outwards through Iraq and southern Turkey thanks to well-established trafficking networks which pass through the whole country and the border areas.[②,③]

Studies argue that this model of governance will soon become unsustainable for ISIL unless the organization succeeds in gaining other territories.④ Firstly, ISIL's oil trade might become scarcer because of terrorists' limited ability to efficiently extract and refine oil, as the organization mostly relies on modular refineries, which are considered as very primitive refining techniques. Secondly, international coalition airstrikes have been hitting hard on oil refineries handled by ISIL. Thirdly, the Turkish authorities made efforts to counter oil smuggling, and the Iraqi Government committed to seize potential ISIL-related shipments of oil products. However, the government of Ankara has not succeeded yet in exerting a tight border control able to block the transit of resources, weapons and individuals. Furthermore, it is essential to identify more accurately traders, carriers, buyers, routes involved in the ISIL-managed oil trafficking.⑤

3) Boko Haram as a symptom of Nigeria's turmoil

The third case we take into consideration is the Boko Haram, which in March 2015 declared its alliance with ISIL.⑥ The uprising of the group in the northeastern part of Nigeria since 2009 has to be framed in the broader national scenario of state crisis epitomized by the situation in the southern Niger Delta region, an area generating the 80% of national income due to its richness in natural resources and therefore extremely attractive for Nigerian

---

① FATF. "Financing of the Terrorist Organisation Islamic State in Iraq and the Levant.", 2015. http://www.fatf-gafi.org/topics/methodsandtrends/documents/financing-of-terrorist-organisation-isil.html.

② Zarate, Juan C., and Thomas M. Sanderson. "In Iraq and Syria, ISIS Militants Are Flush With Funds." The New York Times, June 28, 2014. http://www.nytimes.com/2014/06/29/opinion/sunday/in-iraq-and-syria-isis-militants-are-flush-with-funds.html.

③ FATF. "Financing of the Terrorist Organisation Islamic State in Iraq and the Levant.", 2015. http://www.fatf-gafi.org/topics/methodsandtrends/documents/financing-of-terrorist-organisation-isil.html.

④ Ibid.

⑤ Ibid.

⑥ NBC News. "Boko Haram Leader Pledges Allegiance to ISIS in New Audio." NBC News. March 7, 2015. http://www.nbcnews.com/storyline/isis-terror/boko-haram-leader-pledges-allegiance-isis-new-audio-n319256.

criminal oligarchies and groups.①

The spread of Boko Haram's influence has its roots in the gradual destabilization of the political scenario favored by the end of the military dictatorship in 1999. This rupture brought to a series of electoral processes that became opportunities for criminal militias to compete for the control over territories and resources.Although Boko Haram is mostly active in the North,his geopolitical goal should be read at a national scale:dismantling the federal union of Africa's most populous country and annihilating both the northernand the southern leaders in order to plunder the richest areas of the country.② Favored by a weak rule of law,Boko Haram has so far financed its terrorist operations through the exploitation of a diverse network of black market trades,including a robust slave market,a territorial system of kidnapping for ransom,and racketeering.③ They obtain weapons by stealing them from the Nigerian army or buying them from corrupt soldiers.④ The option of entering Boko Haram or other criminal gangs is especially attractive to Nigerian youth as it represents an alternative to a widespread unemployment context.⑤

The geopolitical goals of Boko Haram combine with strong ideological claims.The myth of Sokoto,dating back to the 19th Century and occupying the Northern lands between the Niger River and the Chad Lake,is still alive in the terrorists' imaginary.The declared objective of Boko Haram is to restore this pre-colonial empire through the imposition of shari'a.⑥

In this case,like in the others we analyzed,the success of the terrorist organization was determined by an initial condition of weak rule of law and quasi-state failure.This was the necessary precondition to trigger the profitable opportunities linked to illicit trades and activities,which were in turn exploited by a terrorist network in order to gain power and further destabilize the initial scenario,fuelling a deleterious vicious circle.

4. Conclusion:less military action but more research and law enforcement

From the analysis of organized crime and from the cases analyzed in relation to interna-

---

① Cholewa,Ewa,and Andrea Romoli."Non È Boko Haram La Vera Minaccia per La Nigeria." Limes.Accessed June 10,2015.http://www.limesonline.com/non-e-boko-haram-la-vera-minaccia-per-la-nigeria/76859.

② De Volder."Boko Haram:Prima Secessionisti Poi Terroristi." Limes 3,Jan,2015.

③ McCoy,Terrence."This Is How Boko Haram Funds Its Evil." The Washington Post,June 6,2014.http://www.washingtonpost.com/news/morning-mix/wp/2014/06/06/this-is-how-boko-haram-funds-its-evil/.

④ De Volder."Boko Haram:Prima Secessionisti Poi Terroristi." Limes 3,Jan,2015.

⑤ Adebayo,Anthony Abayomi."Implications of 'Boko Haram' Terrorism on National Development in Nigeria:A Critical Review". Mediterranean Journal of Social Sciences 5:16(2014):480.

⑥ De Volder."Boko Haram:Prima Secessionisti Poi Terroristi." Limes 3,Jan,2015.

tional terrorism it is clear that the illicit trade is at the center of their development. Its main facilitator is the fragility of the states where they develop. Just because this could be a cause and/or an effect enters in the vicious circle and should be considered. Disrupting resources could be the right process to dismantle the criminal organizations, terrorists included. We argue that disrupting illicit trade opportunities is a more efficient counter-crime and counter-terrorism strategy than the mere repression of groups exploiting such chances. Recent studies have pointed out the importance of tackling the preconditions easing terrorism and crime such as poverty, inequality, and low opportunity costs for illicit activities rather than adopting a criminalizing or military approach.① This strategy significantly reduces the costs suffered by populations affected by the war and by the spread of criminal and terrorist groups, by regenerating a damaged socioeconomic tissue.② In this sense, we believe that the reduction of opportunity approach is the most efficient long-term antidote to the spread of criminal and terrorist groups, and is the only option able to break the vicious circle of conflicts, illicit trade opportunities, and the rise of criminal and terrorist groups. The United Nations Security Council in its Resolution 2199 of February 2015 considered with attention the interruption of financial flows as one of the instruments for combating terrorism. This resolution is an advanced step conceptually and culturally in the reduction of opportunities approach. It moves more towards the resources than towards the people, that are still considered as a target by military forces.

Developing this approach requests more research in the understanding of the financial flows (where they start and where they go, together with their dimension), learning more about the organizations operating in the area and focusing on their income. This understanding should be translated into action, which means closing and/or reorienting the loopholes that produce illicit trades and developing situational prevention measures to contrast what makes illicit trade profitable and attractive.

Dealing with illicit financial flows is also the task defined by target n. 16. 4 of the UN Post development agenda, which by 2030 aims at "significantly reduce illicit financial and arms flows, strengthen recovery and return of stolen assets, and combat all forms of

① Khan, Alam, and Mario Arturo Ruiz Estrada. "The Effects of Terrorism on Economic Performance: The Case of Islamic State in Iraq and Syria (ISIS)". Quality & Quantity, May, 2015, 1-17. doi: 10.1007/s11135-015-0226-9.

② Ianchovichina, Elena. "The Economic Impact of the Syrian War and the Spread of ISIS: Who Loses & How Much?" Text. Voices and Views: Middle East and North Africa. December 18, 2014. http://blogs.worldbank.org/arabvoices/economic-impact-syrian-war-and-spread-isis-who-loses-how-much.

organized crime" (United Nations 2014).[①]

This is a joint task of research and law enforcement action. It means more applied research and more innovative investigation carried out by law enforcement. Both these two components have a challenge in front of them: change how they behave, and consequently change their expertise and training. In the future this will allow to reduce the military approach and component in favor of a more civil one. This will produce benefits for all: less economic, social and human costs and higher effectiveness in dismantling criminal and terrorist organizations.

---

① United Nations, "Open Working Group Proposal for Sustainable Development Goals", 2014. https://sustainabledevelopment.un.org/focussdgs.html.

恐怖主义商业:基于ISIS的个案分析

路易丝·谢利(Louise Shelley)[①]

恐怖分子有商人的功能。他们寻求产品组合、专业服务,进行成本效益分析,使用税收策略,还会进行供应链的开发。[②] 他们会谋求市场操纵、战略联盟、竞争优势、机会目标,并设法高效地利用新方法和新技术。他们通过国际网络来寻找途径以获取最佳的人力资源。ISIS就体现了这些特点,但它只是众多拥有这些属性的恐怖组织中的一个。不过,它是这些恐怖组织中最具规模的一个。

恐怖分子总是寻求新的方法来获取资金。在这个方面,他们与跨国企业一样,需要从事多种经营才能在全球经济下继续生存。为了生存,他们需要如同最灵活的企业那样,具有前瞻性、流动性和灵活性。我们必须像关注商人一样重视他们的能力,而不能像那些只关注于恐怖主义融资的学者那样,仅仅探测他们以往的资金流。

一、利用相对优势

恐怖分子会利用自己的相对优势。靠近自然资源的恐怖分子会将自然资源作为

---

① 路易丝·谢利(Louise Shelley),美国乔治·梅森大学公共政策与国际关系学院教授,奥马尔·L.和南茜赫斯特讲席教授,恐怖主义、跨国犯罪和腐败研究中心主任。

② 想要进一步了解更多的分析内容请看 Louise I.Shelley, *Dirty Entanglements: Corruption, Crime and Terrorism*, Cambridge: Cambridge University Press, 2014, 173-217。

商品来为自己提供活动经费,靠近军火库的恐怖分子会成为武器商,在边境区域的恐怖分子会向跨境的商品流征收税费。他们利用着自己所处的关键位置的优势。例如"基地"组织(Al-Qaeda),他们从事着钻石贸易,尤其是在塞拉利昂、利比里亚和坦桑尼亚。① 哥伦比亚革命武装力量(FARC)和哥伦比亚民族解放军(Ejército de LiberaciónNacional,National Liberation Army,or ELN),在哥伦比亚的不同区域中,采用区域控制的手段来勒索钱财并主导了对能源设施的袭击②,这样的情况也出现在了阿尔及利亚,以及 ISIS 与"博科圣地"控制的区域中。

位于象群和犀牛群附近的恐怖分子和叛乱组织,为了猎取象牙和犀牛角而对这些动物进行大规模的屠杀,这对生态系统造成了不可逆转的破坏。2015 年 9 月发行的《国家地理》杂志证实了其早先出版的一份关于恐怖分子与苏丹政府成员一道参与非法象牙贸易的调查③,并指出了恐怖分子与腐败官员在其中发挥的作用。美国是第二大象牙进口国。他们的财富正在为恐怖主义筹资提供帮助。

二、固定的供应链

恐怖分子十分关心其产品的供应链,因为他们需要确保货物在不受损害的情况下被安全及时的送达。恐怖分子主要关心那些像麻醉药品、伪造的药物、香烟(这是许多恐怖组织的生命线)和昂贵的改道货物,比如石油,这样的非法货物的供应链。

恐怖分子通过控制供应链来获取大量的金钱,这些供应链用来传递他们的货物,例如毒品,恐怖分子也会通过对途经其控制的边境区或者领地的其他人的走私行为进行征税,以此来获得大量的金钱。对途经商品课税是他们筹集资金的关键。我们已经知道,有组织犯罪集团对贸易的勒索已经到了一个十分严重的时期,这就是为什么他们要如此大量地参与到船运和卡车运输之中的原因了。存在于许多不同大洲的

---

① Global Witness,"For a Few Dollars More:How Al Qaeda Moved into the Diamond Trade",April 2003,http://www.globalwitness.org/library/few-dollars-more;Greg Campbell,*Blood Diamonds:Tracing the Deadly Path of the World's Most Precious Stones* (Boulder,CO:Westview Press,2002);Douglas Farah,*Blood from Stones:The Secret Financial Network of Terror* (New York:Broadway Books,2004).

② FrédéricMassé and Johanna Camargo,"ActoresArmadosIlegales y Sector Extractivo en Colombia", V informe del Centro Internacional de Toledo para la Paz (CITpax) ObservatorioInternacional, 2012, 49, http://www. toledopax. org%2Fuploads%2FActores _ armados _ ilegales _ sector _ extractivo. pdf. http://www. askonline. ch/fileadmin/user _ upload/documents/Thema_Wirtschaft_und_Menschenrechte/Bergbau_Rohstoff/Gold/Actores_armados_ilegales_sector_extractivo.pdf.

③ Bryan Christy,"Tracking Ivory", National Geographic, September 2015, 30 – 59; Kasper Agger and Johnathan Hutson,Kony's Ivory:How Elephant Poaching in Congo Helps Support the Lord's Resistance Army,June 3,2013,http://enoughproject.org/reports/konys-ivory-how-elephant-poaching-congo-helps-support-lords-resistance-army.

恐怖组织也都通过对供应链的利用以及对交易活动的征税来获取利润。但这一发现在反恐组织中还没有获得应有的重视。

恐怖分子总能通过对那些将合法或非法的产品运经其控制的领地的供应链征税来获得收益。通过腐败官员和暴力行为,恐怖组织会逐渐对国家造成破坏并且逐渐在关键的边境区域、港口和其他交通枢纽中扩大自身实力。因此,恐怖组织已经从有组织犯罪集团中学到了控制领地的重要性,同时,在日益全球化的经济形势下,他们已经开始学会利用企业对远距离商品运输的需求。

三、固定的人员

正如接下来需要进一步讨论的那样,ISIS 已经发展出了一个国际化的成员招募模式。其采用了新型科技,比如利用推特来识别潜在的新成员。然后他们会根据地理特点将独特的信息发送给所要招募的成员,让他们为自己战斗,或者唆使女性加入他们并为他们提供资金支持。其通讯系统和市场策略在某些方面就像是跨国公司一样。

四、恐怖分子商业活动的多样性

各种恐怖组织不会都采用同样的方式来进行商业活动。文化、历史以及地理条件造成了各个恐怖分子之间独特的筹资方式。例如在中东地区,从有文字记录以来,贸易一直是其经济的重心,贸易和来自贸易的税收是 ISIS 以及其他像 PKK 这样存在于该区域的恐怖组织的主要资金来源。阿富汗和安第斯山脉长期存在着毒品种植现象,这导致了那里的恐怖组织依赖种植业和毒品来筹措资金。在非洲,人类的统治力远超过其他动物,这使人成为了统治者,在那里对动物器官的贸易成为了恐怖主义的重要资金源。

恐怖分子挑选所要实施的犯罪时,不仅看其所能带来的利润和进入该类商业领域的难易程度,也会考虑该犯罪活动的竞争程度和花费在腐败官员上的成本。① 而对于有些恐怖分子来说,对被侦查到的风险和资产损失风险的评估结果也是其所需要

① *Fondeo del terrorismo*, *Infolaft*, 1, no.4, 2009, 10-15, reveals that FARC's financial records calculated their expenditures for corruption as a cost of business.

考量的内容。像商人一样，恐怖分子也会利用自己的战略优势。了解一个恐怖组织在融资结构方面的比较优势，是判断该组织的持续性并制定消减其收益的策略的关键。

五、恐怖分子利用犯罪来为自己的活动筹措资金

恐怖分子将犯罪作为一种获取收益和后勤保障的手段，他们也会利用犯罪渠道来进行资金转移。罪犯会为他们提供犯罪工具，例如伪造的文件、新的身份以及在需要时对恐怖分子进行跨境运输。[①] 他们也会成立一些机构以帮助恐怖分子转移资金和洗钱。罪犯通过贿赂官员为恐怖分子及其商品提供安全的过境通道。恐怖组织的犯罪支持结构，要么包括了轻微的刑事犯罪人，要么包括了发达的犯罪组织，就像那不勒斯的克拉默组织一样[②]，它们通过合法辅助者的服务来获得强化，这些辅助者可以是银行家、律师和公司，他们有意或无意地帮助着恐怖主义实施犯罪。[③] 腐败的军事人员充当了罪犯和恐怖组织的军火供应商。[④] 也有其他的辅助者能够向犯罪领域提供服务，最为突出的是贩毒分子和进行军民两用核材料运输的人。

六、产品组合

恐怖主义几乎使用了所有已知的犯罪活动来进行筹资。对犯罪活动的选择能够反映出恐怖组织的地理位置、成员数量和犯罪盈利能力。挑选何种犯罪是根据其逃避侦查或起诉的能力、接触腐败官员的能力以及获得利润的能力而作出的。通过敲

---

① C.J.de Poot and A.Sonnenschein, *Jihadi Terrorism in the Netherlands*(The Hague: WODC, 2011), 109-10.

② Roberto Saviano, *Gomorrah*, trans.from the Italian by Virginia Jewiss(New York: Farrar, Straus, and Giroux), 2007, 181-86.

③ Mark Pieth, ed., *Financing of Terrorism* (Dordrecht, Netherlands: Kluwer Academic, 2003); Nikos Passas, "Terrorism Financing Mechanisms and Policy Dilemmas", in *Terrorism Finance and State Responses: A Comparative Perspective*, ed.Jeanne Giraldo and Harold Trinkunas(Stanford, CA: Stanford University Press, 2007), 30, which discusses how the 9/11 hijackers used the established banking system.The nuclear proliferation of the A.Q.Khan network was facilitated by businessmen in Europe.Rebekah K.Dietz, Illicit Networks: Targeting the Nexus between Terrorists, Proliferators and Narcotraffickers, (Monterey, CA: U.S.Naval Post Graduate School, 2010), http://www.dtic.mil/dtic/tr/fulltext/u2/a536899.pdf; *IISS Nuclear Black Market Dossier: A Net Assessment* (London, 2007), 43 - 64, http://www. iiss. org/publications/strategic-dossiers/nbm/nuclear-black-market-dossier-a-net-assesment/.

④ 柬埔寨军队的情况对此进行了很好的说明。见 David Capie, "Trading the Tools of Terror: Armed Groups and Light Weapons Proliferation in Southeast Asia", in *Terrorism and Violence in Southeast Asia: Transnational Challenges to States and Regional Stability*, ed.Paul J.Smith(Armonk, NY: M.E.Sharpe, 2005), 191.

诈和绑架,恐怖分子能够将普通市民和企业作为自己的猎物。通过信用卡滥用和其他金融手段来操纵市场,他们就能够对那些合法金融机构实施欺诈行为。① 现如今,大量非法活动汇聚于供应链之中,并受到同一个运输辅助者的掌控。

除了这些高利润、大规模的犯罪活动,恐怖分子与叛乱分子也会参与到其他不同种类的犯罪行为中,包括早些年,恐怖分子和游击队员所使用的那些犯罪行为,比如绑架、勒索和抢银行。② 而由于对信用卡犯罪和网络诈骗的依赖,他们一直处于科技的前沿地带。他们会使用新技术,比如利用加密货币(比如比特币)进行资金转移。同时他们也能够利用暗网来进行对话通讯和商品贩卖,而我们却无法侦查到这些。

还有许多其他形式的非法活动,它们已经成为了恐怖主义的生命线,比如走私古董和艺术品、跨境走私货物、交易假冒商品和改道商品。这些犯罪中有许多都与合法经济存在着联系,所以我们可以有效地利用来自商界的信息对恐怖主义进行打击。自然资源的非法贸易,如石油、黄金等也为恐怖主义提供了资金支持。③ 像黄金、钻石这样的商品尤其需要受到重视,因为其只需极小的重量就能带来极高的固有价值。还有一些犯罪活动,例如人口走私与贩卖,它们有"两种用途":既能产生收益又能帮助恐怖组织进行工作人员的转移。恐怖分子已经发展出了一套完美的生产线,其涉及所有的犯罪,从最基本的犯罪到最复杂的犯罪全都包含其中。

七、小规模的非法贸易对资助恐怖分子方面所发挥的主要作用

涉毒恐怖主义概念的提出意味着我们已经开始关注像毒品贸易这样大规模的筹资方式。但是在美国、欧洲、南非和中东地区,恐怖分子正越来越多地使用小规模的非法贸易来为自己筹措资金,其交易的商品包括了假冒产品、燃料、香烟、食品、药品、纺织品和服装。另一种具有军民两用的双重用途的犯罪——武器贸易,在北非地区

---

① Matthew Levitt and Michael Jacobsen, *The Money Trail: Finding, Following and Freezing Terrorist Finances*, Policy Focus 89 (Washington, DC: Washington Institute, November 2008), 50-51, http://www.washingtoninstitute.org/policy-analysis/view/the-money-trail-finding-following-and-freezing-terrorist-finances, and Rohan Gunaratna, Inside Al Qaeda: Global Network of Terror (New York: Columbia University Press, 2002), 63-65; de Poot and Sonnenschein, Jihadi Terrorism in the Netherlands, 111.

② R.T.Naylor, "The Insurgent Economy: Black Market Operations of Guerrilla Organizations", Crime, Law and Social Change 20, no.1 (1993): 13, 20.

③ 对地下黄金的讨论,可见 R.T.Naylor, Wages of Crime: Black Markets, Illegal Finance, and the Underworld Economy, rev.ed. (Ithaca, NY: Cornell University Press, 2004), 196-246; for extractive industries, such as oil, see Massé and Camargo, "ActoresArmadosIlegales y Sector Extractivo en Colombia".

十分普遍，特别是在利比亚，其武器流出的情况十分严重。① 总的来说，这些活动的收益相当可观，其主要的竞争对手是毒品贸易，但是相比于毒品贸易来说，其被起诉的风险却又低得多。

在美国，非法烟草贸易中产生的资金会被运出美国以资助中东地区的恐怖组织。ISIS 从欧洲招募的新成员通过这些非法贸易产生的收益来支付他们前往 ISIS 的旅费。发生在欧洲的恐怖袭击，例如对往返于布鲁塞尔和巴黎的火车展开的袭击，其中参与实施的恐怖分子都有实施小规模非法贸易的背景。参与杀害查理周刊漫画家的卡拉奇兄弟组织成员中的一人就曾进行过假冒耐克球鞋和走私香烟的买卖。纽约警察局（NYPD）已经开始关注一些小规模的犯罪，比如香烟走私，这些犯罪会为各种不同的恐怖组织提供资金来源。

八、专业服务

当恐怖分子充当犯罪企业家的时候，他们就需要各种各样的项目服务。② 他们需要有会计、银行家和律师。同时，他们也需要有腐败官员和来自商界的辅助者的帮助，辅助者中有些也许并不知情，但通常情况下以知情者为多。因此，恐怖分子有许多方式可以介入合法经济。但他们也还是需要来自犯罪领域的专业服务，因为他们需要来自人口走私者、"无法追踪的通信技术方面上的专家、伪造者和洗钱者"所提供的服务。③ 如果不雇佣这些专家，他们就无法发挥自己的商业功能。④

作为恐怖主义企业家，他们总是在寻觅新的生产线，并努力学习从某一区域中获得的区域性成功经验，并将这些成功经验复制到其他地方。因此，著名的毒枭恐怖分子——哥伦比亚革命武装力量（FARC），实际上也有许多不同种类的商业活动，他们甚至参与了碳氢化合物的开发。和商业世界的情况一样，多样性也是恐怖主义企业

---

① Global Initiative on Transnational Crime, "Libya: Criminal Economies and Terrorist Financing in the Trans Sahara", May 2015, http://www.globalinitiative.net/libya-criminal-economies-and-terrorist-financing-in-the-trans-sahara/; International Crisis Group, "Tunisia's borders: Jihadism and Contraband", Middle East/North Africa Report, N°148, (2013) 31.

② SherzodAbdukadirov, "Terrorism: The Dark Side of Social Entrepreneurship", *Studies in Conflict and Terrorism* 33, no.7(2010): 603 - 17; Douglas Farah, "Fixers, Super Fixers, and Shadow Facilitators: How Networks Connect", 2012, http://www.strategycenter.net/docLib/20120423_Farah_FixersSuperFixersShadow.pdf.

③ *Organised Crime in Australia Key Trends* 2008, 2, http://www.crimecommission.gov.au/publications/organised-crime-australia/organised-crime-australia-2008-report; Farah, "Fixers, Super Fixers, and Shadow Facilitators".

④ 对一个在新西兰奥兰克的为有组织犯罪分子以及恐怖分子提供帮助的辅助者的分析，见"Offshore Registration Business Halts Operations", June 28, 2011, http://www.reportingproject.net/occrp/index.php/en/ccwatch/cc-watch-indepth/930-offshore-registration-business-forced-to-halt-operations.

家能够继续生存的关键。

恐怖主义企业家，与其同行们一样，面临同一个问题——专业服务的维护。这些服务提供商帮助他们转移资金、腐化官员以及获取伪造的文件。

九、基于 ISIS 的个案分析

2014 年 ISIS 在伊拉克逊尼派的迅速传播，在某种程度上，可归因于伊拉克战后初期所制定的大量考虑不周的决策。废除伊拉克军队，对伊拉克复兴党的严厉清洗，在伊拉克战后将复兴党成员与恐怖分子一并关押，以及马利基政府的腐败，这些决策引发了逊尼教徒们极大的愤怒。这些愤恨在叙利亚混乱局面这样一个有害的环境下得以继续发酵，而叙利亚的混乱也为 ISIS 的产生提供了帮助，这是一个脱离美国和北大西洋公约组织控制的情况。

ISIS 之所以能战胜伊拉克安保部队，是因为它吸收了伊拉克"基地"组织的技术和那些在走私和非法贸易方面有着丰富经验的萨达姆·侯赛因政府的前高级官员。犯罪活动带来的利润和对于腐败的有效利用使得 ISIS 拥有了大量坦克，其拥有的坦克数量甚至超过了一些北大西洋公约组织的主导成员国所拥有的。ISIS 拥有当代复杂的武器装备，并且他们也会利用先进的媒体宣传以及推特和其他社交方式的信息传递，来进行国际化的成员招募。

美国和北大西洋公约组织成员一直在关注那些与国家相关的问题，然而现在中东地区的威胁主要来自于像 ISIS 这样的非国家行为者。这种新型的威胁并非来自国家，而是来自那些像跨国非法企业一样的犯罪化恐怖组织。如今我们所面临的挑战，不仅是要切断他们的资金源，还要破坏他们的全球招募策略、他们的市场以及他们的国际信息传递机制。打击恐怖主义就要像打击商业竞争对手一样。这要求我们的政策不仅只是依靠军事力量，还要依靠政府部门之间以及政府部门与私营部门之间的相互合作。

ISIS 在伊拉克逊尼教派中的快速发展使得美国政府感到震惊，他们完全没有预料到伊拉克安保部队会如此快速而彻底地被瓦解。逊尼派成员和无家可归的复兴党人在这十年中所积累的愤恨也使得他们不愿意与 ISIS 为战。此外，当地军队的腐败也进一步导致逊尼派成员无法得到所需的保护。

然而，如果分析人员已经关注过犯罪与恐怖主义的关系以及腐败所带来的腐蚀性影响的话，那么他们就不会对于 ISIS 的崛起感到惊讶。当我在 2013 年 10 月对自己的书《肮脏的纠缠:腐败、犯罪和恐怖主义》("Dirty Entanglements:Corruption,Crime and Terrorism")进行总结时,就曾根据与军事人员(大多数来自最高决策层)、政策顾问和当地专家进行的大量的访谈进行了预测,认为世界稳定的最大威胁来自叙利亚。大概九个月之后,ISIS 就从叙利亚里走了出来并开始接管了伊拉克逊尼派。这为 ISIS 的运作提供了一个庞大且相当安全的基地。

十、战后政策

伊拉克战后,逊尼派成员控制了军队以及萨达姆·侯赛因时期的政府机构。复兴党控制了权力杠杆。为了确保侯赛因及其中坚分子不会再次掌权,美国军方领导层和美军在伊拉克的联盟都作出了巨大的努力,以解散那些曾为萨达姆统治提供过帮助的机构。伊拉克陆军于 2013 年 5 月被解散,这个决定在实施之前根本没有经过仔细的分析。五年以后,事实证明,那些曾领导过军队的逊尼派人员带来了一场剧烈的叛乱。[①]

由美国牵头的联盟驻伊拉克临时管理当局(CPA)促成了一个清除复兴党的综合性政策的提出。这与第二次世界大战后德国对废除纳粹所做的努力截然不同,在德国废除纳粹的过程中,他们仔细地回顾了政府的过去,并且他们也并非要清除有关纳粹的一切人员,而伊拉克的清除复兴党行动则太过于彻底,甚至并没有进行个人的审核。当然,这使得逊尼派成员被大量地清除,只要逊尼派成员有在政府行政部门工作的经历,他就会成为被清除的对象。没有经过听证和正当程序就开始大量地解雇前复兴党成员,这使得他们的怨气不断地滋生,也导致了一个毫无功能性可言的政府的产生。[②]

贝卡营(Camp Bucca),一个曾经关押过 10 万囚徒的大型监狱,是 ISIS 的发源地。在《肮脏的纠缠:腐败、犯罪和恐怖主义》一书中,我就曾说过,监狱已经不再是一个控制系统,它已经成为了犯罪与恐怖主义进行互动的大本营。在 2007 年,贝卡营就提供了这一功能,当时在这个过度拥挤的监狱中充斥着大量极端主义者。[③] 囚犯们依据其所信仰的宗教而被隔离开来:逊尼派教徒与逊尼派教徒被分在一起,什叶派教徒与什叶派教徒被分在一起。这导致了被监禁的前复兴党人和宗教极端分子产

---

① http://www.nytimes.com/2008/03/17/world/middleeast/17bremer.html? pagewanted=1&_r=0&hp.

② http://www.nytimes.com/2008/03/17/world/middleeast/17bremer.html? pagewanted=1&_r=0&hp.

③ http://www.independent.co.uk/news/world/middle-east/camp-bucca-the-us-prison-that-became-the-birthplace-of-isis-9838905.html.

生了一个怪异的融合，而这些极端主义者正是如今的ISIS。这些前复兴党人在萨达姆时期积累了多年管理伊拉克的行政经验，而恐怖分子正需要从这些前复兴党人那里获取这些行政管理技能。被监禁的复兴党人正因自己被监禁而愤怒不已，此时他们发现那些虔诚的极端主义者有着与自己相同的目标。因此，ISIS通过吸收前高级政府官员获得了大量拥有精湛技艺的人，其拥有的高级技能人员的数量甚至超过了“基地”组织和那些先于ISIS出现的其他组织。

ISIS的领导人阿布·巴克尔·巴格达迪(Abu Bakr al-Baghdadi)就曾在贝卡营中生活了数年。他在监狱中享有很高的地位，大家需要他来调停纠纷。狱中，他所获得的便利给了他接近其他囚犯的机会，而这些囚犯们在日后也都成为了ISIS的领导人。在ISIS的25个高层领导人中，就有17人曾在2004年至2011年间遭受过监禁。①

伊拉克战争后，在马里奇的统治下，伊朗支持的什叶派获得了压倒性的力量。这使得大量的逊尼派成员十分愤怒，因为在萨达姆·侯赛因时期，他们已经习惯了对政治力量的掌控。在马里奇政府的统治下，伊拉克的石油收益大部分落到了什叶派成员手中，北方的库尔德人也分到了很小的一部分，而逊尼派成员却几乎什么也没有得到。逊尼派十分愤怒，他们的怒火导致了宗教暴力事件和我们今天所看到的冲突，也同样导致了逊尼派成员不愿为了保卫伊拉克而与ISIS交战。

不愿分享税收只是马里奇自身腐败的其中一个方面。② 他将政府高层的位置给了自己什叶派的密友，令逊尼派领导人被边缘化，还使得大片领地范围内的人民享受不到政府所提供的基础服务，如今这些地方已经被ISIS所控制。阿拉伯之春运动开始不久后，逊尼派地区就开始了对马里奇政府的抗议活动。但是反对者却被标以了恐怖分子的标签，遭到了残忍的对待。被ISIS接管的前一年，那里又产生了一波大规模的抗议马里奇政府浪潮，但是这次抗议也遭到了伊拉克安全部队的野蛮镇压。这些事件是了解为什么逊尼派地区的战斗性不断上升的关键。

在这一背景下，伊拉克军队在逊尼派区域中对ISIS采取武装抵抗的最终失败，就不这么令人惊讶了。对于逊尼派成员来说，一个是位于巴格达的腐败且残暴的政府，另一个是位于ISIS的同样腐败且残暴的政府，他们只是在两害之中选择其一罢了。③ 而

---

① http://www.theguardian.com/world/2014/dec/11/-sp-isis-the-inside-story.

② http://foreignpolicy.com/2014/06/19/how-maliki-ruined-iraq/.

③ 2011年美国撤军之后，马里奇对逊尼派领导人的政治边缘化，以及伊拉克安全部队所受到的宗教控制，共同促使了一场反政府抗议活动的产生，该活动主要发生在像安巴尔和萨拉赫丁这样的逊尼派区域中。2013年4月，伊拉克安全部队在企图清除抗议者位于哈维贾(Hawija)的大本营时，对平民实施了杀戮。以此为导火索，这次抗议活动催生出了一个有组织的、公然以武装反对伊拉克政府的反对党。详情请见 http://www.understandingwar.org/report/beyond-islamic-state-iraqs-sunni-insurgency#sthash.GoorCeTO.dpuf.

最终他们选择了 ISIS,因为他们不想因支持马里奇政府而丧命。

此外,叙利亚是 ISIS 的孵化场所。伊拉克战争期间,阿萨德政府为极端主义者提供了庇护并允许他们进行训练、获得武器和筹措资金。阿萨德在当时坚信自己可以控制这些人员。但是当叙利亚内战爆发时,他的幻想就破灭了。混乱为各种极端组织提供了进行整合的机会,并最终使得如今被广为人知的 ISIS 组织形成了,同时,混乱也为新成立的 ISIS 提供了进一步扩张的机会。ISIS 首先扩张到了伊拉克,如今已经扩展成为从阿富汗到北非的各种组织,最近其势力甚至一度扩展到了西非地区。

十一、犯罪企业

ISIS 之所以能成功获取人员、武器和资金,原因在于它发挥着企业的功能。事实上,它是已知的最具规模的恐怖主义企业。犯罪与腐败是其获取武器、增加收益和保证自己在各区域间移动性的关键因素。为了确保日常工作的正常进行,ISIS 会寻求产品组合,正如上文提到的,他们会获取全球化的专业服务、形成战略同盟、抓住机遇并进行技术革新。大量的收益使得 ISIS 既可以从利比亚购买武器,又能够从美国向叙利亚反叛军所捐赠的武器中获得一定数量的美军武器。

ISIS 已经成功掌握了现代市场的销售技术,他们不仅会利用社交媒体来传播自己的暴行,还会用它来进行人员的招募。在那些能够很容易地与 ISIS 所控制的领土取得联系的国家中,招募工作进行得尤为顺利。在欧洲,ISIS 所赞助的社交媒体很聪明地将招募对象选定为被剥夺公民权利或是不再对未来抱有幻想的年轻人。很多被招募者都是被阿拉伯帝国的神秘所吸引的,ISIS 向他们灌输这么一个思想:这里是一个天堂——相比于他们所正在遭受的边缘化的生活来说,这里是一个理想的地方。

为恐怖组织实施极端暴行的成员都有犯罪经历,最近发生在法国和丹麦的恐怖袭击就凸显出了这一特点,发动这些袭击的 ISIS 支持者们都有犯罪前科。阿保·伊萨(Abo Isa),ISIS 所招募的一名瑞典士兵,其在瑞典时就曾三次入狱,其中包括因暴力犯罪而入狱,不仅如此,在他那些来到叙利亚的瑞典同胞中,至少有 8 人有犯罪记录。[①] 对恐怖组织的领导层来说,这无可厚非。虽然组织需要为这些意识形态狂热分子支付旅途费用,但是这也为组织带来了拥有犯罪经验的外国成员,例如以假名“谢赫”(Sheikh)闻名于世的格鲁吉亚人达尔罕·巴提拉什维利(Tarkhan

---

① http://www.ctc.usma.edu/posts/the-swedish-foreign-fighter-contingent-in-syria.

Batirashvili)和因非法藏匿武器而被捕的阿布·奥马尔·舒斯哈尼(Abu Omar al-Shishani)。巴格达迪位于伊拉克和叙利亚的25名副手中,有大约三分之一的人曾有在萨达姆·侯赛因统治时期为军队效力的经历,而几乎所有的人都曾受到美军的监禁,而在监狱中,他们往往都是与如今已成为ISIS成员的那些恐怖分子和叛乱分子关押在一起。很多侯赛因政府的成员都有走私以及从事其他非法活动的经历,因为他们要依靠这些非法活动来使政府能够继续勉强地维持下去。

ISIS也会利用自己的地理位置优势。恐怖主义企业与犯罪企业的不同之处在于,犯罪只是他们用来达到自己的政治目标和经济目标的手段。比如说,对社会成员实施绑架,这能在败坏社会道德的同时产生收益。ISIS是集成了多种犯罪的经济体,其资金来源比伊拉克的那些恐怖组织以及周边的那些国家都要更加丰富。

ISIS能够通过非法烟草贸易、手机贸易、古董交易、偷渡及走私人口、来自其控制下的油田的石油贸易、绑架勒索和向所占领的社区征税来获得资金。销售护照以及假冒的文件和药品可以为士兵们提供资金和旅费。将这些商品从叙利亚走私到土耳其能得到巨额利润。根据现在情况的估计,燃料走私数量已经涨了三倍,香烟的走私数量也有所增长,手机的走私数量也已经翻了五倍。① ISIS会根据国家所在的地域和古董的类型,对走私古董课以20%到50%的赋税。② 在进入叙利亚之前,外国士兵们会在土耳其售卖自己的护照,这能够产生数千美元的收益。这些形式的非法贸易对恐怖分子有着特别的吸引力,因为这些非法贸易难以市场饱和、缺乏法律规制、竞争也不激烈,并且比起那些被高度监控的犯罪,如武器交易和麻醉品交易,执法机关对其的关注度也不高。

美国引导的轰炸行动削减了ISIS的部分石油收入,在过去,这一部分的收入每天至少可达100万美元。因此如今ISIS正通过对"captogon"(一种在海湾地区被广泛销售的合成毒品)交易进行征税来产生更多资金。在海湾地区,制止毒品的流动几乎是不可能的,不过好在从这种贸易中产生的收益十分有限。

ISIS也有进行战略联盟的能力,他们会与其他恐怖组织建立联系并帮助他们进行宣传和成员招募活动。许多存在于非洲和中东的恐怖组织都是从奥萨马·本·拉登的"基地"组织总部中发展出来的。如今,"基地"组织仍旧存在于阿富汗和巴基斯坦的边界区域中。但是"基地"组织有很多的分支,其中最为有名的是:北非的马格里布"基地"组织(AQIM,Al Qaeda of the Mahgreb in North Africa),以也门为根据地的阿拉伯半岛"基地"组织(AQAP,Al Qaeda of the Arab Peninsula)和ISIS的前身伊拉

---

① http://blog.oup.com/2014/11/corruption-smuggling-turkey-government/.

② http://www.nytimes.com/2014/09/03/opinion/isis-antiquities-sideline.html.

克“基地”组织(AQI)。当然,还有其他一些较小的恐怖组织也活跃于这些区域之中,它们根据自己所扎根的社会的文化、历史和宗教传统的不同而形成自己的特点。2015 年 3 月上旬,非洲有四个组织公然宣布效忠 ISIS,这里面就包括了存在于尼日利亚北部以及其周边国家的“博科圣地”组织。而那些在 2015 年 3 月中旬对突尼斯巴尔杜博物馆发起袭击的恐怖组织,也都已经宣布对 ISIS 效忠。

ISIS 对周边国家人民的暴行已经令一些以前并不积极打击 ISIS 的政府开始采取行动。将约旦飞行员活活烧死的行为以及在利比亚海岸对埃及基督徒的斩首行为都极大地刺激到了中东地区的一些国家。约旦政府对 ISIS 的轰炸以及埃及政府在利比亚对 ISIS 的轰炸,都显示出这些国家已经深知 ISIS 所能带来的威胁。而这些空袭行动也得到了美国的火力支持。但是光是用军事力量并不能消除 ISIS 的存在,因为 ISIS 还有向其占领区域的市民们提供服务的职能。

由于 ISIS 需要大量的资金来控制其所占领的区域,再加上各国军队对其的打击,最终 ISIS 定然难逃被消灭的命运,但是这并不能解决那些动荡区域中长期存在的暴力和恐怖主义问题。这些动荡区域从西非开始延伸,然后穿越北非和中东一直延伸至巴基斯坦,甚至可能抵达中亚地区。这些区域存在如此多腐败而独裁的政府,他们不能满足市民的需求,以至于其国内的大片区域都成为了极端主义和恐怖主义的发源地,也导致了这些区域长达几十年的动荡。而且,这些区域中还存在着许多潜在的恐怖主义成员,特别是那些处于社会边缘并且失业的青年人,他们会离开这里并接受暴力组织的雇佣。

ISIS 的个案研究表明,国际社会正面临着一个新的挑战,这一挑战并不是来源于哪一个国家而是来源于那些强有力的非政府行为者,像恐怖分子、叛乱分子以及跨国罪犯。仅仅通过军队,甚至是多国的联合军事行动,都不足以应对这一挑战。新型的恐怖主义和极端暴力是一个犯罪问题、发展问题、腐败问题,一个由对未来不抱希望的年轻人所带来的问题,也是一个极端宗教观念的问题。而如今,巨大且不断增长的全球非法经济正在为恐怖主义提供着资金和便利。

将 ISIS 作为企业来进行打击可能将是今后打击恐怖主义的一个主要模式。这种方法要求我们能够切断其资金来源,并限制其获取维持组织所需的人员以及武器。幸运的是,这种方法正在全世界范围内得到推广。在 2014 年 11 月,联合国安理会一致通过了一个针对恐怖分子融资的重要决议——2195 号决议。随后又在 2015 年 2 月通过了一个针对 ISIS 的资金支持的决议——2199 号决议。该决议肯定了各种犯罪活动是恐怖分子筹集资金的生命线。因此,许多国家已经着手开始通过完善立法以及政府机构来解决恐怖主义融资问题。

但是，目前我们还不能完全解决恐怖主义融资问题。如果全球社会都开始解决腐败问题，那么我们就将在防止个人参与暴力型非政府组织方面迈出重要一步。腐败会使国家的资源流失并引起人民的愤怒从而迫使他们成为恐怖组织的爪牙。我们必须更进一步确保，腐败官员不会将钱财藏到庇护所中，从而对市民的就业和未来发展造成破坏。

如果能够切断恐怖主义与其传统资助者间的联系，并减少恐怖主义的犯罪融资，那么就可能在未来对限制恐怖主义产生巨大的帮助。这样一个打击恐怖主义的策略并不仅仅依赖于军队手段或是外交手段，更多的是要求政府各部门间的跨部门合作，尤其是执法部门、财政部和发展署之间的合作。

但是未来数十年里，我们所面临的巨大挑战并不是仅靠政府就能应对的，这还需要整个社会的通力合作，包括政府、企业、研究员、记者以及公众的积极响应。

我们需要企业来识别那些支持恐怖主义的非法贸易，并进而确保这些贸易不会帮助到那些为恐怖主义提供资金的财务活动。打击 ISIS 的商业途径方面，应该有西方企业的参与。烟草业可以跟踪非法烟草贸易情况的起伏。能源和药品公司可以监督其产品在恐怖主义控制区域的运输。运输公司可以洞察到非法贸易的发展，而保险公司则对绑架有着极强的洞察力。这其中的关键是公私合作，因为非法经济总与合法经济存在着交叉。公司企业要搜集、分享有关非法贸易路线、走私货物和关键辅助者的信息。他们可以警告消费者不要去购买那些为恐怖主义提供资金的假冒商品和走私商品。

我们也需要研究员来识别那些非传统型的威胁。通过国际协作，他们能够了解这些威胁的发展趋势并提供独立的分析。他们需要采取行动以防止年轻人被犯罪和恐怖组织所雇佣，并同时为其他的社会成员提供金融替代品。研究员也需要动员市民去对抗恐怖分子的暴行，并教育小孩恐怖行为是与社会规范和社会价值相背道而驰的。

我们还需要记者来分析并帮助群众发挥其政治意愿。他们应该努力揭露政府官员和辅助者的腐败。当全球社会都承诺会尽力解决腐败问题时，这些打击恐怖主义的策略才能得以很好地实施。相比于已经投入了大量人力物力却没有带来长期稳定的大规模军事行动，这些策略所需的费用要小得多。如果我们把恐怖分子看成有创造性并有极强适应性的犯罪企业，或许我们将会有更大的机会来战胜恐怖主义。毕竟，只有当企业遇见一个成功的竞争者时，才会最终破产。

十二、我们能够做什么

1. 强化公私合作，利用合法商界的洞察力

在处理恐怖分子融资以及恐怖主义商业方面，企业界的洞察力是十分重要的。下面的例子就说明了这个观点：

耐克公司就曾警告过法国政府，有一名卡拉奇兄弟会的成员参与了耐克仿冒品的买卖，并且其正在转移款项。但在当时，这一信息并没有得到重视。而后来，该名卡拉奇兄弟会成员杀害了查理周刊的漫画家。

跨国烟草公司的洞察力就曾帮助我们成功追踪并冻结了用于大规模杀伤性武器项目的资金。在另一个距今更近的案例中，美国当局就曾受到警告，由美国军方代表所统一销售的香烟正被运往国外，用以资助中东的恐怖主义组织。

跨国制药公司发现有人在中东地区通过假冒其产品而获得资金，这使得政府进一步意识到假冒处方药对于恐怖主义融资的重要。国际刑警已经开始与商界合作来进行信息的搜集与整合。

虽然国际刑警已经能够很好地运用企业的信息，但是目前仍然没有一个系统的方法来促进世界各个地区间的合作。这种打击恐怖主义的方式，目前并没有完全地发挥作用，还需要进一步地推广。

除了搜集情报，许多企业依靠其所拥有的具有强大分析能力的团队，还可以发现恐怖分子融资的趋势与模式。如今，一些企业已经开始与国际刑警合作来完成一些共同的项目，以帮助打击全球恐怖主义，但是我们还需要更多用来促进企业合作的项目。这是个必须被填补的空白，因为公私合作是打击恐怖主义的关键。

2. 追踪恐怖分子犯罪及资金的警务模式的实施——将成功的执法模式复制到其他地区

由于城市的规模、经济实力以及经济与人口的多样性，纽约和洛杉矶已经成为了恐怖主义的重要经济来源。洛杉矶成为了千禧年炸弹袭击的目标而纽约也遭受了“9・11”恐怖袭击带来的毁灭性的打击。这两个城市都已经成功开展了一些项目，并利用自己的资源来追踪与恐怖主义有关的资金，以此来打击犯罪和恐怖主义。在《肮脏的纠缠：腐败、犯罪与恐怖主义》中，我对来自洛杉矶警察局的大量犯罪案例进行了讨论。洛杉矶警察局一直以在洛杉矶范围内的那些为巴萨耶夫（世界上最致命的恐怖袭击之一——俄罗斯别斯兰恐怖袭击的责任人）提供资金帮助的汽车盗窃行为为目标。通过与政府部门领导者的讨论，我们发现这种方法用在打击恐怖主义融资以及恐怖主义商业上也十分有效。尽管2015年，在西欧地区发生了大量由参与恐怖主义的犯罪人所实施的致命袭击，但是目前这一方法还没有被用在西欧地区中。我们需要重新定位警务活动，以使洞察犯罪和反恐能够很好地结合在一起。

3. 针对日用消费品的非法贸易

对像伪造的药品、食物、酒精、手机、烟草这样的日用消费品交易所作出的惩罚是十分有限的，这使得这些领域已经逐渐成为了恐怖分子的重要资金来源。我们需要优先在这些领域中来打击恐怖主义的融资活动。同时我们也需要重视这些非法贸易形式与其他恐怖主义资金来源的衔接，而这些其他恐怖主义资金来源包括毒品、野生动植物、偷渡和贩卖人口。只有重视网络分析，重视各种不同形式的犯罪的衔接，我们才能高效地利用手头上的资源。

4. 针对恐怖主义辅助者

打击辅助者，应该要在对抗恐怖主义的过程中受到更进一步的重视，这些辅助者包括会计人员、银行家、洗钱者和运输专家。这其中的一些辅助者甚至可以进行跨国运输和财产购置，因为目前并没有制定出一些有效的反制措施来打击这些恐怖主义辅助者。

5. 控制加密货币

比特币和虚拟世界中的其他一些未经规范的货币的兴起，促进了这类交易的发展。加密货币被越来越多地用于网上支付和暗网交易之中，这使得追踪变得更加困难。这些交易的进行会依据暗网位置的不同而采用不同的语言，有英语、中文和其他语言。这些货币可以为全球不同地区的非政府行为者提供进行非法活动的便利，也会为一些企图规避法规的法人提供开展非法活动的帮助。许多国际融资活动能够脱离国家法律规范的规制，这是非法贸易得以扩张的重要力量。因此，我们需要尽快发展我们的法律体系来增强对加密货币的管理。

6. 支持那些为识别恐怖主义融资和恐怖主义商业新趋势所做的研究

国际社会对恐怖主义融资趋势以及恐怖主义商业发展所做的独立研究太过有限。其中的许多还将重点放在了特定区域以及特定产品上，然而恐怖主义的融资活动已经跨越了各个大洲，其贸易活动也涉及多种不同的产品。从根本上理解这些现象，是能够系统阐释那些有效打击恐怖主义的政策的前提条件。

（阮重骏 译）

The Business of Terrorism:A Case Study of ISIS

Louise Shelley[①]

Terrorists function as business people. They seek a product mix, professional services, conduct cost-benefit analyses, employ tax strategies, and exploit supply chains.[②] They seek market dominance, strategic alliances, competitive advantage, targets of opportunity, and try to employ innovation and technology effectively. They seek ways to obtain access to the best human capital through their global networks. ISIS illustrates all these concepts but it is only one of many terrorist groups that share these attributes. It is just the typical of these.

Terrorists are always looking for new ways to fund themselves. In this way, they resemble multi-national businesses that need to diversify to survive in the global economy. To survive, they are proactive and are fluid and flexible, like the most nimble of businesses. We must appreciate their capacity as business people and not just explore their past streams of funding as one does if one discusses only terrorist financing.

EXPLOITING COMPARATIVE ADVANTAGE

Terrorists exploit their comparative advantage. Terrorists near natural resources use these

---

① Louise Shelley, University Professor and Omer L. and Nancy Hirst Endowed Chair and Director, Terrorism, Transnational Crime and Corruption Center, School of Policy, Government and International Affairs, George Mason University.

② For more in depth analysis of this see Louise I. Shelley, *Dirty Entanglements: Corruption, Crime and Terrorism*, Cambridge: Cambridge University Press, 2014, 173-217.

commodities to fund their activities, those near weapons stockpiles become weapons traders, and terrorists in border areas tax the cross-border flow of goods. They take advantage of their critical location. For example, Al-Qaeda, was involved in the diamond trade, particularly in Sierra Leone, Liberia, and Tanzania.① The FARC and the Ejército de Liberación Nacional (National Liberation Army, or ELN) use their territorial control in different regions of Colombia to extort money and to lead attacks against energy infrastructure,② such as has also been seen in Algeria and in territory controlled by ISIS and Boko Haram.

Terrorist and insurgent groups, located near populations of elephants and rhinoceroses sought for their horns and tusks are leading to the mass slaughter of these animals and irreversible damage in ecosystems. The September 2015 issue of *National Geographic* confirms earlier published research on the involvement of terrorists in the illicit ivory trade, along with members of the Sudanese government,③ pointing to the role of both terrorists and corrupt officials in this trade. The US is the second largest importer of ivory. Its economic powers is helping to fund terrorism.

SECURING SUPPLY CHAINS

Terrorists are very concerned about their supply chains—as they need to ensure the safe and timely delivery of goods without disruption. Terrorists are concerned with supply chains for illicit goods, such as narcotic drugs, counterfeit pharmaceuticals, and cigarettes (which are the lifeblood of many terrorist organizations), or high-value diverted goods, such as oil.

Terrorists make substantial money by controlling supply chains for delivery of their products, such as drugs, as well as by taxing the smuggling of others that pass through borders or territory that they control. The ability to tax the transit of commodities is one key to their fi-

---

① Global Witness, "For a Few Dollars More: How al Qaeda Moved into the Diamond Trade", April 2003, http://www.globalwitness.org/library/few-dollars-more; Greg Campbell, *Blood Diamonds: Tracing the Deadly Path of the World's Most Precious Stones* (Boulder, CO: Westview Press, 2002); Douglas Farah, *Blood from Stones: The Secret Financial Network of Terror* (New York: Broadway Books, 2004).

② Frédéric Massé and Johanna Camargo, "Actores Armados Ilegales y Sector Extractivo en Colombia", V informe del Centro Internacional de Toledo para la Paz (CITpax) Observatorio Internacional, 2012, 49http://www.toledopax.org%2Fuploads%2FActores_armados_ilegales_sector_extractivo.pdf. http://www.askonline.ch/fileadmin/user_upload/documents/Thema_Wirtschaft_und_Menschenrechte/Bergbau_Rohstoff/Gold/Actores_armados_ilegales_sector_extractivo.pdf.

③ Bryan Christy, "Tracking Ivory", National Geographic, September 2015, 30–59; Kasper Agger and Johnathan Hutson, Kony's Ivory: How Elephant Poaching in Congo Helps Support the Lord's Resistance Army, June 3, 2013, http://enoughproject.org/reports/konys-ivory-how-elephant-poaching-congo-helps-support-lords-resistance-army.

nancing. Organized crime groups' extortion of trade has been known for a significant period, which is why they are so deeply involved in ports and the trucking industry. Yet terrorist groups on many different continents also profit from exploiting supply chains and taxing trade. This insight has not merited sufficient attention from the counter-terrorism community.

Terrorists often generate revenues by taxing the supply chains that move legitimate and illegitimate products across territory they control. Through corruption of officials and application of violence, terrorist groups undermine the state presence and bolster their own in key border areas, ports, and other transport hubs. Therefore, they have learned from organized crime the importance of controlling territory and have capitalized on the corporate world's need to move commodities long distances in the increasingly globalized economy.

SECURING PERSONNEL

ISIS, as will be discussed more, has developed an model of international recruitment of personnel. It uses new technology such as twitter to identify potential recruits. Then it deploys geographically distinct messaging to recruit personnel to fight for it, or for women to join and provide support functions. Its communications and marketing strategy in some respects mirrors that of multi-national companies.

HETEROGENEITY OF TERRORIST BUSINESSES

All terrorist groups do not function the same way in business. Cultural, historical and geographic conditions shape their approach to terrorist financing. For example, in the Middle East where trade has been at the heart of the economy since the first recorded language, trade or taxing trade is the major funding source of ISIS and other groups such as the PKK operating in the region. The long-standing growth of drugs in Afghanistan and in the Andes has contributed to a reliance on crop production and drugs in terrorist financing. In Africa, where man's dominance over animals has been a hallmark of rulers, trade in animal parts becomes an important funding source for terrorism.

Terrorists choose the crimes they will commit not only by profitability and ease of entry into this business sector, but also by the extent of competition in this sphere of criminal activity and the costs of corruption.① Yet determinations of risk of detection and asset loss are

---

① *Fondeo del terrorismo*, *Infolaft*, 1, no.4, 2009, 10–15, reveals that FARC's financial records calculated their expenditures for corruption as a cost of business.

also associated with the calculations of some criminal-terrorists.Terrorists exploit their strategic advantages, just as do business people. Understanding the comparative advantage of a terrorist group within this financing framework is key to determining their sustainability and deriving strategies to deprive them of revenues.

TERRORISTS USE CRIME TO FUND THEIR ACTIVITIES

Terrorists use crime as a means to generate needed revenues, to obtain logistical support, and use criminal channels to transfer funds. Criminals provide operational tools, such as falsified documents, new identities, and transit across borders to terrorists in need.① They also provide mechanisms through which terrorists can move and launder funds. Criminals can pay off officials, thereby providing terrorists and their commodities safe passage across borders. The criminal support structures can include either petty criminals or developed crime groups, such as the Camorra in Naples,② complemented by the services of facilitators from the legitimate world, such as bankers, lawyers, and corporations that intentionally or inadvertently assist in the perpetration of terrorism.③ Corrupt military personnel can serve as suppliers of weapons to criminal and terrorist groups.④ There are also facilitators that serve the criminal world, especially drug traffickers and those moving dual-use materials.

PRODUCT MIX

Almost every known form of criminal activity has been used to fund terrorism. The choice of criminal activity reflects the geographic location of the group, its human capacity, and the profitability of the crime. Crimes are selected based on the ability to evade detection or

---

① C.J.de Poot and A.Sonnenschein, *Jihadi Terrorism in the Netherlands* (The Hague: WODC, 2011), 109–10.

② Roberto Saviano, *Gomorrah*, trans.from the Italian by Virginia Jewiss (New York: Farrar, Straus, and Giroux), 2007, 181–86.

③ Mark Pieth, ed., *Financing of Terrorism* (Dordrecht, Netherlands: Kluwer Academic, 2003); Nikos Passas, "Terrorism Financing Mechanisms and Policy Dilemmas", in *Terrorism Finance and State Responses: A Comparative Perspective*, ed.Jeanne Giraldo and Harold Trinkunas (Stanford, CA: Stanford University Press, 2007), 30, which discusses how the 9/11 hijackers used the established banking system. The nuclear proliferation of the A.Q.Khan network was facilitated by businessmen in Europe. Rebekah K.Dietz, Illicit Networks: Targeting the Nexus between Terrorists, Proliferators and Narcotraffickers, (Monterey, CA: U.S.Naval Post Graduate School, 2010), http://www.dtic.mil/dtic/tr/fulltext/u2/a536899.pdf; *IISS Nuclear Black Market Dossier: A Net Assessment* (London, 2007), 43–64, http://www.iiss.org/publications/strategic-dossiers/nbm/nuclear-black-market-dossier-a-net-assesment/.

④ Illustrative of this is the Cambodian military. See David Capie, "Trading the Tools of Terror: Armed Groups and Light Weapons Proliferation in Southeast Asia", in *Terrorism and Violence in Southeast Asia: Transnational Challenges to States and Regional Stability*, ed.Paul J.Smith (Armonk, NY: M.E.Sharpe, 2005), 191.

prosecution, access corrupt officials, and obtain profits. Terrorists prey on ordinary citizens, as well as smaller and larger businesses through extortion and kidnapping. They commit fraud against legitimate financial institutions through credit card abuse and other financial manipulation of markets.[①] Many of these illicit activities converge in supply chains and are handled by the same transport facilitators.

Apart from these high-profit and large-scale sources of criminal activity, terrorists and insurgents participate in a diverse range of criminal actions, including ones used by earlier generations of terrorists and guerillas, such as kidnapping, extortion, and bank robbery.[②] But they also are at the forefront of technology, relying on credit crime and Internet fraud. They also use new technologies such as cryptocurrencies (such as bitcoin) to move money. The dark web is used to communicate undetected and to sell commodities.

There are many other forms of illicit activity that have become the lifeblood for terrorism, including art and antiquities smuggling, cross-border smuggling of goods, trade in counterfeit and diverted goods. Many of these crimes intersect with the legitimate economy and information from the business world can be used effectively to counter terrorism. Illicit trade in natural resources, oil, gold, and other commodities also provides funding.[③] Commodities such as gold and diamonds are particularly sought because they have great inherent value and limited weight. Some activities, such as people smuggling and trafficking, are "dual use:" they both generate money and provide terrorist groups the ability to move operatives. Terrorists have developed a full product line that ranges from the most basic to the most sophisticated crimes.

PRIME ROLE OF SMALL-SCALE ILLICIT TRADE IN FUNDING TERRORISTS

The concept of narco-terrorism had meant that we have focused on such large financial generators as the drug trade. But increasingly smaller-scale illicit trade in commodities such

---

① Matthew Levitt and Michael Jacobsen, *The Money Trail: Finding, Following and Freezing Terrorist Finances*, Policy Focus 89 (Washington, DC: Washington Institute, November 2008), 50-51, http://www.washingtoninstitute.org/policy-analysis/view/the-money-trail-finding-following-and-freezing-terrorist-finances, and Rohan Gunaratna, Inside Al Qaeda: Global Network of Terror (New York: Columbia University Press, 2002), 63-65; de Poot and Sonnenschein, Jihadi Terrorism in the Netherlands, 111.

② R.T.Naylor, "The Insurgent Economy: Black Market Operations of Guerrilla Organizations", Crime, Law and Social Change 20, no.1 (1993): 13, 20.

③ For a discussion of the underworld of gold, see R.T.Naylor, Wages of Crime: Black Markets, Illegal Finance, and the Underworld Economy, rev.ed. (Ithaca, NY: Cornell University Press, 2004), 196-246; for extractive industries, such as oil, see Massé and Camargo, "Actores Armados Ilegales y Sector Extractivo en Colombia".

as counterfeit goods, fuel, cigarettes, food, medicine, textiles and clothing are used by terrorists to fund themselves in the United States, Europe, North Africa and the Middle East. Weapons trade, another dual-use crime is particularly prevalent in North Africa, particularly flowing out of Libya.① In aggregate, the funding from such activities is substantial, and rivals that of drugs, but has much lower risk of prosecution.

Money generated by illicit trade within the US from the illicit cigarette trade is sent out of the United States to fund terrorist groups in the Middle East. ISIS recruits from Europe can fund their voyages to join ISIS through the revenues generated from illicit trade. Terrorist attacks in Europe such as the train attack between Brussels and Paris have been perpetrated by terrorists with backgrounds in small-scale illicit trade. One of the Kouachi Brothers who killed the cartoonists of Charlie Hebdo had traded in counterfeit Nike sports shoes and smuggled cigarettes. This phenomenon is not confined to Europe. The New York Police Department (NYPD) is focusing on many smaller scale crimes, including cigarette smuggling, that are used by many diverse terrorist groups to fund themselves.

PROFESSIONAL SERVICES

Terrorists, when functioning as criminal entrepreneurs, require a variety of services.② They need accountants, bankers, and lawyers. But they also need corrupt officials and often witting and unwitting facilitators from the corporate world. Therefore, they have multiple forms of interaction with the legitimate economy. They also require professional services from the criminal world as they retain the services of human smugglers and specialists in "non-traceable communications, forgers, and money launderers."③ Without hiring this expertise, they cannot make their business function.④

---

① Global Initiative on Transnational Crime, "Libya: Criminal Economies and Terrorist Financing in the Trans Sahara", May 2015, http://www. globalinitiative. net/libya-criminal-economies-and-terrorist-financing-in-the-trans-sahara/ ; International Crisis Group, "Tunisia's borders: Jihadism and Contraband", Middle East/North Africa Report, N°148, (2013) 31http://www.crisisgroup. org/~/media/Files/Middle%20East%20North%20Africa/North%20Africa/Tunisia/148-tunisias-borders-jihadism-and-contraband-english.pdf.

② Sherzod Abdukadirov, "Terrorism: The Dark Side of Social Entrepreneurship", *Studies in Conflict and Terrorism* 33, no.7 (2010): 603–17; Douglas Farah, "Fixers, Super Fixers, and Shadow Facilitators: How Networks Connect," 2012, http://www.strategycenter.net/docLib/20120423_Farah_FixersSuperFixersShadow.pdf.

③ *Organised Crime in Australia Key Trends* 2008, 2, http://www. crimecommission. gov. au/publications/organised-crime-australia/organised-crime-australia-2008-report; Farah, "Fixers, Super Fixers, and Shadow Facilitators."

④ For an analysis of an Auckland, New Zealand, facilitator for organized criminals and terrorists, see "Offshore Registration Business Halts Operations", June 28, 2011, http://www.reportingproject.net/occrp/index.php/en/ccwatch/cc-watch-indepth/930-offshore-registration-business-forced-to-halt-operations.

As terrorist entrepreneurs, they are always looking for new product lines and seek to learn from regional successes in one area that can be transferred elsewhere. Therefore, the FARC in Colombia, known as narco-terrorists, are really a much more diversified business that even generated income from the exploitation of hydrocarbons. Diversification is as much a key to survival as it has been to the business world.

Terrorist businessmen share a key concern of their counterparts—the retention of professional services. These service providers allow them to move their money, corrupt needed officials, and obtain falsified documents.

Case Study of ISIS

The ISIS's sweep through Sunni Iraq in 2014 resulted, in part, from many poorly conceived policy decisions dating to the earliest days of post-invasion Iraq. The abolition of the Iraqi army, the badly executed process of de-Baathification, the incarceration of Baathists and terrorists together in post-invasion Iraq, and the corruption of the Maliki government all resulted in enormous anger among the Sunni population. These resentments fermented in the toxic brew of Syrian chaos that incubated ISIS, an environment outside the control of the United States and NATO.

ISIS overcame the Iraqi security forces because it combined the skills of al Qaeda of Iraq with those of top former officials of Saddam Hussein, experienced in smuggling and illicit trade. The profits of its criminal activities and effective use of corruption has equipped ISIS with more tanks than those deployed by some leading NATO members. ISIS has recent and sophisticated weaponry, and recruits personnel internationally through advanced media campaigns and messaging through Twitter and other forms of communication.

The United States and NATO members have focused on the problems associated with state actors whereas the threat in the contemporary Middle East comes significantly from non-state actors like ISIS. This new kind of threat that does not come from countries but from criminalized terrorist groups behaving like multinational illicit businesses. The challenge is not only to cut off their funds but also to undermine their global recruitment strategies, their marketing, and their international messaging. They need to be countered as one would a business competitor. This requires policies that are not dependent solely on military force but on diverse branches of government working together in cooperation with the private sector.

ISIS's rapid advance in Sunni Iraq was surprising to the U.S.government, which did not expect the complete and immediate collapse of Iraqi security forces. Yet the resentments among the Sunni population and the displaced Baathists accumulated for over a decade, made them unwilling to fight ISIS. Moreover, the corruption of the military in the region, moreover, made it incapable of defending the Sunni population.

Yet if analysts had focused on the relationship of crime and terrorism and the corrosive impact of corruption, they would not have been as surprised by the rise of ISIS.

As I was concluding my book "Dirty Entanglements: Corruption, Crime and Terrorism" in October 2013, I predicted—based on extensive interviews with military personnel (many in top decision-making positions), policy advisers and local experts in the region that the greatest threat to global stability would come out of Syria. Approximately nine months later, ISIS left Syria and took over Sunni Iraq. This gave ISIS an enormous and relatively secure base for its operations.

Post-invasion policies

In pre-invasion Iraq, the Sunni population dominated the military and the governance structures of Saddam Hussein's Iraq. His Baathist party controlled the levers of power. To make sure that Hussein and his ruling elite never returned, much effort was made by U.S. military leadership and the coalition in Iraq to disband the structures that helped Saddam rule. The Iraqi army was dissolved in May 2003, a decision that was never carefully analyzed before implementation. Five years later, it was already clear that the Sunnis who had once led the army would become a powerful insurgency.①

The Coalition Provisional Authority (CPA) in Iraq, led by the United States, promoted a comprehensive policy of de-Baathification. Unlike efforts to de-Nazify Germany after World War II, in which officials' pasts were carefully reviewed and not everyone was removed, de-Baathification in Iraq was sweeping and without the vetting of individuals. Rather, there were mass removals of Sunni personnel, the only individuals with experience in governmental administration. Wholesale dismissals of former Baathists without hearings and due process fostered resentment and resulted in a non-functional government②.

Camp Bucca, a huge prison that once held 100,000 prisoners was the genesis of ISIS. In

① http://www.nytimes.com/2008/03/17/world/middleeast/17bremer.html? pagewanted=1&_r=0&hp.
② http://www.nytimes.com/2008/03/17/world/middleeast/17bremer.html? pagewanted=1&_r=0&hp.

"Dirty Entanglements," I explain that prisons are no longer institutions of control, but corporate headquarters for crime-terror interactions. Camp Bucca served this function when, in 2007, the overcrowded facility was filled with extremists.① Prisoners were separated along religious lines: Sunnis together and Shias together. From this came the strange merger of incarcerated ex-Baathists with the religious extremists that is now the contemporary ISIS. The extremists acquired administrative skills from the former Baathists who had years of administrative experience governing Iraq under Saddam. The jailed Baathists, angry at their incarceration, found common cause with the religious extremists. Hence ISIS, incorporating former senior government officials, has more highly skilled personnel than al-Qaeda and any other organizations that preceded it.

The leader of ISIS, Abu Bakr al-Baghdadi, spent years in Camp Bucca. He assumed a position of authority within the prison and was called on to mediate disputes. His incarceration gave him access to prisoners who became the leaders of ISIS. Seventeen of the 25 top leaders of ISIS spent timein prisons between 2004 and 2011.②

In post-invasion Iraq, the Iran-supported Shiites assuming disproportionate power under Maliki. Mainly Sunnis, accustomed to political power under Saddam Hussein were deeply resentful. Under the Maliki government, the oil revenues of the Iraqi state went to the Shia population and a small percentage went to the Kurds in the North, but the Sunnis received almost nothing from the central government. Sunni anger was so strong that it contributed to the sectarian violence and conflict that we see today, and the unwillingness of Sunni citizens to defend the Iraqi state against ISIS.

The failure to share revenues was only one element of Maliki's corruption③. Top positions were given to his Shia cronies, Sunni leaders were marginalized, and basic services were not provided to the population of the large territory now governed by ISIS. Protests against the Maliki government began in the Sunni region shortly after the start of the Arab Spring. But protesters were branded as terrorists and treated brutally. In the year before ISIS' takeover, there was another wave of mass protests against the Maliki government that was met by brutal suppression by Iraqi security forces. These events are key to understanding the rising

---

① http://www.independent.co.uk/news/world/middle-east/camp-bucca-the-us-prison-that-became-the-birthplace-of-isis-9838905.html.

② http://www.theguardian.com/world/2014/dec/11/-sp-isis-the-inside-story.

③ http://foreignpolicy.com/2014/06/19/how-maliki-ruined-iraq/.

militancy in Sunni areas.

In this context, the failure of the Iraqi forces in the Sunni region to take up arms against ISIS is hardly surprising. For the Sunnis, it was a choice between two bads:[①] a corrupt and brutal government in Baghdad and ISIS. They chose ISIS because they would not die to support the Maliki government.

Again, Syria was the incubator for ISIS. During the war in Iraq, Assad's government gave extremists shelter and allowed them to train, receive weapons and generate funds. Assad must have believed he could control these elements. But that illusion was shattered when the Syrian civil war began. The chaos provided a place for various extremist groups to congeal in the organization now known as ISIS and to prepare for its next phase of expansion. That expansion, initially to Iraq, now extends to groups from Afghanistan to North Africa, and most recently to West Africa.

A criminal business

ISIS has succeeded in acquiring personnel, weapons and funds because it functions like a business. In fact, it is the typical terrorist business known. Crime and corruption have been key to its acquisition of weapons, revenue generation and mobility across the region. To ensure its ongoing operations, ISIS seeks a product mix, acquiring professional services globally, forming strategic alliances, seizing targets of opportunity and making innovative use of technology as mentioned earlier. Significant revenues have allowed ISIS to buy weapons from Libya as well as obtain a good percentage of U.S. weapons donations to the Syrian rebels.

ISIS has successfully adopted the techniques of modern marketing, using social media to not only convey its brutality but also to recruit. This recruitment has worked best in countries where individuals can easily access ISIS' controlled territory. In Europe, ISIS-sponsored social media cleverly recruits among the disenfranchised and often disenchanted youth. Many recruits have been drawn to the mythical idea of the caliphate, sold to them as a paradise—an ideal that contrasts with the marginalized lives they are currently living.

Many fighters have criminal pasts, contributing to the particular violence of the group,

① After the U.S. withdrawal in 2011, Maliki's political marginalization of Sunni leaders and sectarian command of the Iraqi Security Forces spurred an anti-government protest movement, primarily in Sunni areas such as Anbar and Salah ad-Din. The protest movements spawned an organized, overt militant opposition to the Iraqi government after the Iraqi Security Forces killed civilians while attempting to clear a protest camp in Hawija in April 2013. See more at: http://www.understandingwar.org/report/beyond-islamic-state-iraqs-sunni-insurgency#sthash.GoorCeTO.dpuf.

highlighted by recent attacks in France and Denmark by ISIS supporters with prison records. Abo Isa, a Swedish recruit to ISIS, had been imprisoned three times in Sweden including for violent crime and at least eight of his Swedish compatriots who also traveled to Syria also had criminal records.[①] This is also true of the leadership. Although the group has its fare share of ideological fanatics, it also includes foreign members that have extensive criminal expertise, such as the Georgian Tarkhan Batirashvili known by his nom de guerre Sheikh Abu Omar al-Shishani who was arrested for illegally harboring weapons. Of Baghdadi's 25 deputies in Iraq and Syria, approximately one-third served in the military during Saddam Hussein's rule, and nearly all were imprisoned by American forces often with terrorists and insurgents who are now in ISIS. Many in Hussein's government had experience in smuggling and other forms of illicit activity that kept his government afloat.

ISIS also capitalizes on its geographic location. What sets terrorist businesses apart from criminal ones is that crime is a means of achieving their political as well as their economic goals. For instance, the kidnapping of community members demoralizes society even as it generates revenues. ISIS is a diversified criminal economy, and its sources of income are more diverse than those of Iraq and the countries that surround it.

ISIS generates money from the illicit cigarette and cell phone trade, antiquities trade, human smuggling and trafficking, sale of the oil from fields they control, extortion and "taxation" of communities they occupy. Sales of passports and counterfeit document and pharmaceuticals provide money and mobility for fighters. Smuggling in some of these commodities into Turkey from Syria has risen dramatically. It is now estimated that fuel smuggling has tripled, cigarette smuggling has increased and cell phone smuggling has risen five fold.[②] Smuggled antiquities are being taxed at rates of 20 to 50 percent by ISIS depending on the region of the country and the type of antiquity.[③] Foreign fighters sell their passports for thousands of dollars in Turkey before entering Syria where the proceeds help fund them and ISIS. These forms of illicit trade are particularly attractive to terrorists because there is less market saturation, less regulation, reduced competition and limited law enforcement focus than other forms of highly policed crime, such as arms and narcotics trafficking.

U.S.-led bombing has slowed some of the oil revenue, which used to total at least a mil-

① https://www.ctc.usma.edu/posts/the-swedish-foreign-fighter-contingent-in-syria.

② http://blog.oup.com/2014/11/corruption-smuggling-turkey-government/.

③ http://www.nytimes.com/2014/09/03/opinion/isis-antiquities-sideline.html.

lion dollars a day. So ISIS is generating more money by taxing the trade in captogon, a synthetic drug sold extensively throughout the Gulf region, where the possibility of stopping drug flows and the profits generated from this trade is limited.

ISIS is also capable of strategic alliances, establishing links with other terrorist groups and helping them publicize and recruit. Many of the terrorist groups operating in Africa and the Middle East evolved out of Osama bin Laden's al-Qaeda central, which still operates in the Afghanistan-Pakistan border area. But al-Qaeda has many offshoots, the best known of which are AQIM (al Qaeda of the Mahgreb in North Africa), AQAP (Al Qaeda of the Arab Peninsula) based in Yemen, and Al-Qaeda in Iraq (AQI), which evolved into ISIS. There are other, smaller terrorist groups that operate in the region too, shaped by cultural, historical and religious traditions of the communities where they are based. In early March 2015, four groups in Africa declared allegiance to ISIS, including Boko Haram in northern Nigeria and neighboring states. Those behind the attack on Tunisia's Bardo Museum in mid-March also professed their loyalty to ISIS.

ISIS's brutality against the citizens of neighboring states has prompted action by several governments in the region that have not previously been active in combating ISIS. The burning alive of the Jordanian pilot and the beheadings of Egyptian Christians on Libya's coast have galvanized several countries in the Middle East. Bombings of ISIS by the Jordanian government and by Egypt inside Libya show that these understand the threat posed by ISIS. Their air strikes are supplementing U.S. firepower. But military force alone is not going to displace ISIS because it provides some services to citizens in areas it occupies.

The heavy financial demands on ISIS to run the territory it occupies, combined with the military campaign against it, may help dislodge it eventually, but these will not solve the long-term problem of violence and terrorism in the unstable region that now extends from West Africa through North Africa, the Middle East and extending to Pakistan and perhaps Central Asia. There are so many corrupt autocratic governments not serving the needs of their citizens that this vast territorial expanse will remain a source of extremism, terrorism, and instability for many decades to come. Moreover, there are many potential fighters, particularly marginalized and unemployed youth, who can be recruited across this large and diverse region to join violent groups.

The ISIS case study shows that the international community faces a new challenge that does not emanate from states but from potent non-state actors, such as terrorist, insurgents and transnational criminals. This challenge cannot be met by military alone, or even military acting in concert with others. The new terrorism and extreme violence is a crime problem, a development problem, a corruption problem, a problem of youths without futures, and one of extremist religious views. And it is funded and facilitated by a large and growing illicit global economy.

Attacking ISIS as a business—may be a model for the future. This approach requires cutting off its funds, and limiting its access to personnel and weapons needed to maintain its organization. Fortunately, this approach is acquiring traction globally.

In a unanimous vote last December 2014, the U.N. Security Council passed an important resolution on terrorist funding, Resolution 2195. A subsequent resolution on ISIS, Resolution 2199, funding was passed in February 2015, affirming that diverse criminal activity was the lifeblood of terrorist finance. As a result, many countries are beginning to develop legislation and mechanisms to address the financing of terrorism.

Addressing terrorist financing is, however, not sufficient. If the global community begins to address corruption, this would go a long way in stemming the flow of individuals into violent non-state groups. Corruption drains countries of resources and makes citizens so angry that they are driven into the hands of terrorist organizations. We must go farther in making sure that corrupt officials do not shelter their money in safe havens, thereby denying their citizens jobs and a future.

If the traditional donors to terrorism are cut off and the criminal financing of terrorism can be reduced, this may help limit terrorism in the future. Such a counter-terrorism strategy is not dependent on the military or diplomacy alone and requires interagency cooperation of other branches of government, especially law enforcement, treasury and development agencies.

Yet the enormous challenges we face in coming decades cannot be solved by government alone. It requires a whole of society approach, including a response . by government, business, researchers, journalists and the community.

Businesses are needed to help identify the illicit trade that supports terrorism and to ensure that it does not facilitate the financial activity that funds terrorism. The business approach to countering ISIS also should incorporate western businesses. The cigarette industry follows the ebb and flow of the illicit cigarette trade. Energy and pharmaceutical companies monitor the movement of their commodities in the region. Transport, companies have insight into the dynamics of illicit trade and insurance companies have insights into kidnapping. Public-private partnerships are key because the illicit economy intersects with the licit. Corporations collect and can share information on illicit trade routes, smuggling shipments, and key facilitators. They can also warn consumers not to purchase the counterfeit and smuggled commodities that fund terrorism.

Researchers are needed to identify non-traditional threats. Through international collaborations they can understand trends and provide independent analysis. Citizens need to act to prevent youth recruitment into crime and terrorism, and to develop financial alternatives for members of the community. They need to help mobilize citizensto resist terrorist violence and teach their children that such activity is against the norms and values of their society.

Journalists need to analyze and help develop political will. They need to expose the corruption of government officials and facilitators. These are strategies that we can work on as a global community that has made a commitment to address these issues. They are less costly than large-scale military operations that have cost vast sums in lives and treasure and have yielded little long-term stability. We may have a greater chance of success in combating terrorists if we respond to them as creative and adaptable criminal enterprises. Businesses can fail if they meet successful competitors.

WHAT CAN WE DO?

1) DEVELOP PUBLIC-PRIVATE PARTNERSHIPS, USE INSIGHTS FROM THE LEGITIMATE BUSINESS COMMUNITY

Insights from the corporate world have been valuable in understanding terrorist financing and the business of terrorism. Illustrative of this are:

Nike warned the French government that one of the Kouachi brothers who later killedthe cartoonists of Charlie Hebdo was engaged in the sale of counterfeit Nikes and was transferring payment. This information was ignored.

Insights obtained from one multi-national cigarette company led to the tracing and freezing of money that could contribute to WMD program. In another more recent case, American authorities were alerted that cigarettes sold en masse out of American military commissaries were being sent abroad to fund Middle Eastern terrorist groups.

Insights from a multi-national pharmaceutical company on terrorism funding in the Middle East through counterfeits of their products have raised awareness of the centrality of counterfeit prescription drugs to terrorist financing.Interpol has begun to work with the business community to receive and integrate their inputs.

While Interpol has successfully used information from corporations,there are no institutionalized means to promote this cooperation in many regions of the world.This is an underutilized approach that must be expanded.

Apart from the intelligence corporations collect,many have strong analytical teams that allow them to see trends and patterns in terrorist financing.Some are already working with Interpol on joint programs that help the global fight,but we need programs tailored to promote corporate partnerships.This gap must be closed.Public-private partnerships are key in creating a counter-terrorism approach.

2)IMPLEMENT POLICING MODELS THAT FOLLOW THE CRIME AND MONEY OF TERRORISTS REPLICATE SUCCESSFUL LAW ENFORCEMENT MODELS TO OTHER LOCALES

Both New York City and Los Angeles because of their size,economic strength and diversified economies and populations are important funding sources for terrorism.Los Angeles was targeted by the Millennium bomber and New York suffered the devastating consequences of 9/11.Both have set up highly successful programs,combining their resources against crime and terrorism to follow the money connected to terrorism.In my book,*Dirty Entanglements:Corruption,Crime and Terrorism*,I discuss the major criminal case initiated by LAPD that targeted a car theft ring in Los Angeles that helped fund Basayev who was responsible for one of the world's most deadly terrorist attacks in Beslan,Russia.Discussions with leading personnel in the departments reveal that this approach is still successfully being used to target terrorist financing and business.This approach has not been used in Western Europe that has seen a number of deadly attacks in 2015 that have been committed by criminals who also engage in terrorism.There needs to be a reorientation of policing to combine the insights of criminal and counter-terrorism policing.

3)TARGET ILLICIT TRADE IN CONSUMER GOODS

The limited penalties attached to trade in consumer goods such as counterfeit pharmaceuticals,food,alcohol,cell phones,cigarettes have made these important growth areas for terrorist revenues.We need to prioritize these areas in counter-threat finance.We also need to focus on the convergence of these forms of illicit trade with other sources of terrorist financing—drugs, wildlife, human smuggling and trafficking. By focusing on network analysis and convergence of different forms of crime, we can make efficient use of existing resources.

4) TARGET TERRORIST FACILITATORS

Targeting these facilitators should be a much more central focus of counter-terrorism efforts—accountants, bankers, money launderers, transport specialists. Some are even able to travel internationally and buy property because there are not effectively coordinated counter-measures against identified terrorist facilitators.

5) REGULATE CRYPTOCURRENCIES

The rise of Bitcoin and other unregulated currencies in the virtual world facilitates this trade. Cryptocurrencies are increasingly being used for payment on the web and on the darknet, making traceability of transactions more difficult. These sales function in many different languages with parts of the darknet in English, Chinese and other languages. These currencies will facilitate the illicit activities of non-state actors in many areas of the world as well as some corporate actors who choose to evade regulation. The possibility of so much international financial activity outside of state regulation is a force in favor of the expansion of illicit trade. Therefore, legislation must be developed rapidly to enhance regulation of cryptocurrencies.

6) SUPPORT RESEARCH TO IDENTIFY NEW TRENDS IN TERRORIST FINANCE AND BUSINESS

The international community presently has too limited independent research on the trends in terrorist financing and the development of terrorist business. Much of it is focused on a specific region or commodity, whereas the financing spans continents and the trade converges with many different products. A basic understanding of these phenomena is a necessary prerequisite for formulating effective policies to counter them.

非法核贸易:行为主体和新兴趋势

路易丝·谢利(Louise Shelley)①

一、引　言

犯罪与恐怖主义相联系所能够带来的最可怕的后果,就是罪犯帮助恐怖分子获得大规模杀伤性武器(WMD)——生物武器、化学武器和核武器。大规模杀伤性武器交易是相当罕见的,其拥有已知的供应商和购买者,与毒品走私、仿冒品贸易以及作为恐怖分子犯罪活动的核心要素的改道商品贸易大不相同。相较而言,我们对运输走私核材料的违法物流如何运作,以及该犯罪如何牵涉那些未经批准而从事核扩散的国家,这两方面都所知甚少。②

大规模杀伤性武器贸易的运营是基于一种特殊的经济逻辑——其得以运营的根本并非基于交易量的大小而是基于其交易物的稀缺性以及交易本身的风险性。非法大规模杀伤性武器贸易导致了最终的不对称威胁。不论是采用核武器、生物武器还是化学武器,大规模杀伤性武器袭击都将造成严重而长期的后果,包括破坏地球的可持续性、人类的生命与健康、物种的多样性。甚至一场比核弹袭击更小规模的袭击都

---

① 路易丝·谢利(Louise Shelley),美国乔治·梅森大学公共政策与国际关系学院教授,奥马尔·L.和南茜赫斯特讲席教授,恐怖主义、跨国犯罪和腐败研究中心主任。

② Lyudmila Zaitseva,"Nuclear Trafficking:20 Years in Review",Contribution to WFS Meeting,Erice,August 2010,http://www.physics.harvard.edu/~wilson/pmpmta/2010_Zaitzeva.doc. August 2010,http://www.physics.harvard.edu/~wilson/pmpmta/2010_Zaitzeva.doc.

需要疏散市民并进行大量而又昂贵的清理工作。①

本文主要关注非法大规模杀伤性武器材料贸易的运输者和辅助者,并考察非国家行为者、腐败官员以及那些有意或无意地进行大规模杀伤性武器材料运输的公司在其中发挥的作用。

二、问题的界定

文中“核材料”(nuclear materials)一词涵盖了包括军民两用核材料在内的各种国际机构所追踪的核产品。在目前所收录的案例中,不仅武器级别核材料的非法交易案例十分稀少,涉及放射性同位素的案例或是被污染的非核材料的案例也十分少有。纳入我们考量的案例也包括了一些低级别核材料贸易,比如天然铀矿石、黄饼、贫化铀以及钍—232 的贸易。②

在本文中,“罪犯”(Criminals)并非简单地指普通罪犯或是跨国罪犯,而是包括那些因腐败行为而触犯刑法的人以及违法的核贸易辅助者。辅助者的行为包括获取、运输、筹资和贩卖核材料。③ 本研究也考证了恐怖分子的作用,他们对犯罪活动的个人承诺以及对犯罪服务的维持都对非法核材料贸易提供了帮助。

三、国际能源组织(IAEA)的数据库以及所指出的未来挑战

在过去,核材料非法贸易的见解来自于对国际原子能机构(IAEA)的数据库以及对那些已被调查与分析的个案。笔者对过去 25 年的数据进行了分析,可遗憾的是,

---

① David Smigielski,“Addressing the Nuclear Smuggling Threat”,in *Transnational Threats Smuggling and Trafficking in Arms,Drugs and Human Life*,ed.Kimberley L.Thachuk(Westport,CT:Praeger Security,2007),57.

② 数据来源于 Lyudmila Zaitseva “Nuclear trafficking:20 years in review”.在 IAEA 所记录的事件中,涉及核材料的仅占 30%——大量的案件涉及放射性同位素以及受污染的非核材料。不过,在近 500 起涉及核材料的案件中,低级核材料案件占了将近 60%,这些低级核材料包括:天然铀、黄饼、贫化铀以及钍—232。根据 Friedrich Steinhäusler and Lyudmila Zaitseva,“Illicit Trafficking of Natural Radionuclides”,*The Natural Radiation Environment:8th International Symposium*(NRE VIII).1034:1.(Melville,N.Y.:AIP Publishing,2008).大约有四分之一的案件涉及像铀这样的天然核素。他们认为,铀之所以能够在全球天然放射性核素走私中占统治地位,其主要原因在于主要的铀开采国家,像是哈萨克斯坦、俄罗斯、乌克兰以及乌兹别克斯坦,都存在着高度的腐败。这一趋势如今在发展中国家的那些新兴的铀开采国家中也同样明显,非洲就是一个很好的例子。

③ 这与 Steinhäusler and Zaitseva“Illicit Trafficking of Natural Radionuclides”中所论述的不同,在该文中他们认为,这项研究也考察了非法核贸易的资金供应情况。

这并不能对我们分析未来所要面对的大量问题与挑战带来帮助。

数据所显示的并不是最新挑战。国际能源组织的数据库并没有收录所有非法核材料贸易案例。根据国际原子能机构非法贸易数据库(以下简称ITDB)提供的数据,从1993年1月至2009年11月,参与国以及一些非参与国总共报告了1773起核走私案件。① 少报、不报、漏报的存在意味着我们对过去所发生的情况不能进行全面的观察。而由于铀矿的采集扩大到了非洲偏远区域,网络空间成为销售核材料的主要渠道,这一问题在未来还会变得更严重。在这样的环境下,侦查与报告将会更难实现。

对参与非法核材料贸易的罪犯,国际原子能机构数据库所能给予我们的认知十分有限。② 而对于恐怖分子以及其通过维持犯罪服务所产生的作用,其所能提供给我们的就更少了。自从所谓的"阿拉伯之春"运动的开始,恐怖分子的非法贸易问题就变得更加严重。而这所谓的"阿拉伯之春"运动,在北非和中东地区蔓延,也引发了其与周边许多国家空前的冲突。

此外,未来的趋势并没有表现得乐观,因为新的挑战正在出现。由于暗网中的非法核贸易存在很强的隐蔽性,所以对这些非法贸易的监测不太可能进入国际原子能机构的数据库。目前,正在非洲进行的开采铀矿贸易正被严重低估,而这一现象在未来还将持续,因为对这些地区缺乏可靠的犯罪报告与分析。中东以及北非地区的数据也有同样的问题。在这些极度混乱的地区里,存在着大量的恐怖主义活动,政府面临严峻的挑战。这些地方没有适当的制度去监督大规模杀伤性武器所带来的挑战,更不必说向国际原子能机构报告了。因此,我们不能简单地利用过去的数据来推测未来的情况。但我们能够预期,那些伴随有肮脏的纠缠(dirty entanglements)的区域,即存在犯罪、恐怖主义、腐败相互作用的区域,将成为未来非法核材料贸易的主要区域。我们还认为,今后更多的交易将通过电脑完成,这是因为进入暗网的加密技术以及安全手段,例如通过TOR,使得用户可以更为隐秘地进行交易。③

---

① Amelia Broodryk and Noël Stott,"Securing Africa's Nuclear Resources", *Arms Control:Africa* 3.1(2011):5-6.此外,斯坦福大学的国际安全与合作中心拥有一个核走私数据库。盗窃以及无主辐射源(Theft,and Orphan Radiation Sources)(DSTO),这里面不仅有政府已经确认并记录在ITDB的数据,还从一些开放性报告中搜集了一些未经确认的事件,在1991—2006年期间其共发现了2440起非法交易案件:"其中盗窃、非法运输放射性材料以及在边界区检测到放射性材料的案件共有1674起,关于所谓的无主资源,即已丢失的放射性资源,被意外地发现或是被送错对象的案件有736起,其中还有35起恶意行为事件,包括故意对人进行核辐射、对住宅和财物进行核污染。"这些信息可以参见Lyudmila Zaitseva,"Nuclear trafficking:20 years in review",但是,笔者也写到,IAEA的数据可能也有缺陷,因为一些重要信息可能没有上报IAEA,或者其数据本身并不足够充分和精确。见Louise I.Shelley,"Trafficking in nuclear materials:Criminals and terrorists", *Global Crime* 7:3-4(2006):544-560.

② Zaitseva,"Nuclear trafficking:20 years in review";Louise Shelley, *Dirty Entanglements:Corruption, Crime and Terrorism*, Cambridge:Cambridge University Press,2014,303.

③ Marc Goodman, *Future Crimes Everything is Connected Everything is Vulnerable and What We Can do About It*(New York:Random House,2015).

四、我们能够从犯罪学以及那些帮助我们理解参与非法核材料贸易的罪犯的执法文献之中了解到什么

非法核材料贸易以及对这种贸易的资助都是由各种罪犯与腐败人士进行的。因此,在其他环境下产生的一些犯罪学理论与概念,有助于我们理解犯罪人以及那些为非法核贸易提供便利的条件与关系网络。我们所选取的概念,例如差别交往、日常行为理论、肮脏聚集、合法与非法的并存、白领犯罪,都将被证明对我们理解非法核贸易中罪犯的作用带来帮助。

差别交往

现代美国犯罪学之父——埃德温·萨瑟兰,发展了两个特别适用于本次分析的概念。第一个概念叫作"差别交往"(differential association),其指出进行犯罪的程度是与违法者的交往强度以及交往持续时间所决定的。① 虽然这一理论形成于美国并适用于美国的情况,但该理论依旧非常适用于非国家行为者参与核材料贸易的情况。监狱,由于其本身性质及牢房结构,更容易产生强烈的相互作用。在监狱中,已经发生过密谋获取核材料的行动。而在冲突地区,人们并肩作战的情况,也是差别交往原则的表现。

黑海区域,自苏联解体以来就成为了争议区,历来是非法核贸易的中心,是俄罗斯大部分核走私活动的货源地或疑似货源地,而高加索地区——特别是格鲁吉亚——则成为了进行运输的关键区域。② 在高加索以及黑海区域中,家庭关系是最为重要的。因此,那里的人不论是与自己亲近的还是较为疏远的家庭成员都会有长期而紧密的联系。

被广为研究的格鲁吉亚走私案件也阐释了差别交往原则。俄国人柯恩·萨格夫,被认为曾效力于苏联的秘密警察部门——苏联国家安全委员会(KGB),其于2006年因试图向一名格鲁吉亚秘密调查员销售100克高浓缩铀(HEU)而遭到逮捕。在随后对萨格夫的关系网的调查显示,他的合作者要么是与其有血缘关系的人,要么就是其亲密的朋友。③

---

① http://criminology.fsu.edu/crimtheory/sutherland.html.

② 对此的讨论可见 Maj.Gen.(ret.) Bruce Lawlor, "The Black Sea: Center of the Nuclear Black Market", *Bulletin of the Atomic Scientists* 67.6(2011): 73-80; Lyudmila Zaitseva and Friedrich Steinhäusler, "Nuclear Trafficking Issues in the Black Sea Region", Non-Proliferation Papers, No.39, April 2014.

③ Alexander Kupatadze, "Organized crime and the trafficking of radiological materials: The case of Georgia", *Nonproliferation Review* 17:2(2010): 219-234; Michael Bronner, 100 *Grams* (*and Counting* ...): *Notes from the Nuclear Underworld* Cambridge, MA: Report for Managing the Atom Project, Harvard University, June 2008.

其合作者间紧密的家族联系是阻碍我们对违法商人的关系网进行充分调查的其中一个元素。

萨格夫的案件是目前最著名的一起有记录的武器级别非法核贸易案件。而本案中出现的犯罪者间存在紧密关系的情况并不罕见,因为非法核贸易要求参与者之间有高度的信任。

日常行为理论

与差别交往相关的另一个概念称为日常行为理论。相比于差别交往,日常行为理论在现代犯罪学者间更为流行。日常行为理论是犯罪机会理论的分支,而犯罪机会理论关注于环境与情景对实施犯罪的影响。[①] 该理论关注于犯罪行为,它认为犯罪行为是人、时间、地点的综合结果。根据这一理论,犯罪的发生必须具备犯罪动机(a motivated offender)、合适的目标(a suitable target)以及有效监控的缺失(the absence of a capable guardian)。根据日常行为理论,一个人越是在日常行为中暴露出违法的生活方式,就越有可能实施犯罪。远离家园也是促使人实施非法活动的重要元素,因为这会使人脱离日常生活的控制机制。[②]

日常行为理论极其适合用于研究非法核活动的参与问题,因为防卫是这一问题的核心。正如美国文献中经常谈到的,防卫的缺乏使得贵重物品缺乏安全,但这并不意味存在着腐败,虽然在这一理论中应用腐败这一概念也是毫无障碍的。

同时拥有核武器项目与核能源计划的国家会严密地守护自己的设施。因此,拥有加工过的核原料的使用权是十分困难的。可是在像苏联的继承国内的那些废弃军工厂和医院中,废弃的放射性材料不可能受到守护,而这些原料带来的威胁只仅仅小于那些被小心管理着的原料。

腐败是苏联和其他很多地区在防卫问题上的致命弱点。如果要求个人对核设施的守护以及国家核项目监管中存在的腐败负责,那么防卫将不会发生任何作用。正如下文将讨论的,在后苏联时期的前十年中,腐败与非法核材料贸易问题广泛存在于俄罗斯的各个阶层。上至政府官员下至底层的守卫都存在腐败。[③] 这给武器级别核材料的安全带来了影响。

日常行为理论的另外两个要素是犯罪的动机及合适的对象,这两个概念都能联系到核材料贸易中。人之所以产生获取或搬运核材料的动力,要么是因为意识形态,要么就是因为非法核贸易能够带来大量资金回报的这一事实或是错觉。后者在格鲁

---

① http://www.popcenter.org/learning/pam/help/theory.cfm.

② http://criminology.fsu.edu/crimtheory/sutherland.html.

③ *Ozerskii vestnik*, July 10, 2004.

吉亚尤为明显，在那里，机会主义犯罪人总是在既没有足够保护，又常常需要承受巨大的个人风险的情况下，依然进行放射性材料的运输，正是因为他们预期能够获得巨大的收益。①

第三个必要条件，合适的目标，也能够完美地应用于核材料贸易。在其他一些应用日常行为理论的情况中，都没有一个如此特定的目标。但是核贸易是如此特殊，以至于其目标的性质反而成为了关键。由于一般人不会住在核材料源附近，因此在核领域，犯罪的实施总是远离于犯罪者的家，这是日常行为理论的另一个重要的关键因素。

肮脏聚集(dirty togetherness)

亚当·坡杰瑞克的肮脏聚集概念，最初形成于波兰，该概念也可应用于非法核贸易方面。② 这一概念能够适用于恶劣环境下，罪犯与恐怖分子的相互作用。坡杰瑞克发明这个词是为了去描述那些小帮派和"在国家缺失以及对国家失去信任的情况下所存在的紧密的关系网"③。而且这个词还可以用来描述大众对于罪犯与恐怖分子长期监禁在一起或是对二者在冲突地区进行合作的看法。正是这些联系，使得罪犯与恐怖分子能够密谋获取核材料并进行核材料的物流运输。

衔接(Convergence)

在2011年，美国政府的犯罪专家们启动了"美国政府关于打击跨国有组织犯罪的战略:解决国家安全的共同威胁"。④ "衔接"这一概念来自执法机关和法律决策团体而非学者。其一提出，就已经成为思考犯罪政策的一个重要且有影响力的概念。正如"衔接"这一概念所被解释的那样:

> 我们以往都是分开打击恐怖主义与跨国犯罪的，对打击这两者我们分别采用一套不同的工具与方法。但是这种古旧的方式可能已经不能应付犯罪、恐怖行为与叛乱这三者关系网的衔接所带来的挑战。包括恐怖组织与叛乱运动团体在内的暴力型非国家行为者，他们为了负担恐怖活动以及购买毁灭性、杀伤性器具的费用而向犯罪网络寻求合作，在一些案例中，他们甚至成为犯罪网络的一部分。恐怖分子以及叛乱分子可以通过开发全球非法市场来保证自己有足够的资

① 基于TraCCC在格鲁吉亚开展的对因为运输低级别核材料而被捕的人的访谈。见Shelley, *Dirty Entanglements: Corruption, Crime and Terrorism* (Cambridge: Cambridge University Press, 2014), p.305; Kupatadze, 226.

② Maria Łoś and Andrzej Zybertowicz, *Privatizing the Police State: The Case of Poland* (New York: St.Martin's Press, 2000), 16, discuss Adam Podgorecki's idea of dirty togetherness.

③ Janine R.Wedel, "Corruption and Organized Crime in Post-Communist States: New Ways of Manifesting Old Patterns", *Trends in Organized Crime* 7, no.1(2001): 10.

④ Strategy to Combat Transnational Organized Crime, July 25, 2011, http://www.whitehouse.gov/administration/eop/nsc/transnational-crime.

金以进行活动、获取武器和其他对其运作起至关重要作用的物资。[①]

虽然这个概念发展于美国，但是世界许多地方的犯罪活动研究专家以及恐怖活动研究专家都目睹并验证了相同的现象。因此，2014 年 12 月下旬，联合国安理会一致通过了两项涉及犯罪与恐怖主义之间联系的决议。首先是 2195 号决议，其专注于恐怖主义、跨国犯罪以及帮助维持冲突、破坏世界秩序的非法贸易活动这三者间的相互关系。[②]

由乍得发起并于 2014 年年末全票通过的安理会 2195 号决议，确定了多种支持恐怖主义的非法贸易形式。根据这项决议，这些不同的非法贸易形式都对恐怖主义的资金支持至关重要。安理会 2195 号决议列举了以下这些作为恐怖主义核心的非法贸易形式：

> 非法交易武器、人口、毒品、古文物，非法交易自然资源，包括黄金、其他贵重金属和石料、矿物、野生动植物、木炭、石油，以及绑架勒索和其他犯罪，包括敲诈勒索和抢银行。[③]

随后安理会于 2015 年 2 月 12 日通过了针对 ISIS 的资金支持的 2199 号决议。该决议的关注点与前者稍有不同，其更关注于恐怖主义的财政支撑机制，包括那些支持恐怖主义的贸易。这个针对 ISIS 的联合国决议不仅关注那些为恐怖主义提供资金的犯罪活动，还特别关注支持 ISIS 的贸易活动以及基于贸易的洗钱行为。[④] 在中东，自古美索不达米亚时代以来，贸易就是金钱与资金流动的核心。因此，决议以贸易为中心是合理的。该决议同时也关注那些对恐怖分子有价值的商品，并要求国家关注本国内用来进行资金转移的商品以及具有的贸易便利。决议十分注重跨国犯罪的作用和来自自然资源的资金支持。[⑤]

犯罪与恐怖主义的衔接以及自然资源贸易在为恐怖主义提供资金方面所起的作用，是非法核贸易问题的核心。下面笔者将展示一些来自全球不同区域的例证，这些例证显示，不论是在非洲、亚洲、欧洲还是中东地区，我们能够发现，非法核贸易可能与世界其他区域的另一种非法活动相衔接。它不是一种独立的犯罪。虽然其总是伴随着其他贵重物品的非法交易，但也并非总是如此。在最近的一起欧洲烟草走私案件中，走私

---

① Michael Miklaucic and Jacqueline Brewer, eds., *Convergence: Illicit Networks and National Security in the Age of Globalization* (Washington, D.C.: NDU Press, 2013), xv.

② www.un.org/press/en/2014/sc11717.doc.htm.

③ 同上。

④ www.un.org/press/en/2015/sc11775.doc.htm.

⑤ UNEP, Monusco and OSESG, *Experts' background report on illegal exploitation and trade in natural resources benefitting organized criminal groups and recommendations on MONUSCO's role in fostering stability and peace in eastern DR Congo*, April 15, 2015.

的香烟被放射性材料所污染,这表明放射性材料很可能会与低价商品一起被运输。①

在2014年6月9日,一名越南烟草走私犯在华沙机场被捕,被捕时其正在走私香烟、放射性金属板和被锶90污染的包裹。这些香烟都有警示图案以及德国和波兰的纳税印花。一份官方报告指出,购买这些香烟的人都将遭受呼吸道烧伤。波兰负责调查恐怖主义的部门对此展开了调查。而德国海关只在2014年10月对此作出了报告,称进入欧洲的假冒香烟可能已经达到了危险的辐射程度。该案例表明,低级别核材料走私会与像香烟这样数量巨大的消费品走私活动相衔接。②

对土耳其非法核贸易案例的分析为衔接现象提供了重要例证。在20世纪90年代早期至21世纪前十年的中期,土耳其存在着大量各类核材料的非法贸易,包括武器级别的核材料。对这些案例的分析表明,核材料贸易并没有特殊的场所,也不存在于特别的犯罪与恐怖组织之中。土耳其发现的大规模杀伤性武器材料,其运输路径常常和毒品贸易、武器贸易以及走私人口的路径相同。在21世纪前期,核材料还被发现与古文物一起运出土耳其。③ 土耳其所观察到的衔接现象表明,当与大量的非法货物一起运输时,核材料以及放射性材料的运输将更加安全,因为罪犯常常会通过贿赂政府官员,以使他们不去理睬这些赃物。④

笔者曾和一位进出口管制违规方面的法律专家讨论过一个案例,该案例中,参与出口管制违规的行为人,同时也是某组织主要的因特网服务提供者。⑤ 这两种现象的衔接并不使人惊讶,因为参与出口管制违规的行为人一般都是为伊朗工作的人员,而伊朗是支持该组织的重要国家。该案例的特别之处在于,不同于前面所讨论的,非法行为的衔接并不仅发生于现实世界,而是同时发生于现实世界与虚拟世界之中。

合法与非法的并存

犯罪分析师已经注意到了非法活动总是很难被发现,因为非法活动总是与合法

---

① Radioactive Cigarettes,"Germany Warns Of Deadly Contraband Shipment",October 13,2014. http://www.worldcrunch.com/culture-society/radioactive-cigarettes-germany-warns-of-deadly-contraband-shipment/health-nicotine-tobacco-cancer-danger-strontium-90/c3s17230/#.VD6dK0iPIjU.

② "Radioactive Cigarettes:Germany Warns Of Deadly Contraband Shipment",October 13,2014,http://www.worldcrunch.com/culture-society/radioactive-cigarettes-germany-warns-of-deadly-contraband-shipment/health-nicotine-tobacco-cancer-danger-strontium-90/c3s17230/#.VD6dK0iPIjU;"Deadly radiation traces found in contaminated imported cigarettes and customs on red alert",Daily Mirror,October 13,2014,http://www.mirror.co.uk/news/uk-news/deadly-radiation-traces-found-contaminated-4427982;the original appeared in German on October 12,2014,"Tödliche Gefahr:Zoll warnt vor radioaktiv verseuchten Zigaretten(Deadly Threat:Customs warn of radioactive contaminated cigarettes)",http://www.bild.de/news/inland/zigarette/warnt-vor-radioaktiven-verseuchten-zigaretten-38112712.bild.html.

③ Interview with former chief of Turkish National Police nuclear smuggling unit 2006.

④ Mahmut Cengiz,*Turkish Organized Crime:From Local to Global*(Saarbrücken,Germany:VDM,2011). Dr. Cengiz worked in the anti-nuclear smuggling division of the Turkish National Police in the mid-2000s.

⑤ Interview conducted at Greenberg Traurig,Washington,DC,December 3,2014.

经济活动结合在一起。从供应链的获取阶段一直到运输和分配阶段，都存在合法贸易与非法贸易衔接的现象。在同一个市场内，合法的供应商可能会同时向合法购买者以及罪犯进行售卖。例证之一就是，在哥伦比亚的美国家电制造商，其不仅会向合法购买者售卖家电，也会向毒品走私犯售卖。毒品走私犯利用洗衣机以及其他的大型家具进行洗钱。故家电卖主同时向哥伦比亚的合法以及非法买家进行了商品供应。[①] 二者的不同之处在于，洗钱者购买大量家电的行为并不符合当时价格水平下的市场需求。

在运输环节，非法物品会与合法物品一起运输，从而将一种贸易掩饰成另一种。举个例子，从哥伦比亚运来的集装箱内，毒品被藏在作为货物的鱼或其他像咖啡这样的食物之中。

经销商可以通过与合法物品一起贩卖来掩饰非法物品的存在，例如在非法贸易中心——法国巴尔贝斯地区。在那里，有营业许可的烟草商店也可能同时贩卖合法的进口烟和从北非和东欧走私的香烟。[②] 这两种商品的区别在于价格的不同，合法香烟的卖价大约是走私烟的两倍。

了解合法与非法并存的现象，是了解获得那些用于像伊朗武器项目这样的军民两用核商品的可能性的关键。笔者通过对大量的调查记录的分析发现，虽然有些供应商会和非法买家串通来进行军民两用核材料供应，但在大多数侦破的案件中，获取军民两用核材料环节并没有供应商共谋参与其中。当然，这也可能是这些非法买家为了努力掩盖自己购买这些产品的主观故意而制造的重要托词所造成的。而非法购买者也常常会设立一个幌子公司，假冒合法买家来欺骗军民两用核材料的供应商。

2012 年美国司法部(DOJ)起诉的关于向伊朗发货的案例就是一个例子。该案中，被告人从 2007 年至 2011 年，与全球各地的企业共发生交易超过 1250 次，获取或者试图获取零部件 105000 件，总价值达 2630800 美元。这些交易遍布不同的行业，并且每笔交易的规模都很小，其中人均利润大概 2000 美元的交易就超过了 1000 笔，这些交易难以受到大出口商的注意。

分割贸易出口也在德国——土耳其研究中被观察到了。在该研究中，伊朗买家进行了大量的贸易出口分割来隐藏最终的买家。这个 2013 年的案例中，我们追踪到零件最终都被运往了伊朗阿拉克的核设施中。调查表明，这些零件制作于印度和德

---

① From a Drug War special that revealed the involvement of top appliance manufacturers in laundering drug money, http://www.pbs.org/wgbh/pages/frontline/shows/drugs/special/us.html. See also the related newspaper article by the show's producer, Lowell Bergman.

② 笔者于 2015 年 3 月在向导带领下对周边国家进行徒步远行时洞察到了这一点。

国，其通过五个独立的空壳公司被发送至伊朗的侨民手上。而这些伊朗侨民正是伊斯坦布尔的幌子公司的建立者。这个紧密的非法网络只由居住在德国或是伊斯坦布尔的伊朗人或伊朗裔的土耳其人组成。在 2010 年至 2012 年之间，走私者共运出冷却设备和其他器械 900 次，其中 800 次的货物来自于印度，另外 100 次的货物来源于德国。伊斯坦布尔的幌子公司使这些出口商品被错误地认为是阀门和排水管固定装置。①

与前面的一个案例一样，该案例揭示，中间商的故意欺骗导致同样的供应源同时被合法买家以及非法买家所使用。德国与伊斯坦布尔的商品流动十分频繁，以至于这些以非法使用为目的的零件可以顺着知名的合法贸易路线来运输，这说明合法货物与非法货物的运输路线时常一致。

白领犯罪

著名的犯罪学家埃德温·萨瑟兰不仅发展了差别交往的概念，也发展了白领犯罪这一概念。该术语创始于 1939 年，其指由商业或是政府的专业人士实施的，以财产为目的的非暴力犯罪，是“被一名在职的受到尊敬的并有很高社会地位的人所实施的犯罪”②。

白领犯罪可以适用于许多的银行家以及包括核材料运输在内的物流运输专家。受国际商业信贷银行(BCCI)、意大利国民劳动银行(Banco Nazionale de Lavoro)或汇丰银行(HSBC)③雇佣的银行家，为核扩散计划获取资金提供了便利。萨达姆·侯赛因时期的伊拉克与全球性的意大利政府银行——“意大利国民劳动银行亚特兰大分行”建立了特殊的联系。该银行处理了数十亿的伊拉克资金，而这些资金中，有一些被用于非法购买。④ 相似的模式也出现在荷兰国际集团(ING)、巴克莱银行、荷兰银行、瑞士信贷和汇丰银行之中。⑤汇丰银行，作为英国主要的银行和伊朗核项目的辅助者，不仅忽视客户的非法活动，还不顾自己承诺的义务，蓄意帮助客户逃避其本国

① UPI, “Nuclear Materials Smugglers Arrested”, March 11, 2013, http://www.upi.com/Top_News/World-News/2013/03/11/Nuclear-materials-smugglers-arrested/UPI-80861362997303/; Nihat Uludag, “Nuclear Operation: Seven Iranians Captured in Simultaneous Operations in Turkey and Germany”, http://www.upi.com/Top_News/World-News/2013/03/11/Nuclear-materials-smugglers-arrested/UPI-80861362997303/.

② https://www.law.cornell.edu/wex/white-collar_crime.

③ J.C.Sharman, The Money Laundry Regulating Criminal Finance in the Global Economy, Ithaca (New York: Cornell University Press, 2011).

④ Matthew Bunn, “Corruption and Nuclear Proliferation”, in *Corruption, Global Security, and World Order*, ed.Robert Rotberg, Washington, DC: Brookings Institution, 2009, 139.

⑤ U.S.Senate Permanent Subcommittee on Investigations, “U.S.Vulnerabilities to Money Laundering, Drugs, and Terrorist Financing”, 117; Javier Serrat, “Financial Interdictions to Curb Proliferation”, July-August 2012, http://www.armscontrol.org/2012_07-08/Financial_Interdictions_To_Curb_Proliferation.

法律的制裁,而且在一些案例中,汇丰银行还积极地参与到客户的犯罪活动之中。[①] 关于其参与伊朗核扩散项目的细节将在之后关于辅助者的章节进行讨论。

高加索地区进行核材料运输的犯罪人和 ISIS 窃取伊拉克大规模杀伤性武器部件的事件,都受到了极大的关注。[②] 这些确实是重要的威胁,但正如萨瑟兰在大约 75 年前所指出的那样,在关注犯罪活动方面,我们总是倾向于不对那些由社会地位较高的人实施的犯罪给予充分的关注。在汇丰银行的案例中,没有起诉任何帮助伊朗筹集核项目资金的人,这证实了萨瑟兰在数十年前所明确提出的观点。

正如我们之前所讨论的,像进口 100000 件配件这样昂贵的运营,对于伊朗来说也是可能的,因为即使被制裁,其也有办法进入国际银行系统。从 2002 年至 2007 年,汇丰银行充分认识到自己正在为伊朗机构处理美金进行转账。[③] 汇丰银行在伊朗商业方面的财务审计表明,"经检查,已鉴定有关伊朗的交易大约 25000 美元,涉及资产超过 194 亿美元。"[④]这违反了国际反洗钱规定的部分条款,因此汇丰银行最终与美国政府达成和解,仅缴纳了略高于 19 亿美元的罚款。[⑤]

此外,汇丰银行的高级官员明知故犯地为这些交易进行掩饰。但其他案例中,银行如果没有经过政府中追踪核扩散者领域的研究员以及专家们的进一步训练及指导,很可能无法识别核扩散的筹资模式,同时也无法阻止对其提供金融便利。[⑥]

核扩散者以及他们的辅助者中有很高地位的人,他们可以是银行家,也可以是运输和物流的专家。企业法人的参与是核扩散挑战中一个十分重要的部分,但是目前大众以及政府都还没有对此有足够的重视,没有去检测出口的货物中是否真的含有诸如铀 235 和铯这样的核材料。非法贸易中,不同参与者所发挥的作用将会在下面章节进行分析。只有通过分析所有的行为主体,我们才能设计出针对非法贸易现在的情况以及未来发展趋势的更为有效的策略。

---

① Kevin McCoy,"HSBC will pay $1.9 billion for money laundering",*USA TODAY*,December 11,2012.http://www.usatoday. com/story/money/business/2012/12/11/HSBC-laundering-probe/1760351/ ; Paul Farrell, James Ball, David Leigh,Juliette Garside and David Pegg,"The HSBC Files." *The Guardian*. February 8, 2015, http://www. theguardian.com/news/2015/feb/09/HSBC-swiss-files-leading-australian-figures-held-offshore-bank-accounts.

② Stephen Hummel,"The ISIL's Theft of WMD Components in Iraq", *CTC Sentinel*,Volume 7,Issue 7(July 2014),p. 1.(*Published by Combating Terrorism Center*)

③ U.S.Senate Permanent Subcommittee on Investigations,Committee on Homeland Security and Governmental Affairs, "U.S.Vulnerabilities to Money Laundering,Drugs,and Terrorist Financing:HSBC Case History",July 17,2012,118,Helping Clients Evade US Sanctions",January 3,2013,http://www.financialtransparency.org-20.

④ 同上,p.120.

⑤ Heather Lowe,"HSBC Deferred Prosecution Agreement":/2013/01/03/the-HSBC-deferred-prosecution-agreement-helping-clients-evade-u-s-sanctions/.

⑥ Sonia Ben Ouagrham-Gormley,"Banking on Nonproliferation:Improving the Efficiency of Counter-Proliferation Financing Policies",*Nonproliferation Review* 19,no.2(2012):241-65.

五、不具有意识形态的罪犯和具有意识形态的罪犯参与非法贸易的特点

在接下来的章节中，我们所分析的犯罪者类别包括：作为罪犯和恐怖分子的非国家行为者，腐败官员和受到国家腐败保护的重要人士，那些为自身利益或国家利益而开展行动的重要辅助者也会被纳入分析的行列。① 在下文，笔者将展示私营企业，比如出口商、银行家、企业，在非法贸易上所发挥的重要作用。

这些参与到非法核贸易中的不具意识形态的罪犯，包括常常不清楚自己所搬运的物品的底层投递员，还有非常高级的官员。要揭露那些参与非法核贸易的高层人士，需要大量的调查，还需要投入大量的人力才能了解他们进行非法核贸易的原由。而这些关键人物还受到辅助者的支持，这些辅助者会为他们提供军民两用核材料或帮助他们运输金钱及物资。

非国家行为者

非国家行为者包括各种准备参与核材料贸易的人。这些人里有供雇佣的轻罪罪犯、犯罪组织成员和那些与新型有组织犯罪业务相关的人。低阶层的人、投机主义者或轻罪罪犯最容易被发现，而更高级别的辅助者却总是隐藏在复杂的幌子公司背后。

恐怖组织也属于这个类别，但是正如先前在关于 2014 年年末至 2015 年年初联合国安理会关于恐怖主义的最新决议那部分章节所讨论的那样，现在对恐怖主义与有组织犯罪进行区分变得越来越困难。虽然许多跨国犯罪仍旧独立于恐怖主义存在，但是几乎没有恐怖组织可以不靠实施犯罪和吸收罪犯来经营组织并负担相关的经费。②

我们可以通过核走私链模型（Nuclear Smuggling Chains Model）③提供的视角，来了解那些与铀走私相关的各种行为主体。对供应者来说，核设施内部人员是保护核

---

① Douglas Farah，"Fixers，Super Fixers and Shadow Facilitators：How Networks Connect"，in *Convergence：Illicit Networks and National Security in the Age of Globalization*，eds. Michael Miklaucic and Jacqueline Brewer（Washington，D.C.：NDU Press，2013），75－95.

② Shelley，*Dirty Entanglements：Corruption，Crime and Terrorism*，chapter 3，97－131；UN Resolutions 2195 and 2199.

③ 该模型是从许多分析非法核/放射性商品流通的资料中推测出来的。这些资料包括：Mike Bourne，"Controlling the shadow trade"，Contemporary Security Policy 32：1（2011）：215－240. Lyudmila Zaitseva and Kevin Hand，"Controlling the shadow trade，Nuclear Smuggling Chains Suppliers，Intermediaries，and End-Users"，American Behavioral Scientist 46：6（2003）：822－844. Mahmut Cengiz，"Various System Methodologies To Analyze Theft and Smuggling of Nuclear Material Cases"，Turkish Journal of Criminology 1：2（2010），http://traccc.gmu.edu/pdfs/publications/weapons_smuggling_publications/cengiz2.pdf.

材料的关键。这在先前日常行为理论中,有关防卫的内容里已经谈论过了。在核材料的储存设施内,这些拥有或能够获得核材料或其他放射性材料使用权的内部人员,属于典型的雇佣人员。从技术员到高层管理者,甚至可能包括军事人员以及警卫,都属于这类人。根据目前的资料,外部人士几乎不可能参与核材料的盗窃行动,这表明腐败以及唯利是图才是问题的根源。①

中间商可以是个人、团体和组织,他们为盗窃的材料找寻潜在的买家,这些人通常可以被分为非专业人士、投机主义商人或厂商、有组织的犯罪集团。有组织的犯罪集团是最受到重视的,因为他们是物流专家,并且他们有现成的设施可以用来运输核材料和放射性材料。至今为止,在我们侦测到的案件中,几乎没有一个案件表明某一有组织犯罪集团与核走私活动有联系;但是,由于有组织犯罪能够轻松地避免自己的非法活动被侦测到,所以我们很难通过侦察到的案件情况来评估其参与核走私活动的真实程度,但是近些年在摩尔多瓦的调查显示出,这一情况确实存在。②

由于核材料的截获多发生在运输阶段,所以我们对核材料的需求方所知甚少。但是大多数反走私项目都是基于这样一个假设:需求的产生,需要具备国家和非国家行为者,还有已建成的投递网络、安全的走私航线和可以藏匿核材料的临时目的地。③

传统的有组织犯罪总是与国家有着共生关系,并且尽力避免与恐怖分子合作。④但是我们在全球观察到的情况是,新型的有组织犯罪已经不再避免与恐怖分子合作了,这使得联合国将跨国犯罪视为一种安全挑战。在过去的十年里,这一现象正日益受到联合国安理会的重视。在 2004 年安理会的决议中跨国犯罪只出现了 4 次,而到了 2014 年这一数字增加到了 30 以上,这反映出国际社会的观点有了重大的改变。⑤如此危险的新型有组织犯罪是什么?笔者在新书《肮脏的纠缠:腐败、犯罪与恐怖主

---

① 根据杰特塞娃(Zaitseva)和汉德(Hand)的著作《核走私供应链、中间商和终端用户》(*Nuclear Smuggling Chains Suppliers, Intermediaries, and End-Users*),"至今已知的所有盗窃武器可用材料的内部人员,都是低调的人,其范围从技术员、海员、工人到低级海军军官。而大部分非武器可用铀的数据也反映出相同的模式。"

② Lyudmila Zaitseva and Friedrich Steinhäusler, "Nuclear Trafficking Issues in the Black Sea Region", pp.11-17.

③ 杰特塞娃(Zaitseva)和汉德(Hand)的著作《核走私供应链、中间商和终端用户》(*Nuclear Smuggling Chains Suppliers, Intermediaries, and End-Users*),归纳出了五种最终用户:正在扩张的国家、恐怖组织、宗教教派、分裂运动者、犯罪团伙及个人。虽然恐怖分子从事核能及辐射能的历史记录数量较少,但是严重的信息偏差以及对其的不了解,使得这一问题变得十分复杂,参见 Sara Daly, John Parachini and William Rosenau, "Aum Shinrikyo, Al Qaeda, and the Kinshasa Reactor", *RAND Documented Briefing* Santa Monica, CA: RAND Corporation(2005).

④ Shelley, *Dirty Entanglements: Corruption, Crime and Terrorism*, p.102.

⑤ Ambassador Ugi Zvekic, Presentation at "Breaking the Chain between Corruption and Organised Crime in the post-2015 Development Agenda", April 14, 2015, United Nations Congress, Doha, http://www.un-congress.org/Sessions/SummaryReport; Global Initiative Against Transnational Organized Crime, "Reinforcing Multilateral Approaches to Transnational Organized Crime by Strengthening Local Ownership and Accountability", 2015.

义》(*Dirty Entanglements*:*Corruption*,*Crime and Terrorism*)中用以下的方式描述了这一问题:

"但这也是一种'新型跨国犯罪'(new transnational crime),其具有更大的规模,其官员的腐败程度也远胜于我们以前所见的一切。其政治影响力与成员数量不成比例,因为其通常根植于那些没有能力也没有意愿阻止其成长的弱小国家。① ……

忠于政府的犯罪集团不再具有优越性。近二十年来,由于冷战的结束以及全球化的兴起,新型跨国犯罪集团在数量以及人数上都急剧增高。② 新型罪犯多存在于冲突地区和处于过渡期的国家之中,他们利用着边界效力的衰退、流动性的增长,以及各种新型交流方式和国际运输的较大便利。他们依靠地下经济、有效政府的缺失以及地方的腐败得以发展繁荣。③ 正如有位学者所说,'恐怖主义网,像黑手党,它的蓬勃发展都是在管理较差的国家之中,而不是在没有管理的国家之中。'④

与其说,许多新型罪犯对国家的持续没有兴趣,倒不如说,破坏国家及其结构的稳定能给他们带来收益。在战争带来的混乱中以及冷酷而又持续的冲突下,这些组织得以成长繁荣,在这些地方,政府无法阻止他们的非法活动,同时腐败更是一种常态。⑤ 在后社会主义世界的那些处于过渡期的国家里,他们也十分繁荣兴盛,在那里旧的标准已经被打破而新的标准还没付诸实践。虽然在20世纪90年代以前还鲜为人知,但如今这些以前南斯拉夫、西非部分地区、苏联的继承国们和阿富汗为基础而建立起来的强大的有组织犯罪集团正在全球活跃着。⑥"

犯罪行为人

一旦了解了新型跨国犯罪的含义,那么新型跨国犯罪的繁荣区域与非法核材料贸易区域之间强烈的相关性就不那么使人惊讶了。了解地理环境和犯罪环境对辨别那些不受制裁的核材料贸易未来的趋势有着至关重要的作用。

---

① 本段来自 Shelley, *Dirty Entanglements*: *Corruption*, *Crime and Terrorism*, p.99, uses ideas from Stewart Patrick, *Weak Links*: *Fragile States*, *Global Threats and International Security* (Oxford: Oxford University Press, 2011), 141-42.

② Saskia Sassen, *Globalization and Its Discontents* (New York: New Press, 1998); James Mittelman, *The Globalization Syndrome*: *Transformation and Resistance* (Princeton, NJ: Princeton University Press, 2000); Moisés Naím, "Five Wars of Globalization", *Foreign Policy*, January 1, 2003; see http://www.foreignpolicy.com/articles/2003/01/01/five_wars_of_globalization.

③ 注意这里说的是管理能力低下的国家而非弱小的国家,因为最弱小的国家并不适宜犯罪组织。见 Stewart Patrick, *Weak Links*: *Fragile States*, *Global Threats and International Security* (Oxford: Oxford University Press, 2011), 3-4.

④ Kenneth J.Menkhaus, "Somalia and Somaliland: Terrorism, Political Islam and State Collapse", in *Battling Terrorism in the Horn of Africa*, ed.Robert I.Rotberg (Washington, DC: Brookings Institution Press, 2005), 45.

⑤ Ivan Briscoe and ElisaDari, *Crime and Error*: *Why We Urgently Need a New Approach to Illicit Trafficking in Fragile States*, Clingendael Conflict Research Unit CRU Policy Brief 23, May 2012, 3, http://www.clingendael.nl/publications/recent/.

⑥ Shelley, *Dirty Entanglements*: *Corruption*, *Crime and Terrorism*, pp.102-103.

侦测到的非法贸易案例中，出现了各种各样的罪犯。正如先前提到的，机会主义犯罪者一直与大量的低级走私案件有所牵连。① 在土耳其，核材料在传统的贩毒网络之中被发现，在这里，跨国有组织犯罪的作用被清楚地呈现了出来。② 而在一些更重大的走私案件之中，还识别出了其他类型的犯罪主体。在苏联，犯罪组织里常常包含有前安全组织成员。③ 先前讨论的柯恩·萨格夫走私高浓缩铀（HEU）案件就能说明这一现象。

全球国际网络促进了跨国犯罪的转移，但还不能被我们完全理解。举个例子，从金沙萨的一个研究型反应堆中窃取的包含少量铀235的低度浓缩铀燃料的成分，随后却被发现到了西西里岛的黑手党手中。④ 我们还不知道，他们到底是通过什么方法将铀运输几千里给一个重要的跨国犯罪组织。非洲的移民群体，同时从事合法和非法的贸易，这体现了核扩散的风险，因为正如前面提到的，非洲是向非法使用者提供或转移铀矿的新兴的重要区域。⑤

在铀矿扩大生产之前，非法核贸易已经成为非洲的一大问题。根据国际原子能组织数据库的数据显示，刚果民主共和国核设施官员参与了2007年3月发生的大规模核材料消失案。⑥ 除该案以外，在1994年至2005年期间，非洲还发生了12起确认过的天然铀走私事件。其中在坦桑尼亚、刚果民主共和国和肯尼亚记录有四起事件，在纳米比亚和南非分别有两起。⑦

犯罪记录中已知的专业罪犯，被指参与了一些最为贵重的放射性材料走私案件，比如走私浓缩铀。⑧ 开始于2011年的摩尔多瓦案件说明了这一点，在该案件中，4.4克武器级铀的样品被查获，据说这只是1千克贮存物中的一部分。⑨ 据称这些是要被运过外德涅斯特冲突区域的核材料，来自俄罗斯和摩尔多瓦的至少6名非国家行

---

① Kupatadze.

② Cengiz,"Various System Methodologies To Analyze Theft and Smuggling of Nuclear Material Cases".

③ Louise Shelley,"Crime,Organized Crime and Corruption",in Return to Putin's Russia 5th edition ed.Stephen K.Wegren(Lanham,Maryland:Rowman and Littlefield Publishers,2013),189-208.

④ Bunn,139.

⑤ 见 Australian Conservation Foundation,"Uranium Undermining Africa",January 14,2014,www.acfonline.org.au/news-media/news-features/uranium-undermining-africa.

⑥ Nwanolue,Bonn Obiekwe Godwin and Victor Chidubem Iwuoha,"Nuclear Politics In Africa:Legal and Empirical Foundations",April 2015,http://nwanoluebog.net/wp-content/uploads/2015/04/Nuclear-Politics-in-Africa.pdf,p.14.

⑦ 同上,p.14.

⑧ Lyudmila Zaitseva and Kevin Hand,"Nuclear Smuggling Chains:Suppliers,Intermediaries,and End Users",*American Behavioral Scientist* 46,no.6(2003):822-44;Zaitseva,"Nuclear Trafficking:20 Years in Review";Lyudmila,Zaitseva,"Organized crime,terrorism and nuclear trafficking",*Strategic Insights* 6.5(2007):1-24.

⑨ NTI Illicit Trafficking Initiatives,NIS Nuclear Trafficking Initiative,2,2011.Illicit Trafficking Incidents Summary Table,http://www.nti.org/analysis/reports/nis-nuclear-trafficking-database/.

为者，打算将手上的这些核材料卖给北非的买家。[①] 摩尔多瓦当局已经确认，这是一个专门从事铀的收购、持有、运输和出售的稳定的犯罪组织。[②] 在 2014 年，摩尔多瓦警方逮捕了 7 人，他们承认走私了 7 盎司铀，据称其价值达 210 万美元。[③]

上面的第二个案件证明了前面提到的观点，摩尔多瓦和河海区域一直是非法贸易的中心。早在 20 世纪 90 年代，该区域就有 130 起以谋利为目的的非法交易案件，这证明该区域存在强大的走私网络。[④] 根据扎特丝娃和斯坦霍斯勒的研究，该地区的官员低估了有组织犯罪的作用。他们的最新研究显示，在乌克兰、格鲁吉亚、土耳其、罗马尼亚和那些有着严重的有组织犯罪问题的国家里，犯罪集团参与核走私活动十分普遍。[⑤]

正如早先提到的，调查员已经在网络世界的“暗网”(dark web)之中，发现非法核材料贸易的存在，在那里人们可以进行匿名的交互行为。正如其名一般，暗网正被罪犯和非法行为者所控制。[⑥] 暗网拥有大量的网站来贩卖你所能想到的一切非法商品，包括人、毒品、武器以及职业杀手。目前的研究显示，有 50000 个网站与人口贩卖有关。[⑦] 在网络世界中，网站的扩增不仅使得生物和化学的大规模杀伤性武器得以售卖，也使得核材料，如钋，得以售卖。[⑧]

俄罗斯的有组织犯罪被认为在大多的世界网络犯罪中扮演着重要的角色。[⑨] 不幸的是，俄罗斯有组织犯罪大量地参与到可访问网络和暗网的情况可能已经与俄罗斯核材料问题相互衔接在了一起。[⑩] 而这些高放射性钋在伦敦，杀死了俄罗斯移民亚历山大·利特维年科。

---

① “Moldova Sentences Would Be Uranium Dealers”, May 25, 2012, http://www.nti.org/gsn/article/moldova-sentences-would-be-uranium-dealers/; Desmond Butler, “Moldova, U.S. Pursue HEU Held by Criminal Organization”, September 27, 2011, http://www.nti.org/gsn/article/moldova-us-pursue-heu-held-by-criminal-organization/.

② Zaitseva and Steinhäusler, “Nuclear Trafficking Issues in the Black Sea Region”, p.17 and the rest of the publication for an excellent analysis of the problem with helpful charts.

③ Mark Hay, “How Worried should we be about Moldova's Recent Uranium Smuggling Bust?” December 11, 2014, http://www.vice.com/read/moldovas-recent-uranium-smuggling-busts-arent-something-to-worry-about-at-least-not-yet-000.

④ Lyudmila Zaitseva and Friedrich Steinhäusler, “Nuclear Trafficking Issues in the Black Sea Region”, p.11.

⑤ Ibid., 12.

⑥ Marc Goodman, *Future Crimes Everything is Connected Everything is Vulnerable and What We Can do About It* (New York: Random House, 2015).

⑦ Larry Greenemeier, “Human Traffickers Caught on Hidden Internet”, February 8, 2015, http://www.scientificamerican.com/article/human-traffickers-caught-on-hidden-internet/; U.S. Department of State, Trafficking in Persons: Filling Knowledge Gaps, January 27, 2015, Washington, DC.

⑧ U.S.-France Cooperative Futures Forum, “Anticipating Transnational Threats and Risks”, April 28-29, 2015, Washington, DC.

⑨ Brian Krebs, *Spam Nation: The Inside Story of Organized Cybercrime from Global Epidemic to your Front Door*, (Naperville, Il.: Sourcebooks, 2014); see also blog Krebsonsecurity.

⑩ 因此，对钋进行广告销售并不足奇，因为这些从国营反应器中取得的高放射钋很可能来自俄罗斯。

恐怖分子

在核武器收购上，恐怖组织已成为国际社会的恐惧之源。但该现象在许多案件中还没有被得到证实。最知名的案件发生在1995年11月，当时俄罗斯车臣分裂组织"将含有70磅铯137和炸药混合物的自制炸弹放置于莫斯科的伊斯曼洛夫斯基公园。最终，反叛者决定不引爆这个'脏弹'而是将其位置告知了国家电视台。"[①]其中的核材料被认为是在苏联解体的混乱时期得到的，当时苏联允许车臣领导人焦哈尔·杜达耶夫保管这些用于制造致命脏弹的材料。[②]

为守护俄罗斯核设施而进行的大量投资已经降低获取武器级别材料的可能性，但是核材料的非法贸易仍旧存在。北高加索地区的犯罪集团已经成功拥有了放射性材料，现在还在不断尝试获取核武器。[③] 2011年，贝尔弗尔科学与国际事务研究中心与俄罗斯科学院的合作研究得出结论，由于"大量军队里的犯罪"和"那些允许恐怖分子携带非法货物从俄罗斯的一个区域穿越到另一个区域的腐败官僚机构和执法机构"的存在，北高加索地区的组织所带来的核恐怖威胁正在增长。[④]

造成该区域风险的是ISIS中的一名领导人，阿布·奥马·阿-什萨尼，其最初是一名来自潘基斯峡谷的格鲁吉亚基督徒，其长期为车臣恐怖分子和伊斯兰激进分子提供庇护。在2014年被宣称杀死以前[⑤]，他在格鲁吉亚成为了一名激进者，还与一名车臣分子结婚并被提升为ISIS的指挥官[⑥]。格鲁吉亚一直是非法核材料的中转站，在此处侦测到的最新案件是在2012年。[⑦] 因此，南北高加索地区的恐怖主义与ISIS恐怖主义之间的联系，增加了我们对这些渠道可能会成为核材料的流通管道的担心。

---

① Allison, 31. This overlooks the Kocaeli case that will be discussed subsequently in the section.

② Allison, 31－32. For a further discussion of Chechen involvement in nuclear terrorism, see Simon Saradzhyan, "Russia: Grasping Reality of Nuclear Terror", Discussion Paper 2003－02, International Security Program, Belfer Center for Science and International Affairs, Harvard Kennedy School, March 2003, http://belfercenter.ksg.harvard.edu/publication/2938/russia.html? breadcrumb=%2Fexperts%2F1897%2Fsimon_saradzhyan%3Fgroupby%3D0%26hide%3D1%26id%3D1897%26back_url%3D%2525252Fexperts%2525252F%26%253Bback_text%3DBack%252Bto%252Blist%252Bof%252Bexperts%26filter%3D2003; Charles D. Ferguson and William C. Potter, *The Four Faces of Nuclear Terrorism* (New York: Routledge, 2005). See Kupatadze, 226.

③ Ibid., p.295.

④ 见 *The U.S.-Russia Joint Threat Assessment on Nuclear Terrorism*, Belfer Center for Science and International Affairs and Russian Academy of Sciences, 2011, http://belfercenter.ksg.harvard.edu/files/Joint-Threat-Assessment%20ENG%2027%20May%202011.pdf.

⑤ "Where has Umar Al-Shishani Gone?", January 1, 2015, www.rferl.mobi/a/26805849.html/.

⑥ Nina Akhmeteli, "The Georgian Roots of ISIS commander Omar al-Shishani", July 9, 2014, www.bbc.ccom/nes/world-europe-28217590.

⑦ Global Security Newswire, "Georgia Conducted 15 Nuclear Smuggling Probes since 2005", December 10, 2012, http://www.nti.org/gsn/article/georgian-conducted-15-nuclear-smuggling-probes-2005-report/. Also, a researcher affiliated with the author has had recent cases officially released by the Georgian government for analysis from this period as part of this study.

各种宗教极端组织，“最突出的是，这些组织都表现出了一定程度的意图，并进行了一定程度的实验和一定程度的规划，以求获取核武器、生物武器以及化学武器。”①许多“基地”组织的分支机构如今活跃在从西非穿越北非、中东直到巴基斯坦的不稳定区域之中。这些恐怖组织，以及像“博科圣地”组织这样最近与ISIS联合的其他恐怖组织，可能会依照奥萨马的1998年宣言，将获取大规模杀伤性武器作为其追随者的宗教责任。②

土耳其的科喀艾里，是一个离伊斯坦布尔不远的人口稠密的城市中心。20世纪初，在那里发生了一起有计划的恐怖行动。该恐怖行动表明，恐怖分子受到了“基地”组织的影响，正在争取进行放射性袭击。该恐怖行动的部分参与者是从阿富汗和巴基斯坦回归的土耳其人，在回来前他们一直与伊斯兰激进分子待在一起。随后发生的事件也使我们看到了宗教极端分子回归现象的致命性，波士顿马拉松投弹者中就有一人曾生活在达吉斯坦；还有，在巴黎发生的查理周刊袭击案中，卡拉奇兄弟组织的其中一员曾生活在也门，并且与“基地”组织也门分支（AQAP）（阿拉伯半岛的“基地”组织）有联系。

大约有40名伊斯兰激进分子的科喀艾里恐怖组织，它来自于土耳其中部科尼亚的保守宗教中心。他们计划袭击一个科喀艾里的工厂，以获取能够制造用于医疗仪器的放射性同位素的医疗设备。由于在袭击发生以前，部署有预防犯罪单位与反恐警察单位的科尼亚警方及时发现并破坏了这次袭击，才使得这次袭击得以避免。在调查期间，警方定位了处于恐怖分子监视下的放射性产品的位置。③

“基地”组织并不是唯一一个在动荡地区中谋求核材料的组织，伊朗支持的什叶派与“基地”组织一样活跃于黎巴嫩和叙利亚，并且也在土耳其东部进行相关的运作。

在叙利亚和伊拉克周围的动荡区域中，腐败现象十分显著。因此，即使在各种条件都处于最好的时期，打击非法核材料贸易的执法能力和情报能力都十分有限。而

---

① 引用于 Rolf Mowatt-Larsen, “Al Qaeda Weapons of Mass Destruction Threat: Hype or Reality”, Harvard Belfer Center, January 2010, 5, http://belfercenter.ksg.harvard.edu/publication/19852/al_qaeda_weapons_of_mass_destruction_threat.html.亦可见 David Albright, Mark Dubowitz, Orde Kittrie, Leonard Spector, and Michael Yaffe, *U.S. Nonproliferation Strategy for the Changing Middle East* (Washington, DC: Project on U.S. Middle East Nonproliferation Strategy, 2013), 103 on the same topic.

② Rahim Kanani, “Al Qaeda's Religious Justification of Nuclear Weapons”, *Huffington Post*, November 19, 2010, http://www.huffingtonpost.com/rahim-kanani/al-qaedas-religious-justi_b_786332.html.

③ 一名调查官曾详细探讨了这次袭击, Anadolou Atayun, “Crime-Terror Nexus: Concrete Examples from the Field”, at Criminal Networks, Smuggling, and WMD Conference, February 25-26, 2010, at Terrorism, Transnational Crime, and Corruption Center, George Mason University, Arlington, VA.亦可见 Shelley, *Dirty Entanglements: Corruption, Crime and Terrorism*, p.308.

在拥有数百万难民的时期这就更为有限了。记录在案的独自生活在土耳其的叙利亚难民就有 180 万[①]，而在周边国家还有更多的难民。这些绝望的人可能会为了获得生活费用而同意干任何事，包括在知情或不知情下进行核材料运输。

中东地区的脏弹问题依然是一个持续的威胁。在 2014 年夏天，ISIS 袭击了摩苏尔，并从摩苏尔大学拿走了 40 千克的铀混合物。这些材料不能用于核装置，因为被夺取的材料是由低级别铀构成的，而低级别铀需要经过大量的程序才能成为核弹——这使得该饱受战乱地区的基础设施得以幸免于难。脏弹的特点是爆炸物中混有放射性材料，生产脏弹是一个更为可能的威胁。如果 ISIS 将偷来的铀用于脏弹上，那么其产生的爆炸将比释放辐射物更加致命。[②] 然而这次袭击带来的象征意义仍旧是十分巨大的。

辅助者

辅助者对于非法网络的运行至关重要。正如道格拉斯·法拉赫说的那样，这些网络，"依靠国际上的'隐蔽辅助者'(shadow facilitators)，他们能够运输武器和商品，进行洗钱和获取伪造的国际文件，比如最终用户证书、护照、营业登记、航运许可和其他所需的文件。"[③]

同一个辅助者常常为多个网络所服务，这些网络会将自己的服务项目进行转包。辅助者能得到很高的收益，其为非法货物的供应链提供了关键节点，这些非法货物包括大规模杀伤性武器以及军民两用核材料。辅助者来自犯罪世界，但他们总是存在于法律不被严格界定以及/或腐败无处不在的世界中。

因帮助转移伊朗、伊拉克以及巴基斯坦的资金而受到罚款的汇丰银行以及其他银行，也应该被看成是超级辅助者。银行虽然没有执行法拉赫所说的全部的辅助者职能，但是他们提供的服务，如财产转移和洗钱，都是核扩散的关键。

早在 2001 年，美国汇丰银行的银行家就违反了反洗钱条例，他们为了清除美国汇丰银行经手的(使用美元的)交易，而掩饰了与伊朗梅里银行有关的所有交易。调查员分析了汇丰银行的内部通讯才使得一切曝光。2001 年 6 月的一封由欧洲汇丰银行客户经理发给与梅里银行有关的某人的电子邮件，指示他们不要输入本次交易的"有关伊朗的客户名"[④]，从而避免留下任何违背美国法律的迹象。

这些系统性的违规行为持续了很长一段时间(2002 年至 2007 年)，而在此期间，

① "ISIL Advances on Syrian city, refugees at border", *Hürriyet Daily News*, June 6-7, 2015, p.9.

② Dina Esfandiary and Matthew Cottee, "The Very Small Islamic State WMD Threat", October 16, 2014, Bulletin of the Atomic Scientists, thebulletin.org/very-sll-islamic-state-wmd-threat7729.

③ Farah, p.78.

④ http://www.treasury.gov/resource-center/sanctions/CivPen/Documents/121211_HSBC_Settlement.pdf, p.1.

汇丰银行清楚地知道这是在为伊朗机构处理涉及美元的财产转移。① 汇丰银行对伊朗业务的财务审计员发现,“经检查,已经确认有关伊朗的交易金额接近 25000 美元,所涉及的资产超过 194 亿美元。”②这违反了国际反洗钱条款中的部分规定,因此银行最终与美国政府达成和解,缴纳了略高于 19 亿美元的罚款。③ 尽管遭到制裁,但是有权使用如此大量的资金还是可以令伊朗进行大规模的采购以支持自己的核项目。

汇丰银行是一个超级辅助者,它不仅为伊朗的核项目提供服务,还帮助那些一掷千金的客户以及腐败的政治家逃税和洗钱。其也曾由于为墨西哥贩毒集团以及其他恐怖组织洗钱而遭到罚款。④

汇丰银行并不是唯一一家因帮助伊朗转移资金而被美国政府调查、指控的银行。在那些被制裁的银行里还包括一些重要的国际银行,比如荷兰国际集团(ING)、巴克莱银行、荷兰银行以及瑞士信贷。⑤

政府官员

各级政府的腐败对核材料的非法贸易至关重要。⑥ 腐败既包括个人的腐败,也包括国家行政机关的腐败。高层官员的腐败会牵涉进大规模发货行为之中,而较为低层官员的腐败则会为获取货源以及运输货物提供帮助。

我们以俄罗斯的案件来进行说明。级别非常高的官员也会利用自己地位来谋取私利。2005 年,瑞士当局应美国政府的要求,逮捕了俄罗斯前原子能部长叶甫盖尼·阿达莫夫,其已被美国法院指控占用 900 万原本用来保卫俄罗斯核设施的美国援助资金,转而用来进行个人投资,而没有去支付给进行安全升级的工作人员。其于 2008 年被引渡回俄罗斯接受审讯,但是经过审讯,其只被判处了缓刑从

① U.S.Senate Permanent Subcommittee on Investigations,Committee on Homeland Security and Governmental Affairs,“U.S.Vulnerabilities to Money Laundering,Drugs,and Terrorist Financing:HSBC Case History”,July 17,2012,118 Helping Clients Evade US Sanctions, January 3,2013,http://www.financialtransparency.org-20.

② 同上,p.120.

③ Heather Lowe, HSBC Deferred Prosecution Agreement:/2013/01/03/the-hsbc-deferred-prosecution-agreement-helping-clients-evade-u-s-sanctions/.

④ Ryan Chittum.“Diamond Dealers in Deep Trouble as Bank Documents Shine Light on Secret Ways”,*International Consortium of Investigative Journalists*, February 9, 2015. http://www. icij. org/project/swiss-leaks/diamond-dealers-deep-trouble-bank-documents-shine-light-secret-ways.

⑤ U.S.Senate Permanent Subcommittee on Investigations,“U.S.Vulnerabilities to Money Laundering,Drugs,and Terrorist Financing”,117;Javier Serrat,“Financial Interdictions to Curb Proliferation”,July-August 2012,http://www.armscontrol.org/2012_07-08/Financial_Interdictions_To_Curb_Proliferation.Sonia Ben Ouagrham-Gormley,“Banking on Nonproliferation:Improving the Efficiency of Counter-Proliferation Financing Policies”,*Nonproliferation Review* 19,no.2(2012):241-65 suggests that some banks were not cognizant and needed more training to identify patterns of proliferation finance.

⑥ Bunn,124-65 provides an excellent analysis of all aspects of the corruption problem and WMD.

而离开了监狱。① 在俄罗斯安全受到威胁的关键时刻，他的腐败暗中破坏了核安全的保障系统。

他的腐败行为并不是唯一的。在后苏联时期开始的几十年里，官员高度的腐败意味着他们对所有在自己控制下的有价值的东西进行了货币化。虽然苏联时期的核设施十分安全，但在苏联解体以后，许多核设施以及武器站都缺乏足够的保护，而在制造以及存储核材料的封闭城市中的那些最高官员，他们的腐败加速了这一问题。② 正如我们在日常行为理论这一块内容中所讨论的，缺乏防护意味着一些官员并没有尽到作为守卫者的职责，反而是将这些在自己控制下的铀作为个人财富的来源。

根据俄罗斯监测机构核安全管理局前局长尤里·维什涅夫斯基所述，2002 年，莫斯科区域内的工厂以及新西伯利亚工厂丢失了"数克武器级别铀以及数千克低度浓缩铀"。③ 这在苏维埃时期根本不可能发生，那时存放有武器级别核材料的设施都被小心地保护着，个人如果违反了苏联核项目相关规范将会受到严惩。但是在后苏联时代，对腐败的调查与起诉锐减到了一个非常有限的数量。④ 因此，与贝卡利亚所倡导的相反，这里既没有刑罚的确定性，也没有刑罚的严厉性。

谚语说得好，"上梁不正下梁歪"（the fish rots from the head）。当核项目的领导人都开始腐败了，那么下面的人就更有可能变腐败。从官僚机构的中层官员直到底层看守核设施或是核设施所在的封闭城市的守卫都可能变得腐败。

在俄罗斯，一名企图接近放置着大规模杀伤性武器设施的封闭城市的走私者诉说了整个经过："我选了一个守卫，然后通过给他香烟和糖果来认识他。一个月之后我们就成了'朋友'，我可以带任何我想带的人进去。当然，我必须严格按照士兵所说的时间进出。"⑤即使被抓住了，贪污所需付出的代价也是微不足道的。人们发现犯走私罪的工人所面对的只是毫无意义的惩罚，而这些惩罚也不足以阻止他们继续走私。

---

① http://www.bellona.org/english_import_area/international/russia/nuke_industry/co-operation/37946; "Russian Ex-nuclear Minister Adamov Released from Prison", April 17, 2008, http://en.rian.ru/russia/20080417/105342331.html.

② 对此提出的预先警告，见 William C. Potter, "Before the Deluge: The Threat of Nuclear Leakage from the Post-Soviet States".

③ Charles Digges, "GAN Says Nuclear Materials Have Been Disappearing from Russian Plants for 10 Years", November 15, 2002, http://www.bellona.org/english_import_area/international/russia/nuke-weapons/nonproliferation/2727Y.

④ Shelley, "Crime, Organized Crime and Corruption".

⑤ Prizrak Usamy brodit po"zapretke", *Chelyabinskii rabochii*, August 12, 2004; research of TraCCC, American University, 2004-5, in which project the author participated.

世界银行将腐败界定为“滥用职权谋取私利”。但这样的界定太过狭隘，因为它没有包括有腐败行为的私人主体。亚洲发展银行对腐败的界定包括了私人的腐败行为。① 在本次研究中，笔者更倾向于使用亚洲发展银行对腐败的界定，这使得腐败的主体包括了腐败的个人以及私营企业，例如前面关于银行业的讨论中所提到的那些银行。

私营企业参与生产军民两用核材料，这对伊拉克的核扩散网络十分重要。在伊拉克的案例中，许多供应商都知道自己的贩卖对象不是一个合法的购买者。公司通过伪造最终用户证书和篡改出口表格来掩饰他们产品的最终收货方。②

该分析说明，法人，不论是幌子公司还是合法企业，都可能是非法贸易的一部分。因此，政府腐败与法人腐败可能会相互衔接，对这一现象笔者在前面的关于犯罪学的白领犯罪原则的章节中已经进行了讨论。

六、总　结

从2014年年末至2015年年初，世界上的许多地区都经历了自第二次世界大战以来从未见过的安全挑战。③ 穿越地中海以及南亚的大量走私者，躲避冲突的难民数量的急剧增长，北非和中东地区持续不间断的冲突，都在威胁着世界的稳定。

由于现在过高的混乱程度，使得以往对罪犯参与核走私的分析，都在判断该种贸易的未来趋势上存在重大的局限性。如今，许多地区要么是没有监督和报告机制，要么就是不受执法机关或情报机关的控制。现在，大多数的监测工作都将重点转到了欧亚大陆、伊朗以及巴基斯坦的非法交易。④ 但是从西非穿过北非、中东直至巴基斯坦的不稳定弧带的形成，尤其在“阿拉伯之春”运动以后，给我们带来了从未有过的

---

① Asian Development Bank, *Anticorruption: Our Framework and Strategies*, 1998, http://www.adb.org/documents/anticorruption-policy.

② Bunn, 130-31.

③ 45th International Peace Institute Vienna Seminar, The United Nations at 70, May 6-7, 2015, discussed this extensively.

④ 例如，Alexander Kupatadze，“Organized crime and the trafficking of radiological materials: The case of Georgia”, *Nonproliferation Review* 17: 2 (2010): 219-234; Special Report: The Khan Network; Kenley Butler, Sammy Salama, and Leonard S.Spector, “Where Is the Justice?”, *Bulletin of the Atomic Scientists*, November-December 2006, 25-34; Mark Hibbs, “The Unmaking of a Nuclear Smuggler”, *Bulletin of the Atomic Scientists*, November-December 2006, 35-41; U.S.Department of Justice, “Summary of Major U.S.Export Enforcement, Economic Espionage, Trade Secret and Embargo-Related Criminal Cases”; Sheena Chestnut Greitens, “Illicit North Korea's Evolving Operations to Earn Hard Currency”, Committee for Human Rights in North Korea, 2014.

挑战。

由于合法和非法的铀矿石采集日渐增多，南非、中非、东非都将成为非法核贸易的组成部分，因此在先前提到的不稳定弧带之外，非洲的其他地区也将越来越多地参与到非法贸易之中。[①] 寻求在官方渠道之外购买铀矿的人，主要是那些拥有大量处理铀矿的生产设备的人。因此，在这些主体中，一些过去就被作为监视对象的人将一直是我们关注的对象。但是非洲不同地区的资源，高度的腐败[②]，以及非洲大陆与日俱增的跨国犯罪者和恐怖组织，造成了未来的严重挑战，我们需要有新的策略来阻止核扩散带来的威胁。尽管部分国际社会有政治意愿，也对重要资源进行了投资，但我们过去在阻止相对容易发现的非洲犀牛角和象牙的非法贸易上所做的努力却一直得不到成功。因此，对更难发现的核材料，例如铀矿石来说，我们的挑战将会更大。

秘密走私者不论是在高加索地区还是在卡迪尔·汗的全球供应链的各个部分之中，要识别这些参与非法核贸易的非政府行为者都是十分困难的。而未来我们所面临的挑战还会更大，因为越来越多的交易将会在暗网上通过密文的控制进行，并且还存在着许多区域，在那里政府与国际社会抗击违法现象的能力明显不足。

由于存在巨大的利润，辅助者遍布世界各地，金融体系依然可以进行大量的非法资金转移，所以未经授权的核扩散国家对军民两用核材料的收购将仍旧是一个问题。因此，不论是在天然核原料领域、加工后核材料领域，还是在销售筹资方面，都存在着挑战。

犯罪学理论帮助我们确定今后需优先考虑的事项，从这些犯罪学理论中，我们能够学到什么？萨瑟兰的单位犯罪（corporate crime）的概念对于我们确定优先级别十分重要。切断核扩散国家的资金和他们获取进行非法核项目所需设备的能力，是至关重要的。

日常行为理论中防卫的概念，促使我们更加重视腐败问题，而不是像过去那样将其重要性最小化。我们需要关注那些无法防卫的区域和那些不能将原料紧锁住的区域，就像我们在俄罗斯所做的那样。我们需要更加关注于如何去解决存在于广阔而又腐败成风的非洲大陆上的这个问题。从事采矿业和运输业的跨国公司之间进行紧密的合作，是解决这一问题的出路之一。目前联合国在非洲大陆上发挥着重要的作

---

① Marta Conde and Giorgis Kallis, "The global uranium rush and its Africa frontier. Effects, reactions and social movements in Namibia", *Global Environmental Change* 22:3(2012):596-610; Ian Anthony and Lisa Grip, *Africa and the Global Market in Natural Uranium: From Proliferation Risk to Non-proliferation Opportunity*. Stockholm International Peace Research Institute(SIPRI), 2013; Taylor Toeka, "Illegal Mining Fuels DRC Conflict", January 12, 2011, https://iwpr.net/global-voices/illegal-mining-fuels-drc-conflict.

② https://www.transparency.org/cpi2014/results.

用，在那里它已深入地参与到许多方面之中。

“衔接”这一概念用于非法核材料贸易上是十分合适的。各种非法产品都能够为那些未经授权的核项目提供资金，而核材料能够与其他非法产品一起运输。抵制核扩散的国家必须与那些抵制其他犯罪和腐败的国家通力合作。联合国安理会通过的 2195 号决议肯定了武器贸易是犯罪与恐怖主义相衔接的其中一环。这些决议为国际社会追查那些与恐怖主义相关的犯罪提供了更大的权力。

（阮重骏 译）

Nuclear Trafficking:Actors and Emerging Trends

Louise Shelley①

Introduction

The most feared outcome of the crime-terror relationship is that criminals will help terrorists acquire WMD biological, chemical, and nuclear weapons. The WMD trade, which is relatively rare, is very different from narcotics smuggling and the trade in counterfeit and diverted goods that are core elements of the criminal business of terrorists, with known suppliers and purchasers. In contrast, relatively little is known about the criminal logistical operations that move trafficked nuclear materials or how the criminal realm intersects with states that engage in unsanctioned proliferation.②

WMD trade operates on a different economic logic—one based not on volume but on scarcity and risk. The illicit trade in WMD leads to the ultimate asymmetric threat. A WMD attack of any kind nuclear, biological, or chemical could have many serious and long-term consequences. These could include undermining the sustainability of the planet, human life, and health and the viability of diverse species. Even a lesser attack than a nuclear bomb

---

① Louise Shelley, University Professor and Omer L. and Nancy Hirst Endowed Chair and Director, Terrorism, Transnational Crime and Corruption Center, School of Policy, Government and International Affairs, George Mason University.

② Lyudmila Zaitseva, "Nuclear Trafficking: 20 Years in Review", Contribution to WFS Meeting, Erice, August 2010, http://www.physics.harvard.edu/~wilson/pmpmta/2010_Zaitzeva.doc. August 2010, http://www.physics.harvard.edu/~wilson/pmpmta/2010_Zaitzeva.doc.

*might require evacuation of citizens and massive and costly cleanup efforts.*①

This article focuses primarily on the movers and facilitators of the illicit trade in WMD materials, examining the role of nonstate actors, corrupt officials, and corporations that unwittingly or consciously move WMD materials.

Defining the Problem

In this paper, the term *nuclear materials* includes the variety of nuclear products tracked by international agencies including the trade in dual-use material. Included are the relatively rare cases of trafficking of weapons-grade materials, but also cases involving radioisotopes, and/or contaminated non-nuclear materials. Cases considered also include trade in low-grade nuclear materials, such as natural uranium ore, yellowcake, depleted uranium, and thorium-232.②

Criminals are defined in this report not simply as ordinary criminals, or transnational criminals, but those who violate criminal law through corrupt behavior or as facilitators of nuclear trade. Facilitators' activities may include obtaining, transporting, financing and selling nuclear materials.③ The study also examines the role of terrorists, their personal engagement in criminal activity, and their retention of criminals' services to assist in the illicit trade of nuclear materials.

IAEA Database and Reporting Challenges for the Future

Insights into illicit trade in nuclear materials in the past have come from analyses of the IAEA database and individual cases that have been investigated and analyzed. Yet analyses of the past twenty-five years, unfortunately, do not help us analyze many of the problems

---

① David Smigielski, "Addressing the Nuclear Smuggling Threat", in *Transnational Threats Smuggling and Trafficking in Arms, Drugs and Human Life*, ed. Kimberley L. Thachuk (Westport, CT: Praeger Security, 2007), 57.

② Based on data presented in Lyudmila Zaitseva, "Nuclear trafficking: 20 years in review." Nuclear materials account for only about 30 percent of the IAEA recorded incidents—most cases involve radioisotopes and/or contaminated non-nuclear materials. Nevertheless, around sixty percent of the nearly 500 nuclear cases involved low-grade nuclear materials, such as natural uranium ore, yellowcake, depleted uranium, and thorium-232. According to Friedrich Steinhäusler and Lyudmila Zaitseva, "Illicit Trafficking of Natural Radionuclides." *The Natural Radiation Environment: 8th International Symposium* (NRE VIII). 1034: 1. (Melville, N.Y.: AIP Publishing, 2008). Approximately one-quarter of cases involve natural nuclides like uranium. They suggest that the reason for uranium dominance in the global trafficking of natural radionuclides is that there is a high level of corruption in major uranium mining countries such as Kazakhstan, Russia, Ukraine, and Uzbekistan. This trend is also apparent in newer uranium extraction sources in the developing world such as seen in Africa.

③ This is different from Steinhäusler and Zaitseva, "Illicit Trafficking of Natural Radionuclides" in that this study also examines the funding for this illicit nuclear trade.

and challenges we will see in the future.

Data reporting challenges are not new. The IAEA database did not capture all the illicit trade that occurred in nuclear materials. According to the IAEA's Illicit Trafficking Database (ITDB), from January 1993 to December 2009, a total of 1773 nuclear smuggling incidents globally were reported by participating states and some non-participating states.① Underreporting and failure to report or detect meant that we only have an imperfect view of what happened previously. But this problem will become even more acute in the future, as mining of uranium ore expands into remote geographical regions in Africa and cyberspace becomes more central to the sale of nuclear materials. Under these conditions detection and reporting will become less common.

The IAEA database has provided limited insight into the criminal involvement in nuclear materials trade.② It provides even less insight into the role of terrorists either acting on their own or through their retention of criminal services. The problem of illicit trade by terrorists has become even more acute since the advent of the so-called Arab Spring that has brought unprecedented levels of conflict to many contiguous countries in North Africa and the Middle East.

Moreover, many future trends will not be as readily apparent because of the locales in which the new challenges occur. The monitoring of illicit nuclear trade on the dark web is not likely to be entered into the IAEA database because of its covert nature. The trade that is now going on from Africa in mined uranium ore is and will remain also significantly underreported because of the absence of reliable crime reporting and analysis from this region. The same can be said for data from the conflict regions of the Middle East and North Africa. In these highly chaotic regions with numerous acts of terrorism and severe challenges to

---

① Amelia Broodryk and Noël Stott. "Securing Africa's Nuclear Resources". *Arms Control: Africa* 3.1 (2011): 5-6. In addition, Stanford University's Center for International Security and Cooperation maintained a Database on Nuclear Smuggling, Theft, and Orphan Radiation Sources (DSTO), which in addition to government-confirmed cases recorded in the ITDB but also collected unconfirmed incidents derived from open-source reports, identified 2440 trafficking cases in the period between 1991 and 2006: "1674 incidents of thefts, illegal movement, and border detections of radioactive materials, 736 cases of the so called orphan sources, which have been lost, accidentally found or misrouted on the way to the recipient, and 35 malevolent acts, such as intentional irradiation of persons and contamination of their residencies and belongings." This information can be found in Lyudmila Zaitseva "Nuclear trafficking: 20 years in review." However, the author has written that the IAEA data may be flawed, with important information unreported to the IAEA or that information is not full or entirely accurate. See Louise I. Shelley, "Trafficking in nuclear materials: Criminals and terrorists." *Global Crime* 7: 3-4 (2006): 544-560.

② Zaitseva, "Nuclear trafficking: 20 years in review"; Louise Shelley, *Dirty Entanglements: Corruption, Crime and Terrorism* (Cambridge: Cambridge University Press, 2014), 303.

governance, there is no system in place to monitor WMD challenges, let alone to report them to the IAEA. Therefore, we cannot easily extrapolate from the past into the future. We can anticipate that regions with dirty entanglements—interactions of crime, terrorism and corruption—will be overrepresented in the illicit trade in nuclear materials in the future. We can also expect that more trade will be enabled by computers, as encryption and secure means of entering the dark web, such as through TOR, guarantee users greater anonymity for trade.①

What insights can be drawn from the criminology and law enforcement literature that would be useful in understanding criminal involvement in the trafficking of nuclear materials?

Illicit trade in nuclear materials and the funding in support of this trade is carried out by a variety of criminal and corrupt actors. Therefore, certain criminological theoriesand concepts developed in other contexts should help us understand the perpetrators, the conditions and networks facilitating illicit nuclear trade. Selected concepts such as differential association, routine activity theory, dirty togetherness, the merger of the licit and illicit, white collar-crime, will be shown to be helpful in understanding the role of criminals in the illicit nuclear trade.

Differential Association

The father of modern American criminology, Edwin Sutherland, developed two concepts that are of particular relevance to this analysis. The first is called *differential association*, by which the extent of involvement in crime is explained by the intensity and duration of the relationship of illicit actors.② Although this theory was developed in and for the American context, it shows significant applicability to the involvement of non-state actors in the trade in nuclear materials. Prison, by its very nature and its cell structure, facilitates intense interactions where plotting on the acquisition of nuclear materials has occurred. But fighting together in a conflict region also illustrates the principle of differential association.

The Black Sea region, a contentious region since the collapse of the Soviet Union, has tra-

---

① Marc Goodman, *Future Crimes Everything is Connected Everything is Vulnerable and What We Can do About It* (New York: Random House, 2015).

② http://criminology.fsu.edu/crimtheory/sutherland.html.

ditionally been at the heart of nuclear trafficking, with Russia being the known or suspected source of most nuclear contraband and the Caucasus area—Georgia in particular—serving as a key transit region.① In the Caucasus and Black Sea Region, family ties are of paramount importance. Therefore, individuals have long and close associations with both immediate and often more distant family members.

The most studied Georgian case of smuggling illustrates the principle of *differential association*. The Russian Oleg Khintsagov, thought to have previously served in the Soviet security police, KGB, was caught in 2006 after trying to sell one hundred grams of HEU to an undercover Georgian investigator. The subsequent investigation of Khintsagov's network revealed that his collaborators were connected by blood or close friendship.② The close family associations of his collaborators were one of the elements that prevented an investigation that fully illuminated the network of the trafficker.

Khintsagov's case is the most known and documented one of illegal nuclear trade in weapons-grade material. Yet the close relationships among perpetrators in this case is not unique because of the need for high levels of *trust* among the participants in diverse forms of illicit nuclear trade.

Routine Activity Theory

Another concept, allied to differential association, called *routine activity theory*, has greater currency among contemporary criminologists than differential association. Routine activity theory is a sub-field of criminal opportunity theory that focuses on the environment and situations that contribute to crime commission.③ The concern of this theory is on the criminal behavior that may result from the intersection of people, time and space. In order for crime to occur, according to this theory, there must be *a motivated offender*, *a suitable target*, *as well as the absence of a capable guardian*. According to routine activity, the more exposed one is to a criminal lifestyle in one's daily activities, the more likely one is to com-

---

① For a discussion, see Maj. Gen. (ret.) Bruce Lawlor, "The Black Sea: Center of the Nuclear Black Market" *Bulletin of the Atomic Scientists* 67.6 (2011): 73–80; Lyudmila Zaitseva and Friedrich Steinhäusler, "Nuclear Trafficking Issues in the Black Sea Region," Non-Proliferation Papers, No.39, April 2014.

② Alexander Kupatadze, "Organized crime and the trafficking of radiological materials: The case of Georgia." *Nonproliferation Review* 17:2 (2010): 219–234; Michael Bronner, 100 *Grams (and Counting ...): Notes from the Nuclear Underworld* (Cambridge, MA: Report for Managing the Atom Project, Harvard University, June 2008.

③ http://www.popcenter.org/learning/pam/help/theory.cfm.

mit crime. Being away from one's home is also a central element that facilitates illicit activity as one is outside the control mechanisms of daily life.①

Routine activity theory is very applicable to the problem of illicit involvement in nuclear activity because the issue of guardianship is at the core of the problem. Lack of guardianship, as it is usually used in the American context, concerns an absence of security for valuable items and does not reference corruption. Yet there is nothing that precludes applying the concept of corruption to this theory.

States that have nuclear programs for both weapons and energy production guard their facilities closely. Therefore, the access to processed materials is difficult. Orphaned radiological materials such as were seen in the Soviet successor states in abandoned military facilities and hospitals were less likely to be guarded, but these sources are less threatening than those that are carefully controlled.

But corruption is the Achilles' heel in the problem of guardianship in the former USSR and in many other locales. If the individual responsible for guarding the facility or having oversight over a country's nuclear program is corrupt, then the role of guardianship is not exercised. The problem of corruption and illicit trade in nuclear materials, as will be discussed, is a problem that was seen extensively in Russia at many levels in the first decade of the post-Soviet period. The corruption that existed both at the level of top officials down to the lowest level guards② affected the security of weapons grade material.

The other two elements of routine activity theory are that there is a motivated offender and a suitable target, both concepts relevant to nuclear materials trade. Individuals are motivated to acquire or move nuclear materials either by ideology or the real or sometimes misplaced perception that trafficking in nuclear materials will result in substantial financial rewards. The latter problem was observed particularly in Georgia where opportunistic offenders moved radioactive materials, often without adequate protections, and sometimes at great personal risk to themselves, because they anticipated significant gains.③

The third requirement of *a suitable target* applies perfectly to the nuclear materials trade. In some other contexts, where routine activity theory is applied, there is not such a specific

---

① http://criminology.fsu.edu/crimtheory/sutherland.html.

② *Ozerskii vestnik*, July 10, 2004.

③ Based on interviews by the TraCCC team in Georgia concerning individuals who have been caught transporting low-level radiation sources. See Shelley, *Dirty Entanglements: Corruption, Crime and Terrorism* (Cambridge: Cambridge University Press, 2014), p.305; Kupatadze, 226.

target. But this trade is so specific that the nature of the target is key. Because most individuals do not live near sources of nuclear materials, another key defining element of routine activity theory is also present. Therefore, the offenses in the nuclear area are most often committed away from the perpetrator's home.

Dirty Togetherness

Adam Podgorecki's concept of *dirty togetherness*, originally developed in Poland, also has applicability to this illicit trade.① This concept can be adapted to the interaction of criminals and terrorists in hostile environments. He developed this term to describe the cliquishness and "close-knit networks in the context of scarcity and distrust of the state."② Yet this term also characterizes the common attitude toward the state of many criminals and terrorists incarcerated together for extended periods, or cooperating in conflict regions. It is these ties that allow them to plot concerning the acquisition and logistics of moving the materials.

Convergence

In 2011, the crime specialists of the United States government launched the U. S. Government's Strategy to Combat Transnational Organized Crime: Addressing Converging Threats to National Security.③ The concept of convergence has been an important and influential concept on thinking of crime policy, especially since it emanated from the law enforcement and legal policy community rather than the academic. As the concept of convergence has been explained:

> The old paradigm of fighting terrorism and transnational crime separately, utilizing distinct sets of tools and methods, may not be sufficient to meet the challenges posed by the convergence of these networks into a crime-terror-insurgency nexus. Violent nonstate actors, including terrorist organizations and insurgent movements, seek to collaborate with criminal networks—and in some cases become criminal networks—in order to finance acts of terrorism and purchase the implements of destruction and killing. Terrorists and

---

① Maria Ło 0 a2d Andrzej Zybertowicz, *Privatizing the Police State: The Case of Poland* (New York: St. Martin's Press, 2000), 16, discuss Adam Podgorecki's idea of dirty togetherness.

② Janine R. Wedel, "Corruption and Organized Crime in Post-Communist States: New Ways of Manifesting Old Patterns", *Trends in Organized Crime* 7, no.1 (2001): 10.

③ Strategy to Combat Transnational Organized Crime, July 25, 2011, http://www.whitehouse.gov/administration/eop/nsc/transnational-crime.

insurgents can tap into the global illicit marketplace to underwrite their activities and acquire weapons and other supplies vital to their operations.[①]

Although this concept has been developed in the American context, there are crime and terror specialists in many parts of the world who have seen and identified this same phenomenon. Therefore, starting in late December 2014, the United Nations Security Council has passed two resolutions unanimously concerning the relationship of crime and terrorism. The first Resolution 2195 focuses on the relationship between terrorism and transnational crime and the illicit trade activities that help perpetuate conflict and undermine the world order.[②]

Resolution 2195 of the Security Council passed unanimously in the final days of 2014, sponsored by Chad, identified diverse forms of illicit trade that support terrorism. According to this Resolution, these diverse forms of illicit trade are crucial to the funding of terrorism. UN resolution 2195 enumerated these forms of illicit trade as central to terrorism.

Trafficking of arms, persons, drugs, and artifacts and from the illicittrade in natural resources including gold and other precious metals and stones, minerals, wildlife, charcoal and oil, as well as from kidnapping for ransom and other crimes including extortion and bank robbery.[③]

A subsequent resolution 2199 on the funding of ISIS passed by the Security Council on February 12, 2015, had a slightly different focus emphasizing the terrorist financial supporting mechanisms including the trade supporting terrorism. The UN resolution on ISIS focused not only on the crimes that generate funds for the terrorist group but particularly on the trade as well as the trade-based money laundering that supports ISIS.[④] In the Middle East, since the times of Ancient Mesopotamia, trade has been at the core of the movement of money and funds. Therefore, it is logical that trade was more central to this Resolution. The second resolution also pays attention to the commodities that may harbor value for terrorists, directing states to concern themselves with trade facilitation and the commodities used to move money. This resolution pays significant attention to the role of transnational

① Michael Miklaucic and Jacqueline Brewer, eds., *Convergence: Illicit Networks and National Security in the Age of Globalization* (Washington, D.C.: NDU Press, 2013), xv.

② www.un.org/press/en/2014/sc11717.doc.htm.

③ Ibid.

④ www.un.org/press/en/2015/sc11775.doc.htm.

crime and the funding provided by natural resources.①

The concepts of the convergence of crime and terrorism as well as the role of the natural resource trade in funding terrorist activity is very central to the problem of illicit nuclear trade. The following examples drawn from different regions of the world: Africa, Asia, Europe and the Middle East suggest that the nuclear materials trade may converge with other forms of illicit activity in different regions of the globe. It is not a stand-alone offense. Even though it is often accompanied by trafficking in other high value items, this is not necessarily the case. A recent cigarette smuggling case in Europe shows that radioactive materials may travel along with less valuable commodities, as was revealed by the contamination of smuggled cigarettes through their interaction with radioactive materials.②

On June 9th, 2014, a Vietnamese cigarette smuggler was caught in the Warsaw airport smuggling cigarettes along with radioactive metal plates and packages contaminated with Strontium 90. The cigarettes had the usual warning stamps along with German and Polish tax stamps. An official radiation report said, that those who would consume these cigarettes would suffer respiratory burns. The Polish department responsible for investigating terrorism launched an investigation. German customs officials reported only in October of 2014 that counterfeit cigarettes entering Europe might be contaminated with dangerous levels of radiation. This case reveals the convergence of the smuggling of low-level nuclear materials with a mass-consumed commodity such as illicit cigarettes.③

Analysis of nuclear trafficking cases from Turkey provides important illustrations of convergence. Turkey in the early 1990s through the middle of the first decade of the 2000s was the site of a significant number of cases of trafficking of different types of nuclear materials, including weapons-grade materials. Analyzing these cases reveals that the trade in

---

① UNEP, Monusco and OSESG, *Experts' background report on illegal exploitation and trade in natural resources benefitting organized criminal groups and recommendations on MONUSCO's role in fostering stability and peace in eastern DR Congo*, April 15, 2015.

② Radioactive Cigarettes: Germany Warns Of Deadly Contraband Shipment, October 13, 2014. http://www.worldcrunch.com/culture-society/radioactive-cigarettes-germany-warns-of-deadly-contraband-shipment/health-nicotine-tobacco-cancer-danger-strontium- 90/c3s17230/#.VD6dK0iPIjU .

③ "Radioactive Cigarettes: Germany Warns Of Deadly Contraband Shipment", October 13, 2014, http://www.worldcrunch.com/culture-society/radioactive-cigarettes-germany-warns-of-deadly-contraband-shipment/health-nicotine-tobacco-cancer-danger-strontium-90/c3s17230/#.VD6dK0iPIjU ; "Deadly radiation traces found in contaminated imported cigarettes and customs on red alert", Daily Mirror, October 13, 2014, http://www.mirror.co.uk/news/uk-news/deadly-radiation-traces-found-contaminated-4427982; the original appeared in German on October 12, 2014, "Tödliche Gefahr: Zoll warnt vor radioaktiv verseuchten Zigaretten (Deadly Threat: Customs warn of radioactive contaminated cigarettes)", http://www.bild.de/news/inland/zigarette/warnt-vor-radioaktiven-verseuchten-zigaretten-38112712.bild.html.

nuclear materials has not been found in distinct locales or among distinct criminal or terrorist groups. WMD materials detected in Turkey usually moved through the same routes as the drug and arms trade and human smuggling. In the early 2000s, nuclear materials were detected moving through Turkey along with antiquities.① The observed convergence in Turkey suggests that nuclear and radiological materials can be more safely moved when they travel along with significant quantities of illicit goods, as bribes have often been paid for officials to look the other way.②

A legal specialist on export control violations discussed a case with the author in which an individual implicated in export control violations was also a major Internet service provider for a terrorist group.③ The convergence of these two phenomena is not surprising, as those who engage in export control violations are often working on behalf of Iran, that is, the key state supporter of this group. What is distinctive about this case is that the convergence of illicit activity is not going on exclusively in the real world as discussed in the previous cases, but represents the convergence of illicit activity in the real and the virtual world.

Merger of Licit and Illicit

Crime analysts have focused on the fact that illicit activity is often hard to detect because it merges with licit economic activity. This convergence of both legitimate and illicit trade can occur along the whole supply chain from the point of acquisition, through the transport and distribution phase. Legitimate suppliers may be selling both to legitimate purchasers and to criminals in the same market. Illustrative of this is that American appliance manufacturers were selling appliances in Colombia both to legitimate purchasers but also to drug traffickers. The drug traffickers were using the washing machines and other large housewares to launder their money. Therefore, the sellers of appliances were supplying both legitimate and illegitimate Colombian purchasers.④ The difference between the two was that the money launderers were buying quantities of appliances that could not be justified by market

---

① Interview with former chief of Turkish National Police nuclear smuggling unit until 2006.

② Mahmut Cengiz, *Turkish Organized Crime: From Local to Global* (Saarbrücken, Germany: VDM, 2011). Dr. Cengiz worked in the anti-nuclear smuggling division of the Turkish National Police in the mid-2000s.

③ Interview conducted at Greenberg Traurig, Washington, DC, December 3, 2014.

④ From a Drug War special that revealed the involvement of top appliance manufacturers in laundering drug money, http://www.pbs.org/wgbh/pages/frontline/shows/drugs/special/us.html. See also the related newspaper article by the show's producer, Lowell Bergman.

demand at existing price levels.

In the transport sector, the illegal is moved along with the legal, thereby masking one trade within another. For example, containers emanating from Colombia have drugs hidden among a shipment of fish or other food, such as coffee.

Distributors can mask the illicit by selling it along with the licit. For example in the Barbès region of Paris, a center of illicit trade, licensed cigarette stores may sell legally imported cigarettes along with smuggled cigarettes emanating from North Africa and Eastern Europe in the same shop.① The difference between the two commodities would be the price, with the legitimate approximately double in cost to the consumer.

Understanding the merger of the licit and illicit is key to understanding the possibility of acquisition of dual-use commodities for weapons programs such as those of Iran. Analyses of the records of numerous investigations by the author reveals that while there are some suppliers who may be complicit in supplying dual use materials to illegitimate buyers, most of the detected acquisitions of dual-use materials were not done with the complicity of the supplier. Rather, they resulted from significant subterfuge engaged in by illicit buyers who went to great efforts to disguise the intended destinations of the products they sought. Often the illicit purchasers set up front companies to pose as legitimate buyers to the suppliers of dual-use materials.

Illustrative of this is a 2012 DOJ prosecution case that concerned shipments for Iran. Defendants from 2007 to mid-2011 defendants obtained or attempted to obtain from companies worldwide over 105,000 parts valued at some $2,630,800 involving more than 1,250 transactions. These transactions were spread across many different businesses and were conducted on a small scale as indicated by the over one thousand transactions which averaged about $2000 apiece, not noticeable transactions for significant exporters.

The segmentation of trade shipments was also observed in a German-Turkish investigation in which the Iranian purchaser did much to hide the ultimate purchaser. This 2013 case traced parts destined for the nuclear facility in Arak, Iran. The investigation revealed that the parts were obtained in India and Germany and sent via five separate shell companies to Iranian nationals who established front-companies in Istanbul. This closed illicit network consisted exclusively of Iranians, as well as a Turk of Iranian origin, residing either in Ger-

① Insight gained by the author in March 2015 on a guided walking tour of the neighborhood.

many or Istanbul. Between 2010 and 2012, the smugglers carried out nine hundred shipments of cooling devices and other apparatuses; eight hundred shipments originated from India and a further one hundred from Germany. The Istanbul-based front companies misidentified the exported commodities as valves and plumbing fixtures.①

This case, like the previous one, reveals that intermediaries' intentional deception resulted in the same supply sources being used by both legitimate and illegitimate purchasers. The movement of goods between Germany and Istanbul is so frequent, that these parts intended for illegitimate use followed a well-known legal trade route reflecting that the licit and the illicit often travel the same path.

White Collar Crime

The distinguished criminologist, Edwin Sutherland, not only developed the concept of *differential association* but also that of *white-collar crime*. The term coined in 1939 refers to financially motivated nonviolent crime committed by business and government professionals, "a crime committed by a person of respectability and high social status in the course of his occupation"②.

The term white-collar criminal applies aptly to many of the bankers, transport and logistics experts involved in the trade in nuclear materials. The Bankers employed at BCCI, Banco Nazionale de Lavoro as well as HSBC③ helped facilitate the financing of proliferation programs. Iraq under Saddam Hussein "established a special relationship with the Atlanta Branch of the Banca Nazionale de Lavoro", a global Italian government bank. It processed billions in Iraqi funds some of which were used for illicit purchases.④ Similar patterns were seen in the behavior of ING, Barclays, ABN Amro, Credit Suisse and HSBC.⑤ HSBC, a major British-

---

① UPI, "Nuclear Materials Smugglers Arrested", March 11, 2013, http://www.upi.com/Top_News/World-News/2013/03/11/Nuclear-materials-smugglers-arrested/UPI-80861362997303/; Nihat Uludag, "Nuclear Operation: Seven Iranians Captured in Simultaneous Operations in Turkey and Germany", http://www.upi.com/Top_News/World-News/2013/03/11/Nuclear-materials-smugglers-arrested/UPI-80861362997303/.

② https://www.law.cornell.edu/wex/white-collar_crime.

③ J.C.Sharman, *The Money Laundry Regulating Criminal Finance in the Global Economy*, Ithaca (New York: Cornell University Press, 2011).

④ Matthew Bunn, "Corruption and Nuclear Proliferation", in *Corruption, Global Security, and World Order*, ed. Robert Rotberg (Washington, DC: Brookings Institution, 2009), 139.

⑤ U.S.Senate Permanent Subcommittee on Investigations, "U.S. Vulnerabilities to Money Laundering, Drugs, and Terrorist Financing", 117; Javier Serrat, "Financial Interdictions to Curb Proliferation", July-August 2012, http://www.armscontrol.org/2012_07-08/Financial_Interdictions_To_Curb_Proliferation.

based bank and facilitator of Iran's nuclear program, was shown to not only ignore the illicit activity of its clients but willfully disregarded its compliance obligations, knowingly facilitating clients' evasion of laws in their home countries, and in several instances, HSBC actively participated in its clients' criminal activities.① The details of its involvement with Iran's proliferation program will be discussed subsequently in the section on facilitators.

Significant attention has been paid to the criminals who have moved nuclear materials in the Caucasus, or to the fact that ISIS has stolen WMD components in Iraq.② These are important threats, but as Sutherland pointed out about 75 years ago, in focusing on criminal activity we tend not to focus sufficiently on the crime committed by high social status individuals. The failure to prosecute anyone in the HSBC case for helping Iran fund its nuclear program is evidence of the point that Sutherland clearly made decades ago.

Expensive operations, involving the importation of one hundred thousand spare parts, as previously discussed, were feasible for Iran, because despite sanctions, it had access to the international banking system. From 2000 to 2007, HSBC bank was fully cognizant that it was processing dollar-related transfers for Iranian institutions.③ A financial audit of HSBC business in regard to Iran observed, "The review identified almost 25,000 U.S. dollar transactions involving Iran, involving assets in excess of $19.4 billion."④ This was part of an overall pattern of noncompliance with anti-money laundering provisions globally, for which the bank eventually settled with the U.S. government for a fine of a little more than $1.9 billion.⑤

Moreover, senior officials in HSBC were knowingly and purposely disguising these transactions. But in other cases, the banks might not have been able to recognize the patterns of proliferation financeand could have prevented this financial facilitation if they had received

---

① Kevin McCoy. "HSBC will pay $1.9 billion for money laundering." *USA TODAY*. December 11, 2012. http://www.usatoday.com/story/money/business/2012/12/11/hsbc-laundering-probe/1760351/ ; Paul Farrell, James Ball, David Leigh, Juliette Garside and David Pegg. "The HSBC Files." *The Guardian*. February 8, 2015. http://www.theguardian.com/news/2015/feb/09/hsbc-swiss-files-leading-australian-figures-held-offshore-bank-accounts.

② Stephen Hummel, "The ISIL's Theft of WMD Components in Iraq", *CTC Sentinel* | Volume 7, Issue 7 (July 2014), p.1. (*Published by Combating Terrorism Center*)

③ U.S. Senate Permanent Subcommittee on Investigations, Committee on Homeland Security and Governmental Affairs, "U.S. Vulnerabilities to Money Laundering, Drugs, and Terrorist Financing: HSBC Case History", July 17, 2012, 118 Helping Clients Evade US Sanctions", January 3, 2013, http://www.financialtransparency.org-20.

④ Ibid., 120.

⑤ Heather Lowe, HSBC Deferred Prosecution Agreement:/2013/01/03/the-hsbc-deferred-prosecution-agreement-helping-clients-evade-u-s-sanctions/.

further training and guidance from investigators and experts in the government tracking of proliferators.①

Proliferators and their facilitators can include high-status individuals. They can be not only bankers but also transport and logistics experts. Corporate involvement represents a very significant part of the proliferation challenge but has not aroused popular or governmental concern to the degree that detected shipments of actual nuclearmaterials, such as uranium-235 and cesium have. The important role of the diverse participants in this illicit trade will be analyzed in the following section. By examining the full range of actors, it is possible to devise strategies to more effectively counter the illicit trade in its present form and in its future directions.

Characteristics of Non-ideological and Ideological criminals engaged in illicit trade:

In the following section, the different categories of perpetrators analyzed will include such non-state actors as criminals and terrorists, as well as corrupt officials and highly placed individuals protected by state corruption. Key facilitators who act for their own profit or state interests will also be examined.② The private sector, as exporters, bankers and corporations will be shown to share an important role in this illicit trade.

Non-ideological criminals engaged in nuclear trafficking range from low-level couriers often unaware of what they are moving to very high-level officials. The unmasking of high-level individuals involved in illicit nuclear trade requires significant investigations requiring the investment of massive manpower to understand their involvement. These key figures are supported by facilitators who provide dual-use materials or help move money or materials.

Non-state Actors

The non-state actors include a diverse variety of individuals ready to engage in the trade in nuclear materials. These include petty criminals for hire, members of organized crime groups, as well as individuals associated with "new organized crime" structures. It is the low-level individuals, opportunists or petty criminals, who are most easily detected whereas

① Sonia Ben Ouagrham-Gormley, "Banking on Nonproliferation: Improving the Efficiency of Counter-Proliferation Financing Policies", *Nonproliferation Review* 19, no.2(2012): 241–65.

② Douglas Farah, "Fixers, Super Fixers and Shadow Facilitators: How Networks Connect", in *Convergence: Illicit Networks and National Security in the Age of Globalization*, eds. Michael Miklaucic and Jacqueline Brewer (Washington, D.C.: NDU Press, 2013), 75–95.

the higher-level facilitators are often masked behind complex front companies.

Terrorist groups also fall into this category but as discussed previously in reference to the recent United Nations Security Council Resolutions on Terrorism in late 2014 and early 2015, it is increasingly hard to distinguish terrorism from organized crime. While much transnational crime still operates independently of terrorism, almost no terrorist group operates without using crime and criminals to finance and operate its organizations.①

The diverse actors associated with uranium smuggling can be understood through the lens of the *Nuclear Smuggling Chains Model*.② On the supply side, insiders in nuclear facilities are key in securing materials. This was referenced previously in the analysis of the guardianship aspect of routine activity theory. The insiders who have, or can gain, access to nuclear and other radioactive material are typically civilian employees at facilities housing nuclear material. They range from technicians to top managers and may include military personnel, and security guards. According to existing data, outsiders are scarcely involved in the theft of nuclear material, reflecting the problems of corruption and profit seeking at the source.③

Intermediaries are the individuals, groups, and organizations that find a potential buyer for the stolen material, and typically fall into the categories of amateurs, opportunistic businessmen and firms, and organized crime groups. Organized crime groups are the greatest concern because they are "the logistics experts" and have established infrastructures that can be exploited to move nuclear and other radioactive material. To date, few detected cases link specific organized crime groups with nuclear smuggling activities; however, because of the ease with which organized crime can avoid detection of their illicit activities, the full magnitude of their involvement is difficult to assess although cases detected and investigated in recent years in Moldova suggest their presence.④

Because most interceptions of nuclear materials are made during the transit phase, much

---

① Shelley, *Dirty Entanglements: Corruption, Crime and Terrorism*, chapter 3, 97-131; UN Resolutions 2195 and 2199.

② This model is extrapolated from a number of sources analyzing illicit nuclear/radiological commodity flows including Mike Bourne, "Controlling the shadow trade." *Contemporary Security Policy* 32: 1 (2011): 215-240. Lyudmila Zaitseva and Kevin Hand, "Controlling the shadow trade, Nuclear Smuggling Chains Suppliers, Intermediaries, and End-Users." *American Behavioral Scientist* 46: 6 (2003): 822-844, Mahmut Cengiz, "Various System Methodologies To Analyze Theft and Smuggling of Nuclear Material Cases." *Turkish Journal of Criminology* 1: 2 (2010), http://traccc.gmu.edu/pdfs/publications/weapons_smuggling_ publications/cengiz2.pdf.

③ According to Zaitseva and Hand. "Nuclear Smuggling Chains Suppliers, Intermediaries, and End-Users", "all of the insider thieves of weapons-usable material known to date were low-key personnel ranging from technicians, sailors, and workers to low-rank naval officers. The data on the diversion of non-weapons-usable uranium largely illustrates the same pattern".

④ Lyudmila Zaitseva and Friedrich Steinhäusler, "Nuclear Trafficking Issues in the Black Sea Region", pp. 11-17.

less is known about the demand side for nuclear materials. But most counter-trafficking programs are based on the hypothesis that demand consists of a combination of nation states and non-state actors with established networks of couriers, secure smuggling routes, and interim destinations that are locales where the materials are unlikely to be detected.①

Traditional organized crime often had symbiotic relations with the state and so refrained from cooperating with terrorists.② But a new organized crime has developed that does not eschew such relationships, a fact observed globally, leading to the United Nations' recognition of transnational crime as a security challenge. In the past decade this phenomenon has become an increasing concern to the Security Council of the United Nations. Whereas in 2004, the Security Council mentioned transnational crime four times in its resolutions, by 2014 the number had risen to over 30, reflecting a profound change in perception by the international community.③ What is the new organized crime that is so threatening? The author has described the problem in her recent book, *Dirty Entanglements: Corruption, Crime and Terrorism* in the following way:

But there is also a *new transnational crime*, whose scale is much larger and whose corruption of officials exceeds anything previously seen. Its political impact is disproportionate to its membership, as it is most often based in weak states that have little capacity or political will to stem its growth.④…

Crime groups with loyalty to the state are no longer ascendant. New transnational crime groups have proliferated in number and membership within the last twenty years as a consequence of the end of the Cold War and the rise of globalization.⑤ The new criminals, many

---

① Zaitseva and Hand, "Nuclear Smuggling Chains Suppliers, Intermediaries, and End-Users" identify five types of end users: Proliferating States, Terrorist Organizations, Religious Sects, Separatist Movements, and Criminal Groups/Individuals. Although the historical record of terrorists pursuing nuclear and radiological capabilities is small in size, complicated by significant information gaps, and not well understood, see Sara Daly, John Parachini and William Rosenau. "Aum Shinrikyo, Al Qaeda, and the Kinshasa Reactor." *RAND Documented Briefing* Santa Monica, CA: RAND Corporation (2005).

② Shelley, *Dirty Entanglements: Corruption, Crime and Terrorism*, p.102.

③ Ambassador Ugi Zvekic, Presentation at "Breaking the Chain between Corruption and Organised Crime in the post-2015 Development Agenda", April 14, 2015, United Nations Congress, Doha, http://www.un-congress.org/Sessions/SummaryReport; Global Initiative Against Transnational Organized Crime, "Reinforcing Multilateral Approaches to Transnational Organized Crime by Strengthening Local Ownership and Accountability", 2015.

④ This paragraph comes from Shelley, *Dirty Entanglements: Corruption, Crime and Terrorism*, p. 99, uses ideas from Stewart Patrick, *Weak Links: Fragile States, Global Threats and International Security* (Oxford: Oxford University Press, 2011), 141–42.

⑤ Saskia Sassen, *Globalization and Its Discontents* (New York: New Press, 1998); James Mittelman, *The Globalization Syndrome: Transformation and Resistance* (Princeton, NJ: Princeton University Press, 2000); Moisés Naím, "Five Wars of Globalization", *Foreign Policy*, January 1, 2003; see http://www.foreignpolicy.com/articles/2003/01/01/five_wars_of_globalization.

based in conflict regions and transitional states, have exploited the decline of borders and increased mobility, diverse new forms of communication, and greater ease of international transport. They thrive in the shadow economy, the absence of an effective state, and endemic corruption.① As one scholar explained, "terrorist networks, like Mafias, appear to flourish where states are governed badly rather than not at all."②

Many new criminals have no interest in the endurance of the state; rather, their profits are made by destabilizing the state and its structures. These groups thrive in the chaos of war, frozen and enduring conflicts, where governments cannot curb their illicit activity and corruption is the norm.③ They also thrive in the transitional states of the postsocialist world, where old norms were destroyed and new ones have not taken root. Powerful organized crime groups based in the former Yugoslavia, parts of West Africa, the Soviet successor states, or Afghanistan are now global actors, even though they were nearly unknown before the 1990s.④

Criminal Actors

Understanding the context of the new transnational crime, it is hardly surprising that a strong correlation exists between the regions where the new transnational crime flourishes and areas where there is an illicit trade in nuclear materials. Understanding the geographic and the crime context is of paramount importance in discerning trends in non-sanctioned trade in nuclear materials.

A diverse array of criminals has participated in detected cases of illicit trade. As previously mentioned, opportunistic criminals have been implicated in many low level cases of smuggling.⑤ In Turkey, where nuclear materials were found within traditional drug trafficking networks, the role of traditional organized crime is clearly present.⑥ Yet in more seri-

---

① Note that these are poorly governed states, but not the weakest states, as the weakest states are not hospitable for crime groups. See Stewart Patrick, *Weak Links: Fragile States, Global Threats and International Security* (Oxford: Oxford University Press, 2011), 3-4.

② Kenneth J. Menkhaus, "Somalia and Somaliland: Terrorism, Political Islam and State Collapse", in *Battling Terrorism in the Horn of Africa*, ed. Robert I. Rotberg (Washington, DC: Brookings Institution Press, 2005), 45.

③ Ivan Briscoe and ElisaDari, *Crime and Error: Why We Urgently Need a New Approach to Illicit Trafficking in Fragile States*, Clingendael Conflict Research Unit CRU Policy Brief 23, May 2012, 3, http://www.clingendael.nl/publications/recent/.

④ Shelley, *Dirty Entanglements: Corruption, Crime and Terrorism*, pp. 102-103.

⑤ Kupatadze.

⑥ Cengiz, "Various System Methodologies To Analyze Theft and Smuggling of Nuclear Material Cases".

ous cases of smuggling, other types of criminal actors have been identified. In the Soviet Union, criminal organizations often have former members of the security apparatus within their ranks.① The previously discussed case of the HEU smuggler, Oleg Khintsagov, is possibly illustrative of this phenomenon.

Global international networks that can facilitate transfers to transnational crime exist but are not fully understood. Illustrative of this, a low enriched uranium fuel element containing small amounts of U-235 stolen in Kinshasa from a research reactor was found subsequently in the hands of the Sicilian mafia.② The means by which this uranium travelled thousands of miles to reach a major transnational crime group is not known. These diaspora communities in Africa that engage in both licit and illicit trade represent a proliferation risk because, as previously mentioned, Africa represents the new area of concern for uranium ore that could be diverted or supplied to unauthorized users.③

Nuclear trafficking has been a problem in Africa even before the expanded production of uranium ore. According to the IAEA database, officials from the DRC nuclear facility were implicated in the disappearance of a significant amount of material in March 2007.④ Apart from this case there were 12 confirmed incidents of natural uranium smuggling in Africa between 1994 and 2005. Four incidents were recorded in Tanzania, in the Democratic Republic of Congo, Kenya, and two each in Namibia and South Africa.⑤

Professional criminals with known criminal records have been identified in some cases of smuggling of the most valuable radioactive materials, such as enriched uranium.⑥ Illustrative of this is a Moldovan case from 2011, in which a 4. 4-gram sample of weapons-grade uranium was seized, allegedly part of a 1-kilogram cache.⑦ It was reputedly transported through the conflict region of Transdniester by at least six non-state actors emanating

---

① Louise Shelley, "Crime, Organized Crime and Corruption", in Return to Putin's Russia 5th edition ed. Stephen K. Wegren (Lanham, Maryland: Rowman and Littlefield Publishers, 2013), 189–208.

② Bunn, 139.

③ See Australian Conservation Foundation, "Uranium Undermining Africa", January 14, 2014, www.acfonline.org.au/news-media/news-features/uranium-undermining-africa.

④ Nwanolue, Bonn Obiekwe Godwin and Victor Chidubem Iwuoha, "Nuclear Politics In Africa: Legal and Empirical Foundations." April 2015, http://nwanoluebog.net/wp-content/uploads/2015/04/Nuclear-Politics-in-Africa.pdf, p.14.

⑤ Ibid., p.14.

⑥ Lyudmila Zaitseva and Kevin Hand, "Nuclear Smuggling Chains: Suppliers, Intermediaries, and End Users", *American Behavioral Scientist* 46, no.6(2003): 822–44; Zaitseva, "Nuclear Trafficking: 20 Years in Review"; Lyudmila, Zaitseva, "Organized crime, terrorism and nuclear trafficking." *Strategic Insights* 6.5(2007): 1–24.

⑦ NTI Illicit Trafficking Initiatives, NIS Nuclear Trafficking Initiative, 2, 2011 Illicit Trafficking Incidents Summary Table, http://www.nti.org/analysis/reports/nis-nuclear-trafficking-database/.

from Russia and Moldova intending to sell their materials to a buyer in North Africa.[①] Moldovan authorities had established that this was a stable criminal group, specializing in acquisition, possession, transport and sale of uranium.[②] In 2014, Moldovan police arrested seven people who admitted to smuggling seven ounces of uranium with an alleged value of $ 2. 1 million.[③]

This second case attests to the continuing centrality of Moldova and the Black Sea Region, as mentioned earlier, to trafficking. This region, since the early 1990s, has had 130 profit-motivated trafficking cases attesting to the presence of strong smuggling networks in the region.[④] Officials in this region, according to Zaitseva and Steinhäusler's research, underestimate the role of organized crime. Their recent analyses show that groups involved in nuclear smuggling were most present in Ukraine, Georgia, Turkey and Romania,[⑤] countries known to have significant organized crime problems.

As previously mentioned, illicit trade in nuclear materials has already been observed by investigators in the "dark web" of the cyberworld in which individuals enter and interact with anonymity. The dark web, according to its name, is now dominated by criminals and illicit actors.[⑥] It contains numerous sites selling every illegal commodity imaginable, including people, drugs, arms, and hit men. Research has already identified 50,000 sites linked to the trafficking of humans.[⑦] In the cyberworld, there is a proliferation of sites offering biological and chemical WMD for sale, but also nuclear material such as polonium.[⑧]

Russian organized crime has assumed a very significant role in much of the world's cy-

---

① "Moldova Sentences Would Be Uranium Dealers", May 25, 2012, http://www.nti.org/gsn/article/moldova-sentences-would-be-uranium-dealers/; Desmond Butler, "Moldova, U.S. Pursue HEU Held by Criminal Organization", September 27, 2011, http://www.nti.org/gsn/article/moldova-us-pursue-heu-held-by-criminal-organization/.

② Zaitseva and Steinhäusler, "Nuclear Trafficking Issues in the Black Sea Region", p.17 and the rest of the publication for an excellent analysis of the problem with helpful charts.

③ Mark Hay. "How Worried should we be about Moldova's Recent Uranium Smuggling Bust?" December 11, 2014, http://www.vice.com/read/moldovas-recent-uranium-smuggling-busts-arent-something-to-worry-about-at-least-not-yet-000.

④ Lyudmila Zaitseva and Friedrich Steinhäusler, "Nuclear Trafficking Issues in the Black Sea Region", p.11.

⑤ Ibid., 12.

⑥ Marc Goodman, *Future Crimes Everything is Connected Everything is Vulnerable and What We Can do About It* (New York: Random House, 2015).

⑦ Larry Greenemeier, "Human Traffickers Caught on Hidden Internet", February 8, 2015, http://www.scientificamerican.com/article/human-traffickers-caught-on-hidden-internet/; U. S. Department of State, Trafficking in Persons: Filling Knowledge Gaps, January 27, 2015, Washington, DC.

⑧ U.S.-France Cooperative Futures Forum, "Anticipating Transnational Threats and Risks", April 28-29, 2015, Washington, DC.

bercrime.[①] Unfortunately, there is a possible convergence of nuclear source material in Russia and the disproportionate involvement of Russian organized crime on both the accessible web and the dark web. Therefore, the advertised sale of polonium is hardly surprising as Russia was the likely source of highly radioactive polonium from state-run reactors that killed the Russian émigré, Alexander Litvinenko, in London.

Terrorist Actors

The role of terrorist groups in nuclear materials acquisitions is a source of great fear to the international community. Yet the phenomenon has not been verified in many cases. The most known case occurred in November 1995 when Chechen separatists in Russia, "put a crude bomb containing seventy pounds of a mixture of cesium-137 and dynamite in Moscow's Ismailovsky Park. The rebels decided not to detonate this 'dirty bomb' but instead informed a national television station as to its location."[②] The material was thought to have been acquired during the chaotic period coinciding with the collapse of the Soviet Union that allowed the Chechen leader, Dzohkar Dudayev, to secure the material for the deadly dirty bomb.[③]

Massive investments made to safeguards Russian nuclear facilities have lowered the possibility of access to weapons-grade materials, but an illicit trade still exists in nuclear materials. Terrorist groups from the North Caucasus have repeatedly sought to acquire nuclear weapons and have succeeded in acquiring radioactive materials.[④] A 2011 joint study by the Belfer Center for Science and International Affairs and the Russian Academy of Sciences concluded that the threat of nuclear terrorism posed by groups from the North Caucasus groups is increased by "widespread crime in the armed forces" and "corrupt bureaucracies and law-enforcement agencies whose personnel allow terrorists to cross from one Russian

---

① Brian Krebs, *Spam Nation: The Inside Story of Organized Cybercrime from Global Epidemic to your Front Door*, (Naperville, Il.: Sourcebooks, 2014); see also blog Krebsonsecurity.

② Allison, 31. This overlooks the Kocaeli case that will be discussed subsequently in the section.

③ Allison, 31 – 32. For a further discussion of Chechen involvement in nuclear terrorism, see Simon Saradzhyan, "Russia: Grasping Reality of Nuclear Terror", Discussion Paper 2003-02, International Security Program, Belfer Center for Science and International Affairs, Harvard Kennedy School, March 2003, http://belfercenter.ksg.harvard.edu/publication/2938/russia.html? breadcrumb =%2Fexperts%2F1897%2Fsimon_saradzhyan%3Fgroupby%3D0%26hide%3D1%26id%3D1897%26back_url%3D%2525252Fexperts%2525252F%26%253Bback_text%3DBack%252Bto%252Blist%252Bof%252Bexperts%26filter%3D2003; Charles D. Ferguson and William C. Potter, *The Four Faces of Nuclear Terrorism* (New York: Routledge, 2005). See Kupatadze, 226.

④ Ibid., p.295.

region to another, carrying illicit cargo."[1]

Compounding the risk in this region is that one of the leaders of ISIS, Abu Omar al-Shishani, was originally a Georgian Christian from the Pankisi Gorge region, a long-term haven for Chechen terrorists and Islamic militants. Radicalized in Georgia, he married a Chechen and rose to be a commander in ISIS[2] before he was allegedly killed in 2014.[3] Georgia, consistently a transshipment point for illicit nuclear materials, had cases detected as recently as 2012.[4] Therefore, the links between the terrorism of the North and South Caucasus and ISIS raise concerns that these channels might be conduits for the flow of nuclear materials.

Diverse religious extremist groups, "figure most prominently among the groups that have manifested some degree of intent, experimentation, and programmatic efforts to acquire nuclear, biological and chemical weapons."[5] Many affiliates of al Qaeda are now active in the unstable region, ranging from West Africa, through North Africa, the Middle East and on to Pakistan. These and other terrorist organizations that have recently allied themselves with ISIS, such as Boko Haram, may follow Osama's 1998 dictum that made it a religious duty for his followers to pursue the acquisition of WMD.[6]

A planned terrorist act in Kocaeli, Turkey, a populous urban center not far from Istanbul in the early 2000s is indicative of al Qaeda influenced terrorists seeking to mount a radiological attack. Some of the participants were Turks who had returned from Afghanistan and Pakistan, after time spent with Islamic militants. The lethality of the returning religious extremists phenomenon has been subsequently observed with the Boston Marathon bombers,

---

① See *The U.S.-Russia Joint Threat Assessment on Nuclear Terrorism*, Belfer Center for Science and International Affairs and Russian Academy of Sciences, 2011, http://belfercenter. ksg. harvard. edu/files/Joint-Threat-Assessment% 20ENG% 2027%20May%202011.pdf.

② Nina Akhmeteli, "The Georgian Roots of ISIS commander Omar al-Shishani", July 9, 2014, www. bbc. ccom/nes/world-europe-28217590.

③ Where has Umar Al-Shishani Gone?, January 1, 2015, www.rferl.mobi/a/26805849.html/.

④ Global Security Newswire, "Georgia Conducted 15 Nuclear Smuggling Probes since 2005", December 10, 2012, http://www.nti.org/gsn/article/georgian-conducted-15-nuclear-smuggling-probes-2005-report/. Also, a researcher affiliated with the author has had recent cases officially released by the Georgian government for analysis from this period as part of this study.

⑤ The quote is from Rolf Mowatt-Larsen, "Al Qaeda Weapons of Mass Destruction Threat: Hype or Reality", Harvard Belfer Center, January 2010, 5, http://belfercenter. ksg. harvard. edu/publication/19852/al _ qaeda _ weapons _ of _ mass _ destruction_threat.html. See also David Albright, Mark Dubowitz, Orde Kittrie, Leonard Spector, and Michael Yaffe, *U. S. Nonproliferation Strategy for the Changing Middle East* (Washington, DC: Project on U.S. Middle East Nonproliferation Strategy, 2013), 103 on the same topic.

⑥ Rahim Kanani, "Al Qaeda's Religious Justification of Nuclear Weapons", *Huffington Post*, November 19, 2010, http://www.huffingtonpost.com/rahim-kanani/al-qaedas-religious-justi_b_786332.html.

where one of the brothers had lived in Dagestan, and more recently in the Charlie Hebdo attack in Paris where one of the Kouachi Brothers had lived in Yemen and interacted with the AQAP (al Qaeda of the Arab peninsula).

The Kocaeli terrorist cell of approximately 40 Islamic militants operated out of the conservative religious center of Konya in central Turkey. They planned to attack a Kocaeli factory for hospital equipment that produced radiological isotopes that were used in its medical equipment. The attack was averted because the Konya police, simultaneously deploying anti-crime and the anti-terrorist units of the police, detected and disrupted the attack before it occurred. During the investigation, the police were able to locate the radiological production site that was under surveillance by the terrorist group.①

Al Qaeda is not the only group in this unstable region seeking nuclear materials, because Shia groups that are supported by Iran are also active in Lebanon, Syria, and are also operating in Eastern Turkey.

Corruption is very pronounced in the unstable region surrounding Syria and Iraq. Therefore, the capacity of law enforcement and intelligence to counteract any illicit trade in nuclear materials is limited under the best of conditions. It is even more limited at a time of millions of refugees. There are 1. 8 million recorded refugees from Syria in Turkey alone② and many more in neighboring countries. These desperate individuals may consent to do anything in return for funds for their survival, including knowingly or unwittingly moving nuclear materials.

The problem of a dirty bomb in the Middle East remains an ongoing threat. In the summer of 2014, when ISIS attacked Mosul, it took 40 kilograms of uranium compounds from Mosul University. These materials could not be used for a nuclear device, because the seized material consisted of low-grade uranium that would need an extensive nuclear program to develop into a bomb—an infrastructure that is fortunately missing from this war-torn region. A more likely threat would be the production of a dirty bomb in which explosives are combined with the radioactive materials. If ISIS used the stolen uranium in a dirty bomb, the ex-

---

① This attack was discussed in detail by one of the investigating officers, Anadolou Atayun, "Crime-Terror Nexus: Concrete Examples from the Field", at Criminal Networks, Smuggling, and WMD Conference, February 25 – 26, 2010, at Terrorism, Transnational Crime, and Corruption Center, George Mason University, Arlington, VA. See also Shelley, *Dirty Entanglements: Corruption, Crime and Terrorism*, p.308.

② "ISIL Advances on Syrian city, refugees at border", *Hürriyet Daily News*, June 6-7, 2015, p.9.

plosion would be more deadly than the radiation released.[①] But the symbolic impact of this attack would, however, be significant.

Facilitators

Facilitators are key to the operation of illicit networks. As Douglas Farah explains, these networks, "rely on international 'shadow facilitators' who can move weapons and commodities, launder money, and obtain the fraudulent international documents such as end user certificates, passports, business registrations, shipping licenses, and other needed papers."[②]

Often the same facilitators are used by multiple networks, which will subcontract their services. Facilitators, who make high-level profits, provide key nodes for supply chains of illicit goods, including WMD and dual-use materials. The facilitators can come from the criminal world, but often they exist in a world where laws are not strictly defined and/or corruption is also pervasive.

HSBC and the other banks fined for their role in moving Iranian, Iraqi and Pakistani money should also be considered as superfacilitators. Banks did not perform all the functions that Farah associates with facilitators. But their service as money movers and launderers is key to nuclear proliferation.

As far back as 2001, HSBC bankers in the U. S. violated anti-money laundering regulations by disguising transactions linked to Iran's Bank Melli in order to clear transactions (in U.S. dollars) through a US-based HSBC bank. Illustrative of how this was done was revealed by investigators analyzing HSBC's internal communications. A June 2001 email from a European HSBC relationship manager to someone associated with Bank Melli instructed them not to input an "Iranian referenced customer name" with the transaction,[③] thus avoiding any sign of a U.S. legal breach.

These systemic violations continued for a significant period (2000 to 2007) with HSBC being fully cognizant that it was processing dollar-related transfers for Iranian institutions.[④]

---

① Dina Esfandiary and Matthew Cottee, "The Very Small Islamic State WMD Threat", October 16, 2014, Bulletin of the Atomic Scientists, thebulletin.org/very-sll-islamic-state-wmd-threat7729.

② Farah, p.78.

③ http://www.treasury.gov/resource-center/sanctions/CivPen/Documents/121211_HSBC_Settlement.pdf, p.1.

④ U.S.Senate Permanent Subcommittee on Investigations, Committee on Homeland Security and Governmental Affairs, "U.S.Vulnerabilities to Money Laundering, Drugs, and Terrorist Financing: HSBC Case History", July 17, 2012, 118 Helping Clients Evade US Sanctions, January 3, 2013, http://www.financialtransparency.org–20.

A financial audit of HSBC business in regard to Iran observed, "The review identified almost 25,000 U.S. dollar transactions involving Iran, involving assets in excess of $19.4 billion."① This was part of an overall pattern of noncompliance with anti-money laundering provisions globally, for which the bank eventually settled with the U.S. government for a fine of a little more than $1.9 billion.② Access to such significant funds allowed Iran to make many purchases, despite sanctions, to support its nuclear program.

HSBC was a superfacilitator as it served not only Iran's nuclear program but also assisted tax evasion and money laundering of high net worth individuals as well as corrupt politicians. It also paid fines for laundering money for Mexican drug cartels and Hezbollah, an identified terrorist organization.③

HSBC was not the only bank to be investigated and charged by the U.S. government for moving money for Iran. Those sanctioned included such major international banks as ING, Barclays, ABN Amro, and Credit Suisse.④

Government Officials

Corruption at all levels of government is key to nuclear materials trafficking.⑤ The corruption includes that of both individuals and administrative bodies of countries. High-level officials are implicated in larger shipments and more low-level corruption facilitates access at the source and in transit.

Illustrative of this are cases in Russia. Very senior officials exploited their positions for personal profit. In 2005, Swiss authorities, at the request of the U.S. government, arrested Russia's former atomic energy minister, Yevgeni Adamov, after he was accused by a U.S. court of appropriating $9 million of U.S. assistance funding intended to safeguard Russia's

---

① Ibid, 120.

② Heather Lowe, HSBC Deferred Prosecution Agreement: /2013/01/03/the-hsbc-deferred-prosecution-agreement-helping-clients-evade-u-s-sanctions/.

③ Ryan Chittum. "Diamond Dealers in Deep Trouble as Bank Documents Shine Light on Secret Ways." *International Consortium of Investigative Journalists*, February 9, 2015. http://www.icij.org/project/swiss-leaks/diamond-dealers-deep-trouble-bank-documents-shine-light-secret-ways.

④ U.S. Senate Permanent Subcommittee on Investigations, "U.S. Vulnerabilities to Money Laundering, Drugs, and Terrorist Financing", 117; Javier Serrat, "Financial Interdictions to Curb Proliferation," July-August 2012, http://www.armscontrol.org/2012_07-08/Financial_Interdictions_To_Curb_Proliferation. Sonia Ben Ouagrham-Gormley, "Banking on Nonproliferation: Improving the Efficiency of Counter-Proliferation Financing Policies", *Nonproliferation Review* 19, no.2 (2012): 241-65 suggests that some banks were not cognizant and needed more training to identify patterns of proliferation finance.

⑤ Bunn, 124-65 provides an excellent analysis of all aspects of the corruption problem and WMD.

nuclear facilities and instead used the funds for his personal investments, rather than paying the workers who were to perform the security upgrades. He was extradited to Russia and tried in 2008 but after his trial, he exited prison with a suspended sentence.① His corruption at a critical time of insecurity of Russia undermined the system of nuclear safeguards.

His corruption was not unique. In the first decades of the post-Soviet period, high-level corruption among officials meant that they monetized anything of value that was under their control. While nuclear facilities were secure in the Soviet period, after the USSR's collapse, many nuclear facilities and weapons sites lacked adequate protections, a problem exacerbated by the corruption of top officials in the closed nuclear cities where the nuclear materials were produced or stored.② This absence of guardianship, as discussed in relation to routine activity theory, meant that some officials did not exercise their responsibility as guardians and used the uranium under their control as a source of personal enrichment.

According to Yury Vishnevsky, the former head of the monitoring agency Gozatomnadzor, plants in the Moscow region and the Novosibirsk plant lost "grams of weapons grade or kilograms of low enriched uranium" in 2002.③ This could not have happened in the Soviet period when facilities containing weapons grade material were carefully guarded and individuals were severely punished for violating norms connected to the USSR's nuclear program. But in the post-Soviet era, investigations and prosecutions for corruption diminished significantly to a very limited number.④ Therefore, unlike Beccaria's recommendation, there was neither certainty nor severity of punishment.

The proverb that "the fish rots from the head" applies here. When the leadership of the nuclear program is corrupt, there is ample possibility of corruption below. This can include officials at the mid-level of the bureaucracy down to the level of the guards who watch the facilities or the closed cities where nuclear facilities were housed in Russia.

In Russia, one smuggler seeking access to a closed city containing a WMD facility explained the process in the following way: "I pick one guard and get to know him, giving him

---

① http://www.bellona.org/english_import_area/international/russia/nuke_industry/co-operation/37946; "Russian Ex-nuclear Minister Adamov Released from Prison", April 17, 2008, http://en.rian.ru/russia/20080417/105342331.html.

② For an early warning about this, see William C.Potter, "Before the Deluge: The Threat of Nuclear Leakage from the Post-Soviet States", http://www.pbs.org/wgbh/pages/frontline/shows/nukes/readings/potterarticle.html.

③ Charles Digges, "GAN Says Nuclear Materials Have Been Disappearing from Russian Plants for 10 Years", November 15, 2002, http://www.bellona.org/english_import_area/international/russia/nuke-weapons/nonproliferation/2727Y.

④ Shelley, "Crime, Organized Crime and Corruption".

cigarettes and candy. After a month of our 'friendship,' I can bring in anyone I want. Of course, I have to agree with the soldier about the exact time of entry and exit." ① The costs of engaging in this corrupt practice if caught were insignificant. People found guilty of smuggling workers faced meaningless penalties that did not deter them.

The World Bank definition of corruption is "the abuse of public office for private gain." But this is too narrow, as it does not include private actors who behave in corrupt ways. The Asian Development Bank definition of corruption includes that of private individuals. ② For this study, I prefer to use the approach of the Asian Development Bank including that of corrupt individuals and also of corrupt private companies such as discussed previously in regard to the banking sector.

Private companies engaged in production of dual use materials were key to Iraq's proliferation network. In the Iraqi case, many suppliers knew that they were not selling to legitimate purchasers. Companies forged end user certificates and falsified export forms to disguise the ultimate recipient of the products they were selling. ③

This analysis illustrates that corporate actors, both front companies and legitimate companies, can be party to this illicit trade. Therefore, there can be a convergence of governmental and corporate corruption, the phenomenon that was discussed previously in relation to the criminological principle of "white collar crime".

Conclusions

In late 2014 and early 2015, many regions of the world experienced security challenges not seen since World War II. ④ The mass smuggling of people across the Mediterranean and South Asia, the enormous growth in refugee populations primarily fleeing conflicts and the presence of ongoing and contiguous regional conflicts in North Africa and the Middle East threatened global stability.

Past analyses of criminal involvement in nuclear smuggling have important limitations in

---

① Prizrak Usamy brodit po "zapretke", *Chelyabinskii rabochii*, August 12, 2004; research of TraCCC, American University, 2004-5, in which project the author participated.

② Asian Development Bank, *Anticorruption: Our Framework and Strategies*, 1998, http://www.adb.org/documents/anticorruption-policy.

③ Bunn, 130-31.

④ 45th International Peace Institute Vienna Seminar, The United Nations at 70, May 6-7, 2015 discussed this extensively.

addressing future trends in this trade because of the extent of contemporary disorder. Many geographical regions are now outside of any monitoring and reporting regimes or control by law enforcement and intelligence bodies. The focus of most previous monitoring efforts has been on trafficking in Eurasia, Iran and Pakistan.① But the arc of instability ranging from West Africa through North Africa, the Middle East and on to Pakistan poses, especially since the Arab Spring, provides enormous challenges not seen previously.

Increasing involvement in illicit trade will also occur in parts of Africa outside this previously cited arc of instability as Southern, Central and Eastern Africa will become parts of this illicit trade, as they have increased legal and illegal mining of uranium ore.② Mined uranium purchased outside of official channels will be sought primarily by those with significant production facilities to process it. Therefore, some of the same actors who have been the subject of scrutiny in the past will remain objects of concern. But the sources in diverse regions of Africa, the high levels of corruption,③ and the increasing presence of transnational criminals and terrorist groups on the African continent, pose future and serious challenges that require new strategies to counter this proliferation threat. Efforts to counter the more visible illicit trade in rhino horn and elephant tusks that both emanate from Africa have been unsuccessful despite the presence of political will in parts of the international community and the investment of significant resources. Therefore, the challenges will be greater with less visible material like uranium ore.

Identification of the non-state actors involved in illicit nuclear trade has always been difficult, whether it was on-the-ground smugglers in the Caucasus or the diverse components of the global supply chain of A.Q.Khan. But the challenges will be even greater in the future, when business is conducted increasingly over the dark web, through encrypted messages, or

---

① For instance, Alexander Kupatadze, "Organized crime and the trafficking of radiological materials: The case of Georgia." *Nonproliferation Review* 17:2(2010):219–234; Special Report: The Khan Network; Kenley Butler, Sammy Salama, and Leonard S.Spector, "Where Is the Justice?", *Bulletin of the Atomic Scientists*, November-December 2006, 25–34; Mark Hibbs, "The Unmaking of a Nuclear Smuggler", *Bulletin of the Atomic Scientists*, November-December 2006, 35–41; U.S.Department of Justice, "Summary of Major U.S.Export Enforcement, Economic Espionage, Trade Secret and Embargo-Related Criminal Cases"; Sheena Chestnut Greitens, "Illicit North Korea's Evolving Operations to Earn Hard Currency", Committee for Human Rights in North Korea, 2014.

② Marta Conde and Giorgis Kallis, "The global uranium rush and its Africa frontier. Effects, reactions and social movements in Namibia." *Global Environmental Change* 22:3(2012):596–610; Ian Anthony and Lisa Grip, *Africa and the Global Market in Natural Uranium: From Proliferation Risk to Non-proliferation Opportunity.* Stockholm International Peace Research Institute(SIPRI), 2013; Taylor Toeka, "Illegal Mining Fuels DRC Conflict", January 12, 2011, https://iwpr.net/global-voices/illegal-mining-fuels-drc-conflict.

③ https://www.transparency.org/cpi2014/results.

in regions where state and international capacity to counter illicit phenomena is distinctly limited.

The acquisition of dual-use materials by unauthorized proliferators will remain a problem as the profits are large, facilitators exist globally and the financial system is still amenable to the movement of significant amounts of illicit funds. Therefore, challenges exist both in the arena of raw, processed materials and in funding to support sales.

What can we learn from criminological theory that can help us prioritize for the future? Sutherland's concept of corporate crime should be central to our priorities. This is crucial in cutting off the ability of proliferating countries to fund and to obtain needed equipment to run their unauthorized nuclear programs.

The concept of guardianship in routine activity theory should force us to focus more on the problem of corruption and not minimize its significance as we have done in the past. We need to focus on areas where there cannot be guardianship and where we cannot lock up at the source like we have done in Russia. We need to focus more on how we address this problem on the vast continent of Africa with pervasive corruption. Part of this will require working more closely with international companies engaged in mining and transport. The United Nations has an important role to play on the African continent where it has been deeply involved in many capacities.

The concept of convergence has applicability in the illicit trade in nuclear materials. Different illicit products can fund the development of an unauthorized nuclear program and nuclear materials can travel in tandem with other illicit products. Those who seek to counter-proliferation must work more closely with those who counter other forms of crime and corruption. The UN Security Council Resolutions 2195 affirm that arms trade is an element of the convergence of crime and terrorism. These Resolutions provide more authority for the international community to pursue the crime linked to terrorism.

责任编辑:张　立
责任校对:陈艳华

图书在版编目(CIP)数据

国际犯罪学大师论恐怖主义犯罪/刘建宏 主编. —北京:人民出版社,2017.4
ISBN 978-7-01-017241-5

Ⅰ.①国…　Ⅱ.①刘…　Ⅲ.①恐怖主义-刑事犯罪-研究　Ⅳ.①D914.04

中国版本图书馆 CIP 数据核字(2016)第 320608 号

国际犯罪学大师论恐怖主义犯罪

GUOJI FANZUIXUE DASHI LUN KONGBUZHUYI FANZUI

刘建宏　主编

人民出版社 出版发行
(100706　北京市东城区隆福寺街 99 号)

北京教图印刷有限公司印刷　新华书店经销

2017 年 4 月第 1 版　2017 年 4 月北京第 1 次印刷
开本:787 毫米×1092 毫米 1/16　印张:13
字数:252 千字

ISBN 978-7-01-017241-5　定价:48.00 元

邮购地址 100706　北京市东城区隆福寺街 99 号
人民东方图书销售中心　电话 (010)65250042　65289539